April, 2001

To/Valerie/John Thompson —

Styles Bridges

Goodfriends from Delmar,
New York and St. Stephen's
Episcopal Church who have
a keen interest in New
Hampshire history, especially
in Dover, New Hampshire where
John Hayes, a scottish ancestor,
who arrived in Dover in 1680.

With my best personal regards,

Jim

*"Men hang out their signs indicative of their re-
spective trades: shoemakers hang out a gigantic
shoe; jewelers a monster watch; and the dentist
hangs out a gold tooth; but in the mountains of New
Hampshire, God Almighty has hung out a sign to
show that there he makes men."*

Daniel Webster

Styles Bridges

Yankee Senator

James J. Kiepper

PHOENIX PUBLISHING

Sugar Hill, New Hampshire

P E R M I S S I O N S
With the exception of the photograph of the Old Man of the
Mountain which appears facing the title page courtesy of White
Mountain Attractions, all illustrations in this volume are from the
archives of the New Hampshire Division of Research Management
and Archives and are used with their kind permission.

Cataloging-in-Publication Data

Kiepper, James J.
    Styles Bridges : Yankee senator / James J. Kiepper.
        p. cm.
    Includes bibliographical references (p.) and index.
    ISBN 0-914659-93-6 (alk. paper)
    1. Bridges, Styles, 1898-1961. 2. Legislators—United
States—Biography. 3. United States. Congress. Senate—Bio-
graphy. 4. Governors—New Hampshire—Biography. 5. New
Hampshire—Politics and government—1865-1950. I. Title.

E748.B842 K53 2001
974.1'043'092—dc21
[B]   00-066889

Printed in the United States of America

To the memory of
Robert Perkins Bass
Governor of New Hampshire
1910-1913
and
Gilbert Verney
Chairman and CEO
Monadnock Paper Mills, Inc.
1948-1978

Contents

Author's Preface

I HAVE WRITTEN THIS BOOK, not only for the general reader, but also in an attempt to involve a new generation of high school and college students in the life and career of U.S. Senator Styles Bridges, and to help promote a fuller understanding of the workings of legislative government. The Bridges biography can be seen as a case study of an individual, a "common man," who served as both governor of New Hampshire (1935-37), and as a United States senator (1937-61). I hope to encourage students to develop a dialogue on the United States Senate, and on key New Hampshire political figures, especially as they relate to their communities.

James J. Kiepper

Delmar, New York
January 2001

ACKNOWLEDGMENTS

I shall always be grateful for the support and interest of the following individuals who supported my preparation of the Bridges biography. They include the late Leon Anderson, political reporter for the *Concord Monitor* and historian for the New Hampshire Lesiglature; Christopher Pratt and Barbara Gesang, who assisted with early drafts of the manuscript; David Carle and John Warrington, who read and commented on revisions of major sections of the book, and who gave invaluable advice on how to capture the essence of Bridges' character and personality. Thanks also to Linda Quinn, who typed many letters and drafts of the manuscript.

At the time of his death, Styles Bridges' papers and memorabilia were sent from his offices in Washington, to his home in East Concord, New Hampshire. There they were stored until early 1967, when the senator's widow, Mrs. Doloris Bridges, appointed me as editor.

I will long remember returning to the Bridges house that summer, opening the barn, and gazing upon box upon box filled with records of over thirty years of public and private papers. It was not until late July that my son, Christopher, and I located the gubernatoral papers (1935-37) on the back wall of the second floor of the barn. These papers were neatly stored in thick-gauged three-drawer file cabinets, untouched since Bridges'rapid move from the State House in Concord to the Capitol in Washington in early 1937.

For their unflagging work in the face of adversity, I am grateful for the assistance of Shirley Kiepper and Stephanie and Christopher Kiepper for their initial assistance in organizing the collection.

The papers were removed from the Bridges' barn to New England College in Henniker, New Hampshire, to the newly built H. Raymond Danforth Library. There they remained until they were transferred to the New Hampshire Division of Records Management and Archives in Concord, as the permanent depository. I am deeply grateful for the cooperation of State Archivist Dr. Frank C. Mevers and his able staff Brian N. Burford, state records manager, and Douglas R. Gourley, research assistant, for their invaluable assistance as I continued my research and preparation of the final manuscript.

In addition, I am appreciative for sabbatical leaves in 1973 and 1986 from my teaching responsibilities at the State University of New York at Albany.

Special appreciation is also given to former congressman Perkins Bass, Robert Bass, current congressman Charles Bass; The Gilbert Verney Foundation, and to Richard Verney, president; The Alex Hillman Foundation, and Rita Hillman, president; and the William Loeb Foundation, Nackey Loeb, president. And most especially to Fred Whittemore, whose generous support made the final publication possible, and to Richard Verney, Chairman and Chief Executive Officer of Monadnock Paper Mills, Inc., for his most kind gift of paper for this book.

In addition, I would like to thank the following individuals for their continuing support of the biography: Doris Bridges, the late sister of Senator Bridges, Bruce Bridges, Henry Styles Bridges, Jr., John Fisher Bridges, Stephen Bridges, Robert Burroughs, Anne Carroll, Eliot Carter, Jere Chase, Joyce Guyer Wiggin, Armand Hammer, Ralph Harper, James Hayes, Andrea Helms, Ted Johnson, Harry Kiepper, Albert McFadden, Fred McFadden, Governor Wesley and Beverly Powell, John Piechnik, Ellen and Barry Proctor, Paul Rinden, Angela and Walter Robinson, George Ruddy, Thomas Shannon, Virginia Turner, William Upton, and John Warrington.

And finally to Anne Lunt for her outstanding editorial comments and to Lex Paradis and Al Morris of Phoenix Publishing for their support and encouragement over many years.

J.J.K.

Foreword

EVEN BEFORE THE Associated Press transferred me from Indianapolis to Washington in May 1957, I was quite aware of Styles Bridges. Anybody who followed national politics knew about the savvy Senator from New Hampshire.

Coming from Indiana, I had covered Senator William Jenner, the Hoosier Red-baiting ally of Joe McCarthy, and I thought of Bridges as a New England variety of the McCarthy-Jenner species. Was I ever wrong! I soon found that he could not be limited to one sector of the Republican ideological spectrum.

He was a subtle, sophisticated political leader, and I find nobody in today's Senate comparable to Bridges. A master of negotiations conducted in his hideaway office just off the Senate floor, Bridges flourished during the heyday of the bipartisan Senate oligarchy. Other oligarchs declined in influence with the advent of Lyndon B. Johnson as Majority Leader in the early '50s, but Bridges maintained his leverage as the Republican leader closest to LBJ.

Covering the Senate for the *Wall Street Journal* starting in 1959, I quickly learned that Styles Bridges could be a reporter's best friend. He knew everything that went on in the Senate, and was surprisingly willing to share this information.

He was the prime Republican power broker in the Senate for decades. But it has been nearly 40 years since Bridges died, and such is the meager memory bank of young journalists that they have no awareness about major figures of even a decade ago. James Kiepper has provided a needed portrayal of a man who was a major political figure of his generation.

There was much about Bridges' background that I learned from this biography. I had not realized how humble was his background, how limited was his education and how mundane was his pre-Senate career (as a county agricultural agent).

Nor did I fully realize that a New Hampshire divided between progressives and the old guard, he was clearly a progressive for much of his career.

Even as Senator Bridges moved to the right, he never became an integral part of the conservative movement. Unlike McCarthy and Jenner, he generally supported the Eisenhower Administration, in 1955 asserting: "I am sure that the New Dealers are not pleased with it, and I imagine that the ultraconservatives are not happy either. In my judgment, the administration is following a constructive middle course." That's where he viewed himself: in the middle of the road.

Bridges was no isolationist. He is depicted in *Styles Bridges/Yankee Senator* on December 7, 1941, Pearl Harbor day, as "berating isolationists for delaying war preparations." Biographer Kiepper correctly portrays Bridges mediating between rival Republican ideological factions. Just before his death in 1961, he saved conservative Senator Barry Goldwater's Senate Republican campaign chairmanship from an attempted liberal coup. But anxious to regain the White House after the 1960 election defeat, Bridges was ready to support not Goldwater but the liberal Nelson Rockefeller for president in 1964.

Styles Bridges would be at home in today's Republican Party, which has lost much of its left wing. His attacks on big government, his call for a balanced budget and his advocacy of military preparedness are so close to today's Republican orthodoxy that he is very much in the party's 21st Century mainstream.

James Kiepper has written a meticulously researched and scrupulously fair biography of this forgotten American that does not hesitate to explore two alleged weaknesses of the statesman.

Bridges is seen as a supporter of Joe McCarthy's excesses. But the release of the Venona decryptions of secret Soviet communications and the release of some Kremlin intelligence files has made clear how deeply Moscow penetrated the U.S. government well into the post-war period. Whatever McCarthy's personal shortcomings (which were fully appreciated by Bridges), his accusations had a basis in fact.

The second alleged weakness is more troublesome. At a Senate salary of $12,500, he apparently left bags of cash to his widow and bequeathed a handsome estate. Was Styles Bridges a crook?

Not by the standards of those days. If he accepted money from advocates of positions he already supported, so did a goodly number of his colleagues. The ranks of Senators who arrived in Washington as poor men and left as multi-millionaires were numerous and led by Lyndon B. Johnson.

I would hope that readers of *Styles Bridges/Yankee Senator* would not worry too much about the Senator's financial balance sheet but appreciate a career dedicated to public service and performed with skill. Just as Styles Bridges would not recognize today's Senate where quality has so sharply deteriorated, contemporary Senators and their aides can benefit from studying one of the chamber's forgotten giants.

Robert D. Novak
Syndicated Columnist
CNN Commentator

Styles Bridges

Prologue

Fall 1942

A STAFF CAR SLOWLY made its way up Pennsylvania Avenue. Rain beat against the windshield, and a streak of lightning momentarily illuminated the deserted street.

"Can't see a thing in this dadgummed blackout," the driver grumbled.

As they passed the capitol building, the Senator in the back seat noted a glimmer of light shining behind the heavy blackout curtains. Someone was working late. In fact, many people were working late in wartime Washington.

The car pulled into the drive on the south side of the White House and stopped as two Marine guards stepped in front of the dim lights. "Halt!"

The driver leaned out of the window, gesturing to the back seat. "It's the senator," he said. "Eight p.m. for the President."

The guard peered into the car, checked his rain-soaked list, and waved them ahead. At the entrance, the car door opened as if by a hidden hand, and the senator slipped out. Waving off the open umbrella waiting for him, he moved into the darkened entryway. An aide appeared from a side office and the two men strode down the long hall. They stopped in front of a door where two others stood—Senator Glass (D-Va) and Senator Nye (R-ND), who nodded their greetings. Words were not necessary.

The sound of clacking typewriters drifted down the hall, somewhere a phone rang. In a moment another man joined them, Senator Kenneth McKellar (D-Tenn), breathless from the short walk. The aide ushered the four men into the Oval Office. President Franklin D. Roosevelt, looking weary, was sitting behind his desk. The honey-rich voice, so familiar from radio and newsreels, greeted them.

"Thank you for coming on such short notice, gentlemen. Sit down. I'm afraid there'll not be much sleep until the war is over." Roosevelt gestured to the newspapers on his desk. The war in the Pacific was going badly. A smug Prime Minister Tojo stared out at them from the front page. "I know I don't have to remind you how important it is to keep this meeting secret."

In spite of the tension in the room and the gravity of the situation, Senator Styles Bridges indulged in a secret smile of satisfaction. Hadn't he been a serious contender to preside in this very room? How many Americans could claim that honor? Now the man sitting across from him—the most powerful man in the United States and his adversary for the last ten years—needed his cooperation. Without the help of Senator Bridges, the construction of America's secret weapon would be in jeopardy. The Manhattan Project, creating the atomic bomb that would bring an end to World War II, and would forever change his future, needed congressional funding. Immediately.

While Bridges waited for the president to speak, his mind wandered back in time. It had been a long journey, from a small farm in New England to the nation's capital—to this very moment. A long journey, and a triumphant one . . .

1

I So Move

"This play is called Our Town. *The name of
the town is Grover's Corners, New Hampshire.
The First Act shows a day in our town. The
day is May 7, 1906. The time is just before
dawn . . ."*

Thornton Wilder

OFF TINY COBSCOOK BAY in the eastern corner of Maine, not far from the Canadian border, is the town of Pembroke. In 1900, four roads led to and from the town:

Going west is Route One that travels on to Machias, Ellsworth, and places of consequence. Heading north is the Charlotte road that makes up inland by farms and across blueberry heaths until it ravels out into trails that wind around timber and lakes of the hunting and fishing country. Eastward the highway soon arrives at Eastport and Calais, small city outposts of a great nation. But the road south follows the gray, rocky, spruce-outlined shore for five miles, stops at Leighton's Point, around which the tides are forever swirling. Set at comfortable intervals along this road are story-and-a-half white clapboarded homes built originally by farmers and men who followed the sea. Many a captain of a small coast-plying schooner settled here, where he could keep a weather eye at the same time on his fields and on the bay and boats.

(Doris Bridges, *Growing Up Down East*, Windswept House: 1997)

Veterans of the Revolutionary War settled this area of rocky soil and deep forests when they were given land grants as a reward for their service—and as an incentive to populate the new nation.

Pembroke, named for the town in Wales, was established in 1774, forty-six years before Maine was made a state. One hundred years after its found-

The Pennamaguan Bay and town of Pembroke, Maine

ing, it was the largest city in Washington County, with a bank, a weekly news-paper, and two hotels serving the stage line that connected it with the world. A cheese factory, a sawmill, and several gristmills employed a number of residents. The largest employer was the Pembroke Iron Works, which at its peak operated around the clock, seven days a week. Its cast iron went into ships—schooners and deep-water barks—that traveled the world, carrying the company name to such exotic places as the Sandwich Islands and Tahiti.

In 1880, the town abruptly stopped growing and began to decline. Several factors were to blame: Produce grown in the more temperate West was cheaper and more easily available than that grown in New England; the great stands of timber had been cut; cement had replaced granite in construction, closing the nearby quarries. The hay crop declined as the internal combustion engine began to replace horsepower. Even blueberry canning ceased to be profitable. By 1890, Pembroke's population had dropped to fifteen hundred; the bank, the newspaper, and other signs of prosperity had vanished.

Those who refused to abandon the town displayed a perseverance and a sense of independence often associated with the frugal and taciturn Yankee character. Among those who stayed "way Down East" were the Fisher and Bridges families.

Family Background

John and Polly Bridges were among the first land-grant settlers in the community overlooking the Passamaquoddy tidal basin, just off the Atlantic seaboard. Their great-grandson, Henry Styles Bridges, for whom the senator would later be named, opened a general store in the town in 1861 during its boom period. Profits from the store led to various investments, including a sardine factory. Two of the four Bridges children died—not unusual in an age when the average life expectancy was forty-five years—leaving one surviving son, Earle, born in 1871, to carry on the Bridges name.

Earle Leopold Bridges was easygoing and, unlike his father, not particularly ambitious. By the time he was twenty-five, the Pembroke general store brandished the sign "H.S. Bridges and Son." The affable Earle had been made chairman of the committee in charge of building the new Odd Fellows Hall in town. He had also been elected as one of the three governing selectmen. Even more important—at least to the eligible girls in town—he was good looking, fun to be with, and he owned a good driving horse.

Alina Rozanna Fisher, an independent-minded schoolteacher three years younger than Earle, caught his eye. He courted her in the traditional ways, but she was reluctant to exchange her freedom for marriage. She loved teaching and knew she'd have to give it up once she was a wife. But Earle prevailed, and on a balmy October day in 1897, they were married in a simple ceremony at her parents' home.

After a honeymoon to Boston, the young couple moved to an upstairs apartment in John and Polly Bridges' large three-story home on an elm-lined hill overlooking the Head of Tide. The arrangement proved to be a good one, holding together the large extended family of grandparents, aunts, uncles, and cousins, including the Fisher relatives.

Bridges' Childhood

On September 9, 1898—a warm, sunny day—Alina gave birth to their first child, a boy. They named him for his grandfather, Henry Styles Bridges. His mother favored the middle name, and from the beginning she called him Styles, rather than Henry.

It was a great time to be born. In June of that year the United States flexed its muscle and defeated the Spanish Empire, ousting it from both Cuba and the Philippines. It was "a splendid little war," boasted future president Teddy Roosevelt, its best-known hero. Victory brought confidence, even bravado. There was nothing that Americans couldn't do. Progress! That's what this country was about in 1898— progress, optimism, prosperity, and a never-say-die spirit. Thomas Alva Edison, Henry Ford, and the Wright brothers were about to fulfill this idea of progress.

Across the nation, young women put their hair up in pompadours and donned shirtwaists, ankle-length skirts, and high-button shoes. They

The Bridges homestead in West Pembroke, Maine in 1906

learned to ride two-wheelers, thought of going to college, and perhaps even of voting. They held their chins up in pert imitation of Gibson Girls, the creation of Charles Dana Gibson depicted in such widely read magazines as *Harper's* and *Collier's Weekly.* Young men, scoffing at the formal frock-coats and silk hats of their grandfathers, wore off-the-rack jackets, shirts with celluloid collars, and jaunty derbies. They planned to go into business for themselves, or join with a manufacturing firm and make lots of money.

Immigrants from southern and eastern Europe streamed into New York City. Some crowded into Providence, Hartford, and Boston; a few ventured farther north in search of work in large mills, like the Amoskeag in Manchester, New Hampshire, which at its peak employed up to 17,000 people. America's ethnic mix was changing.

In 1901, just days before the plump and blond Styles was three years old, President William McKinley was shot while attending the Pan-American Exhibition in Buffalo, New York. The new president, Republican Theodore Roosevelt, brought an unprecedented vigor to the nation. His ideas, and the ideas of those around him, including humanitarian Jane Addams and conservationist Gifford Pinchot, influenced generations of public servants. TR's brand of progressivism drew hundreds of bright young people into government service, promising them the opportunity to "make things better."

One of these young progressives was Robert Perkins Bass, who would soon become governor of the Granite State. In 1910, Bass entered the first direct primary election as a Republican candidate, and won. Calling himself a "Roosevelt Republican," Bass won the governorship on a progressive platform—the only Republican candidate for governor to win in any state east of the Mississippi in 1910. It was, as the pundits say, shades of things to come in New Hampshire politics.

There was no problem that couldn't be solved—from the exploitation of children to public drunkenness, from the preservation of parkland to fairness in business—by legislation. Heretofore, government had been seen as a distant overlord; from the turn of the century until the 1980s, it would be seen as an instrument for good, for progress. Those who stood in the way of progressivism were considered reactionaries, selfish and uninterested in the public good.

At this time, three future political leaders of the United States were all growing up in Maine, only a few miles from one another, under vastly different circumstances. A little over twelve miles south of the Bridges' small family farm, was the Campobello estate of the Roosevelt family, where a young Franklin Delano Roosevelt spent his summers at the family "cottage." A hundred miles farther south, at Seal Harbor, stood the massive complex of the 107-room Rockefeller summer home, with its 44 fireplaces, 22 bathrooms, and two elevators, and a commanding view of the Atlantic. There Nelson Rockefeller, who would court Senator Bridges during the presidential nominating process decades later in 1960, grew up among the splendor of one of America's richest families.

While progressives mobilized for reform, two more children were born in the Bridges home in Pembroke, Doris in 1900 and Ronald in 1905. In her unpublished memoirs, *We Three*, Doris recalled: "Although Styles was a year and a half older, from the time I was two and a half, I was as big as he was. He was a slender, average-sized little boy built on small neat bones in the pattern of his Bridges forebears."

Styles carried with him a heavy dose of responsibility, conscientiously watching out for the younger children. From the very beginning, Doris claimed, Styles was quite shrewd in sizing up people and manipulating them to obtain what he wanted. When Alina handed out treats for the children, she appointed Styles as the divider of the cookie or the orange. Noticing that Styles always enjoyed the larger portion, she sat them down and talked to them about being unselfish and offering someone else the bigger piece. The next day she offered the youngsters a plump date-filled cookie with the proclamation: "Here, Styles, you and Doris may have this if you divide it nicely." Styles politely declined the duty saying, "I'm going to let Doris do the 'viding." Pleased that her words had taken root, Alina passed the treat to Doris. Watching her daughter "clumsily separate the cookie into two unequal parts and conscientiously, but wistfully, pass

Class president and captain of the Pembroke High basketball team, 1916

Ten-year-old Styles Bridges and his white Wyandotte hen

Styles with Ronald and Doris in 1908

the bigger piece to Styles, she realized that this time we had both been outsmarted."

Although he diligently kept an eye on his younger siblings, Styles proved willing to manipulate them to serve his wishes.

The severity of Pembroke winters prevented the children from using their playroom in the northwest corner of the house. In January and February, Alina allowed them to move their toys into her bedroom, which was heated by a register and the sun's rays pouring in through a bay window. Doris recalled how they staked out their territory:

> Delighted with the prospect, Styles and I raced into the chilly playroom and filled our arms with our favorite possessions. Then Styles went ahead into the bedroom and looked the situation over. The tall golden oak head-board of our parents' double bed was across one corner. Styles darted behind it, exclaiming gleefully, "This is going to be *my* place. This is the best place in the whole room!" Whereupon I, conscious of so often having come out on the little end of things, shouted, "No! No! I want it! I want it!" At that, Styles, again with an expression of cherubic goodness, said pleasantly, "All right Doris, you can have it. I don't mind." Then while I was arranging my toys in the dark corner behind the headboard, he happily settled in the sunny bay window.

Styles, at a very young age, knew how to work a room.

The children attended the nearby Head of the Tide School, where they were drilled in the three Rs. Only the first floor of the two-story wooden building was used for the school, with all six grades in one room, heated by an iron stove. The second floor was used for town meetings as Liberty Hall. The little school produced some outstanding citizens. William R. Pattangall became chief justice of the Maine Supreme Court, and Charles Best, who graduated the year before Styles Bridges, was the co-discoverer of insulin.

Earle Bridges was not a typical Yankee businessman. He freely passed groceries out to customers, never pressing them for payment. By Doris' account he was a warm, loving father and husband, and Styles doubtless felt very close to him. Occasionally the boy accompanied his father on business to Portland, then replayed the event with Doris.

When Styles was nine, his father fell ill with an undiagnosed sickness; probably heart trouble, although there is some suggestion of alcohol problems in the family. He continued to work at the store, collapsing on the sofa as soon as he got home. On the Fourth of July, a fire destroyed much of the business section of Pembroke—fourteen buildings went up in flames. Earle helped fight the fire, and soon afterward became seriously ill. He died on July 22, 1907. Alina was devastated. On the day of the funeral, Doris recalls, a two-seated, horse-drawn carriage "appeared with [Alina] looking very strange, white and frozen and dressed all in black, and Styles, red-eyed, crumpled in the corner of the back seat." When the family re-turned from the funeral, Alina went to the house filled with friends and relatives as Styles slipped off to the barn by himself. Alina felt as if her whole world had fallen apart. Nine-year-old Styles became "the man of the family." His childhood days were over.

The next few months were a nightmare, as lawyers came and went. "We hated the sight of them," wrote Doris. An inventory of the store was made. "Mother came to realize that when matters were finally settled and all bills paid, there would be little or nothing left. She faced the situation squarely. She had the home and Father's insurance, and she could teach school. Even if teachers did receive only seven or eight dollars a week, she could probably make out with the house, the woodlot and apple orchard, some hens and a cow."

Styles was the only one of the three children to fully appreciate what was happening. Young Doris, still unsure of where her father was, saw his hat and coat hanging in the hall, noticed his cufflinks and collar buttons on the bureau, and asked her mother about him. Alina retreated to her room, "and Styles would turn on me furiously, 'Keep still, Doris! Can't you stop talking!' and then rush off somewhere himself."

The youngster accepted his new role. "No one ever had to remind him of the chores to be done. Woodboxes and water pails were kept filled; the hens were fed and the eggs gathered; the cow was turned out to pasture and brought in again; and every night before going to bed, he checked to see that the doors were locked." Styles also took on odd jobs around town.

Never a healthy child, he came down with scarlet fever in the fall of 1908. He used the time in quarantine to read the *Boston Post*. The front-page stories on the presidential race between William Howard Taft and William Jennings Bryan nurtured his budding interest in politics. He would then move on to the sports pages, where he could savor the exploits of the Boston Red Sox. Once he recovered, his sister recorded, "Styles went his own way, tended strictly to business, and left the socializing to others." He spent much of his free time hiding out and reading—*The Youth's Companion*, novels by Horatio Alger, and other inspirational material. When he acquired copies of *The Boys of '76* and *Stories from American History*, he read them repeatedly, until he knew them by heart and the books were in tatters.

In 1912, when he was fourteen, Styles was sent to a Boston specialist for operations on his throat and nose, probably to remove adenoids and tonsils. After that, he put on weight, becoming husky and strong, and also became socially outgoing, more willing to have fun—sledding in winter, swimming in summer, singing in the Methodist Epworth League, and at-tending moving-picture shows or sporting events in Eastport. One movie

*Pembroke High class of 1916 aboard a steamer from Eastport to Boston for their
senior class trip. Styles is at extreme left.*

he saw that deeply impressed him was D.W Griffith's classic spectacle
Birth of a Nation, a sweeping saga about the development of modern-day
America, from the wreckage of the Civil War and the turbulence of Reconstruction. It was a landmark, controversial film, which President Woodrow
Wilson declared "was like history writ with lightning." One can imagine a
wide-eyed young Styles Bridges, himself a budding student of American
history, mesmerized before the big screen in the days before television and
computers, watching as this story of his nation's history unfolded before him.

While attending Pembroke High School, Styles increased his livestock
to include hens, a Jersey cow, a pig, and a heifer calf. He also worked part
time at the sardine factory and occasionally served as an assistant at the
post office. In his spare time, he played on and captained the Pembroke High
basketball team, enjoyed wagon rides with his teammates to play at other
schools, and kept a close eye on the workings of the town government.

In 1915-16, Styles was elected president of his senior class, which consisted of eleven students. Except in history and current events, he had not
been an outstanding student. He did, however, excel at rhetoric. His mother, too, was an outstanding public speaker and taught her children and students to present themselves with confidence and flair. Styles' brother, Ronald,
later used his public speaking skills to become a successful lay preacher and
the national moderator of the Congregational Church.

"Winning Out" was Styles' selection for his graduation address to the
undergraduates of 1916. He told his classmates that perseverance and self-

*Styles Bridges (at rear), instructor of the Sanderson Academy stock judging team, 1919.
The team won first honors in every stock judging contest entered.*

betterment were important. "Backbone without brains will carry against brains without backbone," he declared, and added, "Don't wait for somebody to give you a lift—do it yourself." When he pounded his right fist into his left hand and shouted, "Remember you are *self* made, or *never* made," the audience applauded long and loud.

War had been declared in Europe in the summer of 1914, but its effects seemed far from the coast of Maine. In 1916 Woodrow Wilson won re-election to the presidency by promising to keep the United States out of the war, and most people believed he would do so. But in a few short years, America found herself embroiled in the War to End All Wars. Maine newspapers carried accounts of the devastation taking place along the front, recounting tales of trench warfare, the horrors of mustard gas, fields of barbed wire guarded by newly developed machine guns. Some of Styles' friends and classmates joined the fray, but the responsibilities of being "the man of the house" kept the young Bridges at home.

College Bound

In an attempt to earn money before leaving for college, Styles worked with great satisfaction in Merle Fisher's grocery store, the same store built by his grandfather and owned and operated by his father. When autumn rolled around, Styles told his mother that Fisher promised him more pay if he stayed. "And you need me here at home. I don't see how you're going to manage with just Doris and Ronald," young Styles reasoned. Alina would have none of it and assured him they would manage. Doris recalled her mother's words to Styles: "You *are going* to college," Alina insisted. "If you stay home this year, you'll never go, and you'll be just another small-town man."

Heeding his mother's warning, Styles enrolled in a two-year course at the University of Maine's College of Agriculture in Orono. Perhaps surprising himself, he became so homesick in Orono that he wanted to abandon the enterprise. Frequently he packed his bag and went to the train station, only to pace the platform all afternoon and trudge back to the campus at dusk. The mere thought of hurting his mother made him persevere.

Styles worked that summer in Gloucester, Massachusetts, at a large market garden farm. He assured his new employers that he could drive a motor car, then set about learning to do so. According to Doris, Styles passed a Sunday in an "out-of-sight corner of the farm, starting, stopping, backing, and turning the truck, until he was sure he had it under control." When delivery time arrived, Styles ably navigated large trucks through Boston traffic.

Styles' best subject at the university was animal husbandry; his only academic subject was English. To help pay his tuition and living expenses, he worked in the university dairy barns, starting his chores at 4:30 A.M., making fifteen cents an hour for his labors.

After two years in Orono, he launched a career in teaching, receiving an appointment as a teacher of agriculture at Sanderson Academy in Ashfield, Massachusetts. He also acted as an athletic coach for the academy and was a consultant to nearby farms.

Styles enjoyed working with farmers more than teaching. After two years at the academy, he took a position as county agricultural agent for Hancock County, Maine. This brought him closer to home, as he settled in Ellsworth in 1920, again visiting farms and meeting farmers. There he organized soil conservation programs, became editor of a farmers' bulletin, and served on the Ellsworth school committee and the local bank board.

Marriage

He also met a pretty young girl named Ella May Johnston from Lamoine, Maine. After a brief courtship, they married. His mother objected to the match. With Doris in the Farmington State Normal School and Ronald about to enter Bowdoin, she felt Styles still owed responsibilities to his own family. However, she bowed to his determination and accepted the marriage.

Early in 1921, Bridges became manager of Thornsen Farms, a thousand-acre enterprise for raising prize Holstein cattle in West Hancock. Henry Styles Bridges, Jr. was born there on July 15, 1921. "I wanted the boy to have a good name; so we chose the best we knew of," Styles wrote to his sister in Boston. "He weighs nine pounds, has blue eyes, lots of hair and is very handsome."

But the euphoria didn't last. The union was not a happy one. Ella, the daughter of a laborer, may not have shared his ambition. Perhaps Styles withdrew into himself, as he had after his father's death; or perhaps, as he was prone to do, he threw himself too deeply into his work. Whatever the reason, Ella sought companionship elsewhere. Styles brought charges of adultery against her, probably as early as 1922. At that time, divorces were difficult to obtain and substantiated proof of guilt was required. The proceedings must have shocked his family and friends, although in typical Yankee fashion, they kept their feelings to themselves. The marriage was formally dissolved in 1924.

After the divorce, Ella wrote to her ex-husband: "Styles dear I can not say more than please forgive me for my wrongs—I am giving my life [their son, Styles Jr.] to you in part payment. I hate to leave my little boy but you can always look after and guide him through life. I pray that god keep you both from harm. '*Goodbye!*'"

Bridges Moves to New Hampshire

Bridges' love of agriculture and an interest in the new farm bureau movement drew him to New Hampshire. The farm bureau movement, part of the Progressive program, sought to use scientific farming methods to increase production. In 1914 Congress created the Agricultural Extension Service, which offered education as well as assistance in the form of machinery and money to farmers. In 1916 the Federal Farm Loan Act passed, offering to underwrite farmers and allow them to buy land and equipment on credit. Eventually farm bureaus offered insurance.

Near the end of 1921, Bridges joined the Agricultural Extension staff at New Hampshire College as a soils and crops specialist, and took up residence in Concord. There he assisted county agents in mapping out demonstration plots, showing farmers new ways to increase their yields. The move to New Hampshire proved critical to Bridges' career. With his unhappy marriage behind him, he resolved to making the most of it. The avenue he chose was politics.

2

The Politics of Organization

"It's restful to arrive at a decision, And rest-
ful just to think about New Hampshire."

Robert Frost

THE 1920s HAD just begun to roar when Bridges left Maine for New Hampshire. The nation had recovered from the devastating effects of World War I in Europe, and Americans wanted, in the words of composer Irving Berlin, "nothing but blue skies, smilin' at me." The good life beckoned from bungalows on Maple Street and high-rise apartments on Michigan Avenue, and especially from offices on Wall Street in New York. As stock prices soared, everyone able to scrape together a few dollars was buying.

Automobiles had become commonplace and airplanes were almost so. Most middle-class families enjoyed such luxuries as a radio, a phonograph, and indoor plumbing. Americans read *The Saturday Evening Post* every week and went to the neighborhood theater to watch Mary Pickford, Douglas Fairbanks, and Buster Keaton.

Two constitutional amendments associated with the Twenties stamped an indelible mark on American culture. The 18th, which went into effect in January of 1920, outlawed "the manufacture, sale or transportation of intoxicating liquors." Although the long crusade for Prohibition had proved successful, no sooner had the amendment been passed than Americans realized that it wouldn't work. "Bathtub gin," organized crime, and widespread corruption followed in its wake.

The 19th Amendment, ratified in August of 1920, gave women the right to vote. With their hair bobbed and their skirts shortened, women enjoyed

16

a new freedom in many aspects of society. Politicians, whether or not they opposed women's suffrage, needed to court this new constituency if they wanted to stay in office.

The pleasantly bland Warren G. Harding of Ohio had been elected president in 1920. Soon afterward, news leaked out that his secretary of the interior had sold oil leases on public land to two businessmen on the sly. In 1923, with the ensuing Teapot Dome scandal threatening his administration, Harding suddenly collapsed and died. The vice-president, New Englander Calvin Coolidge, was sworn in as the twenty-ninth president. Known for his plain talk, his Yankee simplicity and personal honesty, Coolidge had strong popular backing, which ensured an easy election victory in 1924.

New Hampshire offered a uniquely congenial environment to Bridges in 1921. One of the smallest states, both in size and population, it was also one of the most democratic. Two-year terms for governors, rather than the more typical four-year term, made state executives immediately accountable. The four-hundred-seat House of Representatives and the twenty-four-seat Senate (known as the New Hampshire General Court) ensured full representation.

Although politics opened its arms most readily to the wealthy and powerful, even in New Hampshire, it also had room for the occasional promising newcomer whose pockets were empty. That Styles Bridges, without family or status, could so swiftly gain admission to the inner circles of Granite State politics indicates that he demonstrated to his mentors that he could play the game very well.

In 1920, the Republican party, which enjoyed great popular support within the state, was split into two factions—the progressives and conservatives, with the latter known as the Old Guard power brokers. The progressives were generally defined as people who oppose overtly powerful interests, have confidence in the public regulatory agencies, and promote humanitarian efforts. They tend to be middle class and educated. The definition of conservatism is perhaps best reflected by U.S. Senator Carl Curtis (R-Neb.), who stated in an interview:

There are many people who make noises like conservatives, but my thought is that it boils down pretty much to issues involving the sovereignty of the State. It involves an element of States' rights. A conservative, to my mind, is a person who is for pay-as-you-go government, against deficit spending, and is clearly for limited federal government. He does not believe that individuals or businesses, in the absence of disaster or misfortune, needs or should have the crutch of the federal government. A conservative believes that free private enterprise does more good things for more people than a socialist government.

During his term as secretary to the New Hampshire Farm Bureau in the early 1920s Bridges visited farmers in every town and village in the state.

Working for the Farm Bureau

Later, these terms would come to define Bridges himself, during his long tenure in the United States Senate. But for now, Styles became identified with the progressives because of his association with the Farm Bureau and the issues it espoused. George M. Putnam, president of the state Farm Bureau in 1921, welcomed Bridges to New Hampshire, and soon gave him increased responsibility. On July 1, 1922, Bridges was elected secretary of the New Hampshire Farm Bureau Federation. After less than a year on the job with the Farm Bureau, Bridges spoke for Putnam to a variety of organizations. While he also had administrative duties, speaking seemed to occupy most of his time—whether to small groups of farmers, on field days where thousands were in attendance, at school graduations, or to farm bureaus in neighboring states. The topics he covered were diverse: farmers and politics, a proposed gasoline tax, alfalfa and milk production, the precipitous drop in farm prices following World War I, insecticides, the future of farming, the importance of women in the Farm Bureau. An article in April of 1937 in *The Country Home Weekly Magazine*, by Arthur C.

Barlett, entitled "A County Agent Goes to Washington," said of Styles: "He frequently admonished farmers, saying: 'We've got to change enough to keep up with the times, or we'll lose all we've built up.'"

Along the way, he met a man whose friendship would be vitally important in the coming years—former New Hampshire governor Robert Perkins Bass. Although born in Chicago, Bass grew up on the family farm in Peterborough. After graduating from Harvard, he became intrigued with the idea of applying scientific principles to farming and forestry, and eventually became president of the American Forestry Association. Elected as a state representative in 1905, Bass went from the house to the state senate before utilizing his progressive platform in a successful run for governor in 1910. As governor, he supported passage of a Workmen's Compensation Act, and pushed for a child labor law. He also established a state Public Service Commission to regulate public utilities and railroads, a radical move at that time.

Editor of the Granite Monthly

The friendship between Bass and Bridges began with their shared interest in farming, particularly scientific advances in agriculture. In 1924, Bass hired Bridges as an aide. In this capacity, Styles became editor of the *Granite Monthly*, a forty-year-old magazine Bass had purchased to promote the Republican party. The periodical also printed recipes, farm news, necrologies, an occasional Robert Frost poem, and other items of local interest. In taking on these new responsibilities, Styles resigned his position with the Farm Bureau. Upon receiving Bridges' letter of resignation, George Putman, who thought very highly of Styles, wrote in response:

> It is with sincere regret that I place [your letter] before our executive committee for action. In your decision to sever your connection as its secretary, the Farm Bureau Federation loses an efficient officer, and an able, sincere, and enthusiastic supporter of the objectives and purposes of the organization.
> The service you have rendered to agriculture is appreciated by farm people in all sections of the State.
> Your resignation is to me, a distinct personal loss. You came to us an entire stranger to take up with me what was to both of us a comparatively new undertaking, and during the year and a half you have acted as secretary, we have worked hand in hand in an honest effort to render helpful service to the farm people of the State, and it is with a feeling of deep personal regret that I present your resignation to our executive committee. I congratulate you on your future prospects, in your new position, and offer to you any further assistance it may be in my power to give.

No one, not even Bridges himself, could imagine just where his future prospects would carry him. For now, Styles threw himself into this new

Poster from the unsuccessful 1926 U.S. Senate campaign of former Governor Robert P. Bass managed by Styles Bridges

position with his characteristic drive and dedication. Young Norris Cotton, soon to be elected as a state representative, was hired to compile articles for the magazine. Bridges and Cotton became lifetime friends, as their political careers meshed and constantly crossed each other in the years ahead.

The 1924 Gubernatorial Campaign

Bridges' work in the 1924 campaign, aided by Cotton, began in the primary. They were to secure the selection of state senator John Gilbert Winant as the Republican gubernatorial candidate over Frank Knox, publisher of the *Manchester Union Leader*. Knox was the Old Guard candidate, and fell under the progressive surge in the primary. After Winant's primary victory, Bridges was given the assignment of handling the unique speakers' bureau, forerunner of the Republican flying squadrons, in which a group of speakers would barnstorm a state or a region, addressing as many people as possible. In a feat which clearly showed his strong organizational skills, Bridges arranged for as many as ten rallies a day during October, as the speakers' bureau criss-crossed the state, drumming up support for Winant. Winant, a handsome former schoolmaster at St. Paul's Preparatory School in Concord, was highly intelligent, but so shy he was almost inarticulate. The strategy was so successful that Winant was elected governor for the first of three terms, in a surprise upset over the incumbent, Democrat Fred H. Brown of Somersworth, a one-time professional baseball player.

The governor's ball and reception following Winant's inauguration was one of the most brilliant in New Hampshire history. Some 1,400 residents passed through the receiving line. Two bands furnished music for dancing under red, white, and blue lights, and the refreshment tables stood beneath bowers of evergreens. Styles Bridges had served on the organizing committee.

Bass was so impressed with Bridges' performance in the 1924 campaign that he made him the agent in charge of supervising the Bass family investments. A year later, Bridges received a commission as a second lieutenant in the Quartermaster Corps of the Army Reserve, something that proved to be an important move politically.

In 1926, Bass, emboldened by the Winant victory, ran for the U.S. Senate in the Republican primary against the Old Guard incumbent, George Higgins Moses of Concord, one of the most powerful men in New Hampshire politics. Bass chose Bridges as his campaign manager. Governor Winant also toyed with the idea of bidding for Moses' seat. His indecision proved fatal for both himself and Bass. By the time Winant became persuaded to run again for governor instead of the Senate, Moses was the favorite for the Senate seat. Huntley N. Spaulding, a wealthy Rochester industrialist and brother of a former governor, mounted a hefty challenge against Winant. On primary day, 1926, the Old Guard swept both nominations by large majorities.

Bridges was bitter and angry about this setback, but he learned from it. The Republican party, he decided, could not afford rancor or recrimination. Party unity must transcend ideology, shifting alliances, and individual ambitions. In later years, he often remained neutral during primary fights and always supported the Republican ticket, regardless of who ran.

After the 1926 election, Bridges settled down to manage Bass' affairs, including his New Hampshire Investment Company. Bridges retained interest in scientific farming, and in 1927 was considered for the position of executive secretary of the American Farm Bureau Federation. At its national convention, he was defeated by only two votes.

Marriage to Sally Clement

More important for Bridges in 1927 was his courtship of schoolteacher Sally Clement of Concord. After meeting her on several occasions, he wrote a recommendation for her to the Concord school board. Their romance blossomed. Bridges' family and friends liked Sally and encouraged the union. An engagement was announced in November, and they were married on June 30, 1928, at the South Congregational Church in Concord.

Soon after they exchanged marriage vows, Bridges returned to the political trail. The 1928 state presidential primary resulted in a slate of delegates to the Republican National Convention pledged to support moderate Herbert Hoover.

Campaigning for Charles W. Tobey

The Old Guard U.S. Senator George Higgins Moses barely won a delegation seat to the convention, leading progressives to believe they could win back the governor's chair. They felt the man to do it was Charles W. Tobey. Tobey, former president of the F.J. Hoyt Shoe Company of Manchester, had served as selectman for the village of Temple and chairman of New Hampshire's Liberty Loan campaign during World War I. (Passed by Congress in April 1917, the Liberty Loan Act approved the sale of Liberty Bonds to raise money for the Allied forces.) His dynamic speaking style elevated him to house speaker and senate president.

Tobey had begun his political career as a progressive in 1913, when he denounced state plans to build a highway that would bypass his town. He pointed out that the bypass would enrich an Old Guard legislator who owned land along the right-of-way. Tobey won his battle, and the highway that eventually bore his name was constructed through Temple. Tobey often tangled with the Old Guard while he was presiding in the legislature. His campaign style was closer to preaching than speech-making; he often quoted the Bible, or Latin and Greek verse, using his rhetoric and passion to sway audiences.

As the progressives united behind Tobey for governor, Bridges was chosen to head the campaign, a major vote of confidence for the thirty-year-old newcomer. It promised to be a tough fight. Senator Moses, determined to win a renomination for Governor Spaulding, did everything in his power to derail Tobey's campaign. He personally rigged the state Republican convention to prevent Tobey from delivering an address. Then he persuaded pro-Moses newspapers to avoid mentioning that Spaulding would be opposed in the primary.

These handicaps made it difficult to organize an effective campaign, but Bridges put his skills and his amicable personality to work. By visiting every town and village in the Granite State while secretary to the Farm Bureau, he was able to build on personal contact for his later gubernatorial race. Everyone knew him as Styles, and in most cases he had a friend for life. His friendliness was tempered with the reserve of the professional politician with one eye on the vote count. Bridges often greeted people by doffing his hat and offering a rustic "How-aya." The greeting was always accompanied by a ready smile, and often with a personal greeting, for another Bridges talent was the ability to recall names and small details in the lives of people he had only met once or twice. And with each such greeting, Bridges knew he had gained a lifelong supporter. By then, too, he had an impressive knowledge of names and political connections to tap. Bridges' organizational talent and Tobey's speech-making style carried the day. Tobey defeated Governor Spaulding by a large majority.

The 1928 campaign gave Bridges a significant base of support and led to his increased involvement in statewide political life. Still a young man, he had many more relationships to cultivate before considering himself ready to run for office, but his course was clearly set toward a career in public service. For a while he made no moves to capitalize on his strength. Instead, he settled back into his position as chief aide to Bass. He did not step completely out of the public eye, however. A 1929 editorial in the *Merrimack Valley Sun* noted wryly:

> I hear that the Republican party in New Hampshire is run by—What is your guess? John Winant, George Moses, Huntley Spaulding, Charles Tobey? I have reliable information acquired at some expense to the effect that the man who pulls the strings in the Republican ranks . . . is Styles Bridges. It is something of a romance that this good looking and attractive young man who came over from Maine to help . . . in Farm Bureau affairs, should not tell John Winant and George Moses to come hither or get thither without an if, yes, or perhaps. If my information is correct, if you

are a good Republican and want to know where you get off, go to Styles and he will tell you.

The Public Service Commission

Perhaps it was that popularity, as well as an appreciation for his work in the campaign, that motivated Governor Tobey to sponsor Bridges for appointive office. In May 1929, John W. Storrs, chairman of the Public Service Commission, announced his retirement, and Tobey nominated Bridges as his replacement.

Governor Bass had established the PSC in 1911, with the immediate goal of reducing the political power of the Boston & Maine Railroad, which had rankled New Hampshire residents with its high-handed tactics. The PSC was instructed to regulate the railroad and other utilities by supervising their rates and financial operations. For instance, the railroad could no longer issue free passes as political favors, and a fair evaluation of railroad property would be required for taxation. The Old Guard, favoring the railroad, repeatedly tried to curtail PSC operations. They immediately opposed Tobey's nomination of Bridges, a progressive, to the commission.

Under the New Hampshire constitution, gubernatorial nominations had to be approved by the executive council. In short order, the power companies and their political allies induced the council to vote down Bridges' nomination.

Furious, Styles wrote in a letter to his brother, Ronald:

> The reason is that the big power interests . . . do not want anyone on the Commission who is honest and who has backbone enough to stand up to them, and they cannot control. The New Hampshire papers are full of it and the big issue of the future here will be Power vs. the People's Rights . . . People tell me that it is rumored on the street that the power interests have made their brags that they would spend $100,000 dollars to keep me from being approved. I expected to have some support in the Council, and on the afternoon before, the reports were that I would be confirmed by three [of the five], but all turned over during the night, or at least before the Council met the next morning. The fight has just started on the thing, however, and promises to become one of the leading issues of the year between the liberal and the old line bunch: the Old Guard championing the power interests and the liberal group standing for the people against the power interests.

Governor Tobey resubmitted Bridges' nomination at once. The council promptly rejected it a second time, even though seven former Republican governors endorsed Bridges. Tobey then made a surprise maneuver: He nominated former Governor John Gilbert Winant for the appointment, and for the first time in Granite State history a former chief executive was voted down. However, the Winant rejection split the Old Guard forces, and the progressives successfully portrayed this rebuff as the use of petty politics to obstruct the functions of a vital state agency.

In the midst of this turmoil, a young Norris Cotton rapped on Governor Tobey's door and informed him that if he submitted Bridges' name once more, it would go through. Tobey did, and Cotton's prediction came to pass. Later, according to Raimond Bowles of Tobey's staff, the governor believed he gathered enough evidence that Bridges informed those on the Public Service Commission that they had a friend in him. This constituted a sellout in Tobey's eyes and the two men were never again friendly.

Early in 1930, Tobey decided not to seek a second term. Winant announced that he would run for governor again. His campaign issue would be the executive council and who controlled it—the people or the Old Guard and their cronies. The Old Guard moved to stop the Winant bid.

Because of his new position, Bridges sat out the 1930 fall election. Winant was elected governor for a second term and the progressives stayed in control of the legislature. The PSC job, guaranteed for six years at a salary of five thousand dollars, gave Bridges a certain amount of security. He continued to assist Bass occasionally during the next few years, but the pair slowly drifted apart after the appointment and as Bridges began to veer to the political right.

Personal and family problems beleaguered Bridges through 1929 and 1930. He had several teeth removed in an effort to improve his health. His brother, Ronald, was rushed to a Boston hospital, desperately ill. Diagnosed with acute arthritis, Ronald would have to contend with the condition for the rest of his life. Their mother, too, became so ill that Doris had to take a leave from teaching to care for her.

Family Concerns

October 8, 1929 marked the birth of Bridges' second son, David Clement. Styles bragged about the newest addition to the progressive cause, and Sally welcomed the chores of motherhood. Homemaking was always first with her, and her skillful management of domestic details complemented Bridges' work habits. For socializing, Sally enjoyed a quiet dinner with friends. Although she often accompanied her husband on political trips, her role was more ornamental than participatory. She sat on the platform with Styles, but brought her knitting bag along and kept to the background.

With David's birth, Bridges' concerns over money increased. Three weeks later, on Black Thursday, October 29, 1929, the stock market crashed. Within months, the Great Depression of the 1930s gripped the nation. Like many Americans, Bridges had invested modest sums in stocks rather than savings. Through his handling of the Bass investments, he joined the vogue of "buying on the margin," and when the value of stocks collapsed, his carefully constructed finances were in ruins. The loss was a crushing blow to Bridges, as it was to thousands of Americans. Norris Cotton recalls that the normally reserved Bridges "sat down and cried like a baby. He said that he had lost everything. It was a terrible blow to him. I think that intensified his desire not to be poor again." With the stock market crash, and the resultant loss of his position handling the Bass family investments, Bridges' job with the PSC became even more important.

As the junior member of the commission, he had to work closely with the other commissioners—former governor Fred Brown and attorney Mayland H. Morse of Concord. (Morse was, in fact, also Maine born, coming from Eastport, ten miles from Pembroke.) Under Bridges' urging, they developed a standard policy of rural electrification.

No one knew better than farm women what stringing power lines across the countryside could mean. Electrification brought electric washing machines, irons, refrigerators, mixmasters, toasters, vacuum cleaners, sterilizers, and other appliances that would ease much of the drudgery of farm life. Bridges understood their needs. He commented to a *Manchester Union Leader* reporter in October of 1934, "When you've gone to bed by candle light and done your morning milking by lantern, you appreciate what power means to common people."

Any hope the Old Guard held that Bridges' appointment would remove him from the political scene died, for commission activities kept him in the public eye. With his support, the PSC implemented electric-rate reductions in urban areas. It also supervised the conversion of plants generating power for electric trolleys from private to public use, as that form of transportation disappeared. Bridges' reputation as an administrator enhanced his political standing through the state.

The Gentleman Farmer

On February 11, 1933, Sally Bridges gave birth to another son, John Fisher Bridges. At about the same time, Henry Styles, Jr., who had returned to Ellsworth with his mother after the divorce, joined the family. Needing more room, the Bridges family moved to a modest white, L-shaped farmhouse with twelve acres of land in East Concord, site of the first settling of Concord in 1727. A poultry flock flourished and a lamb was added now and then.

Bridges pictured himself as a gentleman farmer and enjoyed telling associates about "life on the farm." A group of Concord businessmen decided to test Bridges' agricultural knowledge and left a pig in a crate inside his garage while the family was away. As soon as he returned home, Bridges constructed a pen. The "gift" was raised and butchered in due time at a weight of 260 pounds. What started as a practical joke soon turned into valuable publicity among rural folk.

Sally comfortably settled into family life at the East Concord house. Flower beds, vegetable gardens, and fruit trees blossomed under her care. She canned vegetables in the fall and knitted year round to provide for her growing family. Dressed in a simple sweater, skirt, and sports shoes, Sally rose from her work in the flower beds alongside the house to exchange greetings with passing neighbors. A story in the *Boston Advertiser* on October 14, 1934, described her tan face, bright eyes, wavy brown hair, and unaffected manner which endeared her to everyone around her.

Country life seemed to agree with Styles, Sally, and their family.

The 1932 election was a grim affair for the Republican party. President Herbert Hoover's efforts to cope with the Great Depression proved ineffective. Unemployment mounted at an alarming rate, and bankruptcies flooded the country. Manufacturing firms cut back on production as consumer demand dropped.

In the summer of 1932, a dramatic and troubling event took place in Washington, one which would change the landscape of American politics. During the hot months of June and July out-of-work veterans, calling themselves the Bonus Army, descended on the capital. They were seeking a bonus promised to them for their service in the First World War. The money was not due to be paid until 1945, but these were desperate men. In his book *Redeeming the Time* (McGraw-Hill, 1987) Page Smith states: "The army was like an assemblage of ghosts." A ragged group, with hollow cheeks and sunken eyes, the Bonus Army represented the true depth of the Great Depression—men for whom work, home, pride, and dignity were but distant memories. By mid-July, the chief of police in Washington reported that some 23,000 veterans, with their families, were encamped on the flats beside the Anocostia River in Washington, living in improvised shacks, with little in the way of sanitation. As the heat of summer spread across the city, Congress recessed without passing the Bonus Army's demands. (In fact, the House had passed a measure calling for early payment of the bonus, but the Senate did not.) Infuriated by their government's seeming lack of compassion, several hundred veterans picketed the White House, while others took over abandoned houses in the area. On July 28, the police were called in to evict the squatters. The veterans pelted the police with bricks and rocks, and the police opened fire on the veterans, killing two and injuring several more. As the situation got further out of control, the police called for army support. President Hoover then ordered Secretary of War Patrick Hurley to remove the men from the abandoned buildings.

As Americans saw the pictures and read the heartrending accounts of the displaced veterans, who were summarily driven from Washington in army vehicles, and dropped by the side of the road to make their way back home as best they could, it marked the end for Hoover and the beginning of Roosevelt's promise of a New Deal.

In that summer of 1932, Democrats nominated New York governor Franklin D. Roosevelt as their standard bearer. He promised much, from full employment to the end of Prohibition. While his platform lacked specifics, he offered a spirit of hope. The electorate was ready for a change, and had given indications along this line in the 1930 election, by electing a Democratic House and reducing the Republican Senate majority to a single member.

In New Hampshire, the unemployment rate was 33 percent. Governor Winant had proposed a four-day work week, with additional hours to be divided among workers in an attempt at job sharing.

In the face of disaster, Republican factors united. Governor Winant and Senator Moses temporarily forgot their differences and joined hands for re-election bids. Because of rivalry among its members in the urban areas, the Democratic party had become rather ineffective. Americans of Irish and French descent opposed each other so vehemently that at times Republicans dominated the voting in their wards. Democrats closed ranks in the 1932 election, however, with the Depression being the dominant issue, and provided a surprise upset.

Democrats slated former governor Fred Brown for the U.S. Senate against George Moses, and Brown defeated the Old Guard champion by a scant 2,100 votes. Governor Winant easily won reelection, and Tobey was elected to Congress, launching his colorful career in Washington. The 1932 election sounded the death knell of the Republican Old Guard, and in the ensuing decade a younger breed of conservatives succeeded Moses and the Old Guard.

While Bridges maintained neutrality in this campaign, it did not stop him from accepting speaking engagements throughout the state, in which he stressed Americanism and emphasized the values of pride in New Hampshire and its way of life. He addressed the Kiwanis, the American Legion, the Odd Fellows, and a variety of other clubs and service organizations in most of which he was an active member.

In the summer of 1933, Bridges assessed his political future. After seeking the advice of Bass and others, he began to put together an organization of his own. He turned to Ted Johnston of Manchester (later known as The Kingmaker), a proven Republican party campaigner, who mustered the support of Ralph Langdell, also of Manchester, and William Jackson of

Nashua. Another valuable campaign ally was Norris Cotton, who had returned to Lebanon to practice law after graduating from Georgetown Law School and working for Senator Moses in Washington.

The only remaining obstacle was Governor Winant. There was talk that he might run for yet another term. Instead, at the behest of President Roosevelt, Winant moved to Washington, where he became the first director of the Social Security system.

Bridges' Goal—the Governor's Office

With the progressive wing firmly with him, Bridges announced for governor on September 14, 1933, more than a year before the election. He explained why he was declaring so early: "I am making this announcement now in order that my intentions may be known. However, it is not my present plan to make an active campaign until shortly before the primaries, and I shall continue to devote my time and energy to the performance of my duties as a Public Service Commissioner."

Despite the announcement that he would not begin campaigning yet, privately Bridges meticulously constructed an organization that proved such an effective instrument in 1934 that it became a model for the rest of his career.

His major problem was money. To start with, according to Ted Johnston, the campaign had only about a thousand dollars on hand. It was in order to cope with this fiscal shortage, that Bridges announced his candidacy early. He wanted time to speak to small groups across the state. This strategy worked well for two reasons. First, meeting in homes, rather than in large halls, saved the cost of rent and other supplies. Second—and even more important—Styles performed better as a speaker when he addressed small groups. He was able to create a sense of intimacy that bound people to him. (This was ironic; according to his sons, that sense of intimacy was never noticeable at home.)

Bridges was not an orator in the classic sense. He did not speak forcefully before large crowds, as Tobey and Cotton did. However, he was in constant demand as a speaker, and by 1934 he had fourteen years' experience appearing before all kinds of groups. He was at his best flashing his friendly grin and discussing issues with a few people at a time. His phenomenal ability to remember names and circumstances was of inestimable value, and his great strength was his ability to speak in terms that people understood, to touch on issues that interested them. He used down-home language and metaphors that farmers and small-town residents understood. Instead of using the press and radio, he spoke directly to citizens. By the close of the campaign, he had made more than three hundred speeches.

Poster from Bridges 1934 gubernatorial campaign

Until May of 1934, Bridges' gubernatorial rival was Francis P. Murphy, a wealthy Nashua shoe manufacturer and a member of Winant's executive council. Then, abruptly, Murphy withdrew his name, and the glib-tongued mayor of Laconia, Charles E. Carroll, also a member of Winant's executive council, announced his candidacy.

Carroll had an abrasive personality. He launched what Bridges labeled a "campaign of vilification." While publicly ignoring Carroll, Bridges warned his supporters, "We cannot take him too lightly because he will stoop to any level to gain his end."

Carroll accused Bridges of campaigning at the state's expense, and not fully tending to his PSC duties. On August 23, 1934, the *Concord Monitor* quoted Bridges' campaign manager, Edgar H. Hunter of Hanover, a former Winant aide: "If we require all public servants to sever their connections with the public payroll before aspiring to political office in the state, we would automatically lose the possible services of some extremely valuable men." Hunter's logic silenced much of Carroll's rhetoric on that issue, but he continued to criticize the Winant administration and Bridges' close association with it.

Carroll's denunciations of the Winant regime won him some support, because it was generally thought that Bridges was controlled by the Winant forces. While Bridges ignored this charge at first, it began to infuriate him. He did not want to be linked to Winant, for he strongly clung to his political independence. Time and time again he asserted, "I am standing absolutely on my own two feet, and I am not obligated to anyone, nor do I propose to be dominated by anyone."

The intensity of the Winant-Bridges accusations lessened when Bridges announced that he favored decentralization of relief programs, a stance that was in direct contradiction to Winant's stand for state supervision of welfare. Bridges, a proponent of "local control," felt the state should play only a supervisory role in many public areas, including welfare.

"Pay-As-You-Go Basis"

Bridges also called for unification of the Republican party and stabilization of New Hampshire's economy. The first point drew the friendly attention of some of the Old Guard forces, as they appreciated the long-range value of party harmony. Bridges also espoused a minimum wage law, unemployment insurance, and the development of recreational and natural resources in the state. Despite promising new programs, he emphasized that a state cannot spend itself out of a depression, declaring, "I am opposed to any increase in the state debt, and I favor a pay-as-you-go basis."

By the time the September 11 primary arrived, Bridges was weary. He had campaigned strenuously in all sections of the state. His efforts were rewarded by a 2-to-1 victory over Carroll, which led to the slogan: "They may sing their Carrolls, but New Hampshire needs its Bridges."

A period of peace within the party followed the primary. Carroll pledged his support to Bridges, as did Moses, who declared, "I am a Republican without prefix, suffix, or descriptive adjective." Bridges was hailed as the "greatest conciliator" the Republican party had enjoyed in many years. After the primary, Styles and Sally slipped away to the international yacht races at Newport, Rhode Island, for a rest.

His Democratic opponent, attorney John L. Sullivan of Manchester, similarly revitalized himself in Bermuda after his own primary battle. A popular and energetic party leader, Sullivan's only weak spot was the French bias against his Irish Catholic heritage. He was an ardent supporter of President Roosevelt and his New Deal, and the national Democratic party contributed generously to his campaign.

1934 Gubernatorial Campaign

The 1934 gubernatorial campaign revolved, for the most part, around the personalities of Bridges and Sullivan. The party platforms were strikingly similar, liberal in tone, focusing on minimum wage, labor conditions, relief, unemployment insurance, and improving the economy. Both men were young and effective speakers: Sullivan with his polished and accurate diction, and Bridges with his down-to-earth forthright phrases, sprinkled with mispronunciations. (Bert Teague, a Bridges' legislative assistant in Washington, recalled years later how the staff vainly tried, in long office sessions, to train Bridges to say "specific," which invariably came out as "pacific.")

Bridges gained attention through a novel "Flying Squadron" technique, organized by attorney Thomas F. Cheney of Laconia, chairman of the GOP state committee. The major Republican candidates toured the state together, appearing at jointly scheduled rallies, saving both time and money. The scheme was copied from the textile union, which sponsored similar units of speakers who visited mills to recruit members.

Cheney also set up additional speaking schedules for Bridges, as many as three a day, excepting Sundays, and he provided notes for Bridges' speeches. The notes consisted of words to remind Bridges of the topics to be covered, along with a punchline for an anecdote to amuse the audience. Sally occasionally accompanied her husband on these sorties, always carrying her knitting bag, with its embroidered hunting scene. Her quiet, homey presence contributed to Bridges' popularity. The perennial knitting bag eventually became a campaign joke, a symbol of Bridges' "good old New England economy" theme.

Bridges' campaign lacked the customary financial resources from outside the state. Roosevelt dominated the national scene, and Republican fund-raising was practically nonexistent. Bridges' own limited finances were also a hindrance. He had to depend almost entirely on volunteer workers. Resourceful as always, he made it part of his campaign strategy to stress that "a poor man" could become governor of the state of New Hampshire, giving voters the impression that "Bridges is a regular guy."

What pleased Bridges most in his first political campaign was the harmony his candidacy created in the Republican party. There was no infighting. As a tribute to his leadership, all seven living former Republican governors publicly endorsed him: Winant, Tobey, Bass, the brothers Rolland H. and Huntley N. Spaulding, Albert O. Brown, and Henry W. Keyes, then serving in the U.S. Senate. They all praised his thrift, political experience, and public service.

New Hampshire's citizenry correctly looked ahead to a close race on November 6. In the final weekend before the voting, a surprise ploy shook Manchester, the state's largest city and a Democratic stronghold. A rumor was circulated that Sullivan had said, with regard to the demands of the French community for another bridge over the Merrimack River, "Let the frogs hop across the lily pads." This rumor was allegedly spread by Bridges' supporters, and with the Tuesday election less than forty-eight hours away, Sullivan never had full opportunity to deny the canard. It hurt him badly at the polls. Bridges defeated Sullivan by only 2,462 votes, and he garnered more votes in Manchester's French-speaking wards than any other Republican on the state ticket. Even twenty-five years later, according to John Warrington, the quotation quickly brought a twinkle to Bridges' eye and an unconvincing denial to his lips.

Bridges was one of only seven Republican governors elected nationwide in the 1934 election. The usually reserved Bridges became so overjoyed, so exuberant as the returns were posted, that he later wrote his brother, Ronald, who was present at the celebration, apparently compelled to explain his uncustomary jubilance, "I am sorry I was not my normal self."

After savoring piles of congratulatory telegrams and letters, and smiling into countless cameras, Bridges prepared to assume the greatest honor and responsibility of his thirty-six years.

3

New Hampshire Orator; We Can't Spend Our Way Out of the Depression

---

*"He who lies beneath surrendered office,
place and power, rather than bow down
and worship slavery."*

Inscription on the statue of John P. Hale,
U.S. Senator from New Hampshire

A S CONCORD prepared to greet its new governor, a blinding snow-storm blanketed the city with a foot of snow. The roads were finally cleared on January 2, as tumbling temperatures placed the capital in winter's icy grip. The next morning, governor-elect Bridges rose to prepare for his trip to Representatives Hall at the State House. Mindful of the primitive heating arrangement in the hall, and his own poor health, Styles slipped on a pair of thick blue woolen socks with his formal attire. When he presented himself to the Bridges women, his mother and sister refused to let practicality overrule good taste. A quick trip to a clothier for proper hosiery preceded their trip to the inaugural.

Bridges' Inaugural

On January 3, 1935, a bright, cold morning, a car turned off North Main Street onto Capitol Street in Concord. It stopped in front of the three-story capital building, and its passenger stepped out. Briskly striding along the freshly shoveled walk, Bridges passed under the granite arch, nodded at

34

Governor Bridges and his family following his inauguration

the bronze statues of Franklin Pierce and Daniel Webster, and proceeded into the building. He hurried by the Hall of Flags, scarcely glancing at the murals of New Hampshire history, and took the broad staircase to the second floor, to the deserted room where the General Court of New Hampshire would soon meet.

There, at twelve o'clock, the state's 64th chief executive was sworn in by repeating these words: "I, Henry Styles Bridges, do solemnly swear and affirm that I will faithfully and impartially discharge and perform all duties incumbent on me as Governor according to the best of my abilities, agreeably to the rules and regulations of this constitution and the laws of New Hampshire. So help me God."

An eighteen-gun salute boomed in the background. The newly sworn Governor Bridges—at thirty-six, the youngest governor in the nation, and the youngest ever elected to that office in New Hampshire—turned to the assembly before him, comprised of members of the legislature, government officials, the press, friends, and family.

Bridges had spent the previous two months preparing for this moment. He began, "While we have many problems to meet, diverse and complex in character, New Hampshire is in better condition to carry forward than many of our sister States. Gathered here today we can rejoice that we still enjoy our traditional form of government and are a solvent people." Bridges identified relief measures as New Hampshire's greatest challenge, with forty thousand people listed on the relief rolls. However, he declared, "I am one of those who do not believe we can spend our way out of the Depression." Careful management of expenditures, with local control and responsibility for relief measures, marked the surest path back to prosperity, he declared. Bridges presented a comprehensive outline of recommendations for resolving the state's problems. His voice was imbued with a confidence that allowed his listeners to take heart.

After his inaugural address, Governor Bridges administered the oath of office to his executive council members: James C. Farmer of Newbury, Lynn Cutler of Berlin, Burt R. Cooper of Rochester, Thomas J. Leonard of Nashua, and Alphonse Roy of Manchester. Members, who are elected on the general ballot, actually share the governor's responsibilities, in addition to advising him. They also have the power of veto over the governor's actions and make appointments to various state agencies.

Then the governor and his council formed a receiving line in the council chamber for a simple reception. Sally Bridges stood on one side of her husband, Alina Bridges on the other. Doris and Ronald were also present. Doris laughed to see outgoing Governor Winant, who later served as Roosevelt's ambassador to England during World War II, wearing the same kind of heavy wool socks with his formal wear that the Bridges women had made Styles remove.

When the reception ended, Bridges signed a paper with a flourish, and handed it to his mother. It read, "The first stroke of the Governor's pen is for you, Mother." She broke into joyful tears. Before his family returned to Maine, the governor presented them with subscriptions to the *Manchester Union Leader*, so they could follow his activities. With the largest circulation in the state, this newspaper would eventually become one of Styles' closest friends. Chicago native Frank Knox was then publisher. He would soon make his mark on national politics.

In 1932, because of the Depression, Winant had canceled the traditional governor's ball. Despite the continuing hard times, however, Bridges decided to hold the affair, although along low-key, frugal lines. The festival would exhilarate Concord residents, who were tired of daily reminders of the grimness of life. The city buzzed with excitement as local shops were jolted out of Depression-induced doldrums by requests for tuxedos, gowns, and accessories.

Bridges' frugality eliminated the traditional buffet, and the punch noticeably lacked the quality promised by its name. Still, the event successfully netted more than eight hundred dollars for charity, and further strength-

Newly elected Governor Bridges and his family in their East Concord home in 1935

ened the bond between the governor and the people. Who wore what was reported in the newspapers the next day, and Bridges received his due: "Governor Bridges wore a clean shave and his black pants, and bowed to all salutations like a graceful door hinge."

Tackling the New Job

Back at the office early the next morning, Governor Bridges went to work on solutions to cope with the state's economic problems. A disturbing discrepancy had developed between income and spending, and stabilization of New Hampshire's finances was a top priority. He found the "financial difficulties were due more to over-estimating revenue than to under-estimating expenditures," and stressed the importance of thrift and the dangers of increasing state indebtedness. He adamantly opposed the new federal doctrine of spending as a means to control or end the Depression.

"I have come to the conclusion that no Governor has ever entered the Governor's chair with such grave responsibilities facing him," Styles wrote to his friend, former governor Robert Bass. For certain, no one had ever entered the governor's chair with so little in the way of personal assets. Because of this, according to New Hampshire's legislative historian Leon Anderson, the 1935 legislature increased the governor's traditional personal contingency fund of $1,500 a year, to $9,000, for Bridges' term only. Unemployment and relief problems harassed the nation, and New Hampshire had its share of suffering. One out of every eleven Granite State citizens was dependent upon relief for a livelihood. Farm prices fell 53 percent between 1932 and 1939.

The mills cut back on production, laying off hundreds of workers, and several small manufacturing plants closed. At that time, New Hampshire ranked second in the nation in the proportion of its working population engaged in manufacturing.

Bridges found thousands of job applications on his desk, and the pile grew daily. For a single state position, there were 172 applications, of whom 135 were on a first-name basis with him. Things were so bad that one day the newly elected governor took more than an hour to cross Main Street between the State House and a restaurant—he was stopped twenty-seven times by people pleading for jobs.

He commented later that his one regret about the governorship was in making appointments to public office. He was forced to reject many qualified individuals, simply because there was so much competition for each available position. With every appointment he made a friend for life, but many more were disappointed.

The problem of unemployment was more than just dollars and cents; unemployment could mean a loss of security, pride, and spirit. When those were gone, communities were hurt by more than just the tangible loss of jobs. Occasionally, Styles attempted to lighten the stress by quoting Mark Twain, who, when asked if there was anything worse than having scarlet fever and diphtheria at the same time, answered, "Why, yes, having rheumatism and St. Vitus dance at the same time."

Most of New Hampshire's fifty-four newspapers were favorable toward the new governor, and they liked his announcement that he would be available daily to newsmen to answer questions. He maintained this openness to the press all his career, learning to genially deflect questions that he didn't want to answer.

Less than two months after taking office, Bridges made his first request to the legislature. The state's emergency relief program had expired in December of 1934, leaving varied debts. Although opposed to borrowing funds and increasing the state debt, he proposed that the state borrow $400,000 to pay off back relief bills, allowing his administration to start with a fresh slate. His council concurred and the legislature readily approved the loan.

Before his inauguration, Bridges had visited Washington, where, he said, "a Republican governor is looked upon as rather a curiosity, since there are so few of them today." His position was all the more conspicuous because he was the youngest governor in the country. There is no question that the decade of the thirties belonged to the Democrats.

The New Deal

Franklin Roosevelt, nominated for president in 1932, said, "I pledge you, I pledge you myself, a new deal for the American people." He gathered around him men and women who possessed ideas about what such a "new deal" should accomplish. FDR's first one hundred days in office produced dozens of programs and agencies—"the alphabet soup approach to government," one critic said. From the AAA to the WPA, all were intended to put people to work and end the Depression. An enormous bureaucracy was created to administer the programs, which most Republicans deplored.

The liberals who flocked to the New Deal's banner were different from the Progressives who gathered around Teddy Roosevelt. Progressivism as a movement had died with World War I. Progressives, whose main goal was to eradicate evil, were idealistic, visionary, white, middle class, and usually Protestant. They exuded a strong air of "Onward, Christian Soldiers!" New Dealers, on the other hand, didn't concern themselves with evil or grand causes. They sought the "quick fix." Secular, pragmatic, and a bit cynical, New Dealers came from every ethnic group and social stratum. It was a difference in both style and substance: Progressives had led the crusade for Prohibition; New Dealers repealed Prohibition as fast as they could.

From the first, Bridges was an outspoken critic of the New Deal, calling it a "perilous panacea." Of Roosevelt himself, Bridges observed that he was charming, gracious, with a winning smile and voice. "There I have to stop. he is a dangerous leader because he has not a definite program, no bedrock convictions, and starts everything he does with a great flourish, but nobody knows where he is going."

Another time Bridges said, "The present passion for change and experiment on the part of the Roosevelt administration will, unless rudely and swiftly checked, plunge the country into bankruptcy and choas. . . . The New Dealers have gone too far left! I think the national administration must turn more to the right."

Bridges' open criticism of the New Deal hurt him when he asked Washington for aid for New Hampshire. In February of 1935, he proposed a $3 million relief program, financed one-fourth by cities and towns, one-fourth by the state, and half by the federal government. This bill was speedily approved by the legislature, but it ran into trouble when it reached the Washington desk of relief administrator Harry Hopkins, Roosevelt's cigar-chomping "czar," who also supervised the Work Projects Administration (WPA). Hopkins protested the payment, pointing out that in New Hampshire persons on relief were not permitted to vote because they were classified as "paupers," according to eighteenth-century English law. (This fact apparently escaped Hopkins when Governor Winant had been the one requesting aid.) Hopkins wrote Bridges, "I will not grant further federal aid to the state of New Hampshire if these discriminatory practices against the unemployed are continued."

The legislature immediately amended the bill to permit relief recipients to vote.

Addressing Other Problems

Bridges' political philosophy seemed to be a blend of conservative and liberal policies. While Styles greatly favored local control of relief measures, he also realized that there should be some centralized authority and supervision to avoid misuse of such funds. Therefore, his $3 million bill called for the creation of a three-member bipartisan Board of Welfare and Relief to set rules and regulations for the program. The members were to be appointed by the governor and the council, and the auditing of the accounts was assigned to the newly formed comptroller's office. Critics said these provisions gave too much authority to the executive group and called the comptroller's accounting system inefficient and wasteful. These objections did not block final enactment of the program, and the funds were effectively channeled into work-making projects throughout the state.

With the pressures for aid temporarily alleviated, Bridges focused his attention on other legislation, turning next to state planning. His objective here was to eliminate inefficient and overlapping procedures and agencies. To that end, he consolidated the State Planning Board and the State Development Commission into a State Planning and Development Commission. Divisions were created to develop specific planning and promotion areas. One was a Division of Industry, established to preserve industries already in the state and to encourage new ones to move in.

To boost state revenue, Bridges decided increased taxation was necessary. A general sales tax and a "luxury" sales tax were the most popular suggestions. He also suggested a head tax, an income tax, a state poll tax, an inheritance levy, and a cigarette tax. The last was sharply opposed, because of overlapping federal and existing state taxes, and it was voted down. The poll tax met the same fate. (Poll taxes, money extracted for the right to vote, were later declared unconstitutional.)

According to many Americans, the ideal system of taxation would be to restrict the federal government to indirect taxes—such as on luxuries and alcohol—allow states to collect income and inheritance taxes, and let cities and towns keep all property taxes. This was not likely to happen. A federal income tax—a so-called "direct" tax—had been instituted in 1913 and could not easily be rescinded. At that time, the state still continued to impose direct taxes upon municipal properties to balance the biennial state budgets. A lottery was also suggested to boost state revenue, but Bridges was firmly opposed to that idea.

Bridges' energy and decisiveness in the first few months of his administration instilled public confidence. He began to hone the political and executive skills that would serve him so well the rest of his life. From his high school years, he had shown an aptitude for the art of politics, winning leadership roles and balancing the needs of the individual against the needs of the group. Now he began capitalizing on his native talent. He was learning when to compromise, and when to stand firm; how to reconcile differing points of view, and how to dig in and work out the details of administering a complicated government program. He used the committee system to accomplish many of his goals.

He devoted upwards of sixteen hours daily to his office. Of necessity, he had to decline some five invitations a day to speak, yet he developed an ability to say "No" in a way that almost sounded like "Yes." He met with an average of twenty-eight people per day, squeezing them into ten-minute appointments. On one particularly busy day, he spoke with 193 persons. It was not unusual for Bridges to seat a caller at his own desk, while he either sat at a small table nearby or restlessly paced the floor.

Bridges continued to rely upon the political wisdom of Robert Bass, the old sparkplug of progressivism. When Bridges' new state Water Resources Board was created, he offered the chairmanship to Bass, then more than three-score years in age. Bass declined for personal reasons, but he considered the offer a personal tribute, thus renewing the warm bond between the two men.

The Textile Industry Crisis

By the winter of 1935, the New England textile industry faced disaster. For years, the number of spindles had increased in the South and declined in the Northeast. Fifteen years earlier, 37 million spindles had operated in New England. By the time Bridges became governor, according to the *Manchester Union Leader*, only 16 million operating spindles remained. Wages for southern textile workers were much lower than in strongly unionized New England. The lower cost of southern goods combined with inexpensive Japanese imports to undercut New England's prices.

The center of the textile industry in New England was the Amoskeag Manufacturing Company of Manchester. At its peak, in the early years of the twentieth century, Amoskeag was the world's largest textile plant. Encompassing thirty major mills, with a total of eight million square feet of floor space, the mills employed up to 17,000 people. In those days, Amoskeag *was* Manchester. When Amoskeag's 1933 net profit of a little over $32,000 dropped to a net loss of over a million dollars in 1934, immediate action was called for. Bridges and a New England delegation of congressmen visited Washington to confer with Interior Secretary Harold L. Ickes and Treasury Department officials. The delegation sought some sort of relief, such as standardization of textile wages throughout the country, restrictions on foreign imports of textile products, along with repeal or reduction of a new federal processing levy on the industry. Their efforts were in vain.

As the textile situation worsened, the New England governors jointly went to Washington to lay their plight before President Roosevelt. They conferred for more than an hour and spent several additional hours with various cabinet officials. Roosevelt promised to make a study of the crisis. Bridges reported upon his return home, "Frankly, I am alarmed and I am bitterly disappointed. I would not say no impression was made on the President and his advisors, but I see no hope of immediate action to meet the crisis that has undoubtedly developed in New England."

As the situation continued to deteriorate, some fifty Congressmen representing eleven states requested another interview with Roosevelt. They made little impact. Bridges declared, "We have heard a good deal from the present national administration about the 'forgotten man.' I hope New England is not destined to become the 'forgotten land.'"

Earlier Bridges had blasted Secretary of Agriculture Henry A. Wallace for calling for a coalition of southern and western states against New England. "Secretary Wallace should be let out for creating sectionalism. . . . He should resign, because his unfair condemnation and criticism of the New England and New Hampshire people is un-American, unpatriotic, and unjust," Bridges stated. Wallace later accused Bridges and other New England leaders of "whining" and "flabbiness." Bridges retorted: "Secretary Wallace does not understand the problem as it is related to the New England people. He is impatient, and is prejudiced against us." When Wallace was appointed chairman of Roosevelt's committee to study the six-state textile plight, the industry's downfall became an imminent reality.

It was no real surprise when the Amoskeag mills closed in late September of 1935. It was initially a temporary action, and reopening continued as a possibility, especially as the U.S. Supreme Court invalidated the Agricultural Adjustment Act, including the processing levy upon the mills. The Amoskeag Company filed for reorganization under the federal bankruptcy act, and workers agreed to lower pay scales to compete with southern mills. Unfortunately, all these efforts proved futile, and in July of 1936, the Amoskeag mills were liquidated, leaving 12,000 workers unemployed. It was a true economic disaster. Men and women whose parents and grandparents had made their living in the sprawling factories, suddenly found their jobs, their way of life, gone—and this in the midst of the Great Depression. It was impossible not to pass the empty, cavernous buildings, with its rows of idle machinery, and not feel a sense of loss, of hopelessness. As optimism waned, the relief rolls swelled.

Fighting for Federal Relief Funds

Meanwhile, the governor continued to labor to combat New Hampshire's unemployment woes. In May of 1935, he wrote to Aubrey Williams, assistant administrator of the federal Emergency Relief Administration, requesting a grant of $20 million for direct relief. Williams replied that he saw no reason for more aid, when the government was already giving New Hampshire large grants for work relief. Bridges then went to Washington with a personal appeal to Williams, which also led nowhere.

At Williams' suggestion, Bridges turned to Harold Ickes and his Public Works Administration (PWA). This gave Bridges momentary hope, but it was dashed as New Hampshire became a victim of a conflict between Ickes and Hopkins. Hopkins' primary object was to furnish jobs; long-lasting community solutions to unemployment were of secondary importance to that goal. Ickes, on the other hand, gave top priority to permanent jobs. This policy pleased Bridges.

Therefore, when Roosevelt approved a fresh PWA program for Bridges, the governor looked to early implementation of his relief hopes. The ax fell, however, when the funds were allocated to Hopkins and his Work Projects Administration, the *WPA*, by some bureaucratic mixup. The alphabet soup form of government apparently confused even its creators. But the mistake was critical for New Hampshire. With the new allocation, Hopkins made his own determination of priorities, and the Granite State was not one of them. The state was awarded only $1,071,424 of the $20 million requested. Such actions prompted cries of partisan politics from Bridges, and many of his constituents agreed. A May 1934 poll in *Literary Digest* showed a 52 percent approval of the New Deal.

By January of 1936, a new poll found three-to-one opposition to the New Deal. Roosevelt had spent almost the same amount of money in the past thirty months, Bridges angrily charged, as had been spent in the entire 124 years between the presidencies of George Washington and Woodrow Wilson. He complained, "We have expended nationally billions and billions of dollars . . . and we have made no progress at all. . . . Our present heavy relief expenditures will be with us for many years to come. Don't let anyone tell you differently."

Roosevelt's 1932 election had been a "ghastly mistake," declared Bridges, which submerged "most of the states in the Union beneath a flood of Democratic debt, doubt, and delay." To underline his accusations, Bridges added, "It has been the attitude of New England businessmen to change from one of hopelessness, to one of aggressive opposition to President Roosevelt and his policies."

In reply to those who demanded that critics of the New Deal should offer alternatives, Bridges did so. He suggested a reduction in federal spending, a sound currency (Roosevelt had proposed going off the gold standard, and in fact did so shortly after taking office), more efficient handling of relief funds, and more recovery and less reform. He presented these alternatives in speeches to the new Young Republican groups that were sprouting up across the nation. His criticism of FDR and the New Deal netted Bridges a great deal of national publicity.

Bridges and His Family

Bridges' policy of frugality applied to himself, as well as to his state. Although he always dressed neatly and kept his shoes shined, people joked that the name "Styles" hardly referred to his attire. Sally Bridges did not charge any purchases, and the family lived entirely within the governor's $5,000-a-year salary.

The governor's wife and children did not see much of him, however. Home-loving Sally was ill at ease in the limelight, and she much preferred the serenity of home and family to the larger world. She often confided to friends, "I did not marry a politician."

At six years of age, David was impetuous, strong-willed, and given to mischievous adventures. He had inherited his father's shrewdness in sizing up people and situations. And although a handsome and lovable youngster, he could be quite contrary, taking unfair advantage of his mother's leniency. John was an appealing toddler, and Styles, Jr., by then a fast-growing adolescent, was a friendly boy, popular at camp and school, and winner of several "all-around-boy" awards. (He was not pleased when photographers insisted on dressing him in knickers to create the illusion of

Governors' fishing trip to Moosehead Lake, Maine in 1935. Standing and flanking an unknown bearded Mainer are, from left, Bridges, James M. Curley of Massachusetts, Louis Brann of Maine, and Jessie Jones of Texas.

three youngsters at play in the home.)

During his first year as governor, Bridges was home for dinner only seven times. Many visits with the family took place at the State House. When Bridges did go home, his inability to relax and his forceful personality dominated the household. He carried his gubernatorial authority into his home—a rearrangement of furniture or a purchase often provoked his anger, if he had not been consulted about it.

Occasionally, the family spent a weekend in a small camp just outside the city on the Contoocook River, and once they attended a family reunion in his hometown of Pembroke, Maine. But work was the most important part of Bridges' life. Attending a Washington conference took precedence over attending Styles, Jr.'s prep school graduation from Brewster Academy in Wolfeboro. Letters to his mother became newspaper articles, and David resorted to mimicking his father in an attempt to win his attention. Asked many years later if his father had a private life, John shook his head. "His private life was his public life," he said.

Bridges had a low resistance to illness and succumbed several times to various ailments during this period, but he continued to govern from his sickbed. Sally was amused on occasion with her husband's lapses into hypochondria, as were members of his staff when they delivered work to his home. The *Exeter News Letter* took his illnesses more seriously, observing in 1935, "When he first offered himself as a candidate we were not sure that we wanted him; now our fear is that we may lose him."

That spring, Ronald Bridges, then thirty years old and happily married, living in Sanford, announced his candidacy for the Republican nomination for Congress, for the First District in the state of Maine. Well educated, having attended Bowdoin and Harvard, Ronald was on leave from a teaching position in Milton, Massachusetts, where his sister Doris was also employed. Despite a campaign zest akin to that of his brother, Ronald lost his bid.

Acknowledging the Political Importance of Women

A dozen years after they had gotten the vote, women were emerging as a factor in public affairs, boosted by Eleanor Roosevelt's activism. Perhaps influenced by his strong mother and sister, Styles had long championed such a development. When a Pittsfield Municipal Court judge retired, Bridges nominated Idella Jenness, a fifty-three-year-old prominent clubwoman, for the post. She was not a lawyer and had never held public office, but she had served as chairman of the state Republican women's division and was a member of the Republican State Committee.

Some men in Pittsfield denounced the Jenness nomination, Bridges granted them a hearing in his office and explained, "It has been my policy to name lawyers in the larger cities. There was no attorney available in Pittsfield, and I thought I would accord your town the honor of being the first in the state to have a woman justice."

Pittsfield citizens should have "the right to decide for ourselves when we want justice administered by a woman," the men retorted.

The Jenness appointment was one way of expressing "Republican appreciation to the fair sex for their splendid cooperation in our political activities," Bridges asserted. Despite the opposition in Pittsfield, he was deluged with endorsements of the nomination from elsewhere. The New Hampshire League of Woman Voters wrote, "The League highly commends your action because the choice was made for qualification." Opposition faded as Victor Trace, whom Bridges nominated for associate judge with Jenness, withdrew his objections. On May 29, 1935, the executive council unanimously confirmed the nomination for New Hampshire's first female judge.

Bridges continued to make history by appointing other women to the highest posts they had ever held in the Granite State. Abby L. Wilder of Concord became director of a new Division of State Employment and Elizabeth R. Elkins of Concord became administrator of a Minimum Wage Division. Bridges also announced his intention to appoint a woman as police commissioner. "It will result in improved conditions and moral standards in the community in which I make the appointment," he asserted. "Women should not be confined to school boards and the legislature."

One of Governor Bridges' goals when he took office was to solicit the state's industrial and business support, well remembering that it had helped Senator Moses maintain his long political leadership career. In this connection, he launched sponsorship of an unemployment compensation law to help jobless workers from going onto welfare rolls in periods of business down-turns. No sooner proposed than done: The legislature readily created an Unemployment Compensation Division (UCD), along with units to promote employment and increase the minimum wage. New Hampshire became the second in nation to have such an agency. The UCD became part of the State Bureau of Labor, with Gordon P. Eager, Bridges' personal secretary, as administrator.

Another project sponsored by the new governor was the Merrimack River Valley Authority, which was organized to construct dams in order to curb flood damage. Undoubtedly Bridges' background as an agricultural agent had shown him the value of water as a natural resource. New Hampshire is sometimes knows as the "Mother of Rivers." The most important river in the state, the 110-mile-long Merrimack, flows from southeast New Hampshire across Massachusetts, to empty into the Atlantic at Newburyport, just south of the Maine border. The MRVA became the largest single federal undertaking in New England, providing six thousand jobs and indirect work to many thousands of other unemployed.

The governor clashed again with New Dealers over control of the proposed MRVA. The *Manchester Union Leader* of March 9, 1935, quotes Bridges: "If projects now under consideration are made possible by federal grants, the federal government should have something to say about how the money is spent," he stated. However, he continued,

I am still, nevertheless, a firm believer in the sovereignty of the states, no matter how much that fundamental American principle may be lost sight of in the period through which we are passing. And I am wholly opposed to any legislation that would make creation of a federal empire in New Hampshire. Such a development as has been proposed would accomplish a great deal of good, but should not force New Hampshire and Massachusetts to surrender their rights.

The 1936 Spring Flood

The destructive power of rivers became evident in the spring of 1936. That winter had been exceptionally cold and snowy. In March, a sudden thaw brought a welcome warmth; but, as so often occurs with early spring thaws, the deep snow melted too rapidly and the rivers rose as their ice covers broke up and piled along embankments. On March 12, the Ashuelot River rose to flood stage in Keene. Bridges promptly ordered the National Guard to help the city's people. Within days, river valleys throughout the state flooded, as ice jams backed up the swollen streams. On March 18, a sudden downpour and rising temperatures broke the ice pilings. Towns along rivers and streams were inundated.

Bridges ordered his entire staff onto staggered shifts to keep his office open day and night. Working closely with the National Guard, which mustered several units into emergency action, he supervised rescue operations from a crisis center in Concord. Rescue workers had to cope with electricity outages, broken water lines, and road blockages. For a time, the Merrimack and Contoocook rivers merged to isolate the capital city—flood waters pulled down electrical and telephone lines and blocked all but one of Concord's highway exits. An old generator was pressed into service, one telephone line was kept open, and ham operators stepped into the communications breach.

A sudden attack of flu forced Bridges to a room at the Eagle Hotel, across the street from the State House. From there, he continued to direct the flood-relief operations. Reports from the stricken areas were staggering. Entire communities were floodbound and factories were devastated, their machinery and inventories destroyed. Highways and bridges were damaged, the railroad systems totally disrupted. Thousands of people had become homeless; but miraculously, no life was lost. Flood damages amounted to about $12 million, not counting the disruption of industry and services. To Bridges' dismay, the state debt climbed.

As the flood waters began to recede, Bridges focused on rebuilding. He wired WPA administrator Harry Hopkins for emergency federal funds. Hopkins replied that his agency would finance repairs to public property, including bridges, highways, and sewer and water systems, as well as public buildings.

Meanwhile, Bridges appointed a committee to assess the damages and the cost of reconstruction. The 120-member group, with thirteen subcommittees, represented all the stricken areas. The *Coos County Democrat* commended Bridges for this action: "We will not have sociologists building dams or economists repairing highways. . . . In spite of all the damages done to bridges, we still have H. Styles very much on the job." Several

The Amoskeag Bridge in Manchester during the disastrous spring floods of 1936

days later, the *Carroll County Independent*, another weekly newspaper, praised Bridges for not making flood relief a political issue, as developed in Massachusetts.

Bridges' ability to act through committees was clearly demonstrated. He won Executive Council endorsement for a special legislative session on May 12, then utilized the committee's findings to win quick enactment of a $2 million bond issue for emergency repairs not covered by the WPA funds. The legislature also voted to continue a penny-per-gallon gasoline tax that had been imposed in 1927 to finance a flood disaster in that year, to pay off the bonds.

The day following the special session, the State House was quiet, as staff and legislators caught up on rest. But presiding in the chief executive office, diligent as ever, was Styles Bridges. As pictures and accounts of the flooding appeared in newspapers across the country, with New Hampshire's young governor directing the relief effort, Bridges garnered national exposure. His name became known not only in the Granite State, but throughout America.

Bridges—A Middle-of-the-Roader

During his two-year term, Governor Bridges fulfilled every plank in his campaign platform except for a new probation system for juvenile delinquents. He sponsored a Milk Control Act and an Agricultural Standards Act;

The house in East Concord where the Bridges family lived during his term as governor

reorganized the state Fish and Game Department; created the position of Special Veterans' Officer in the Welfare Department, and revamped the state's old-age assistance program, so that New Hampshire became the first state in the nation to qualify for participation in the new federal Social Security program. He was credited with modernizing the Labor Department, which had been "in the same groove for thirty years." Bridges also won legislative approval of a State Cancer Commission, which became the first of its kind in the country. He kept his constituents informed through frequent radio programs. Near the end of his term, a newspaper editorialized: "Probably no more forward-looking legislation has been put on the statute books of New Hampshire in the history of the state, than in the Bridges administration."

Styles had his own view of his accomplishments: "In the old days it used to be that the Governorship was one of the highest honors the state could bestow, but hell, it's getting to be also a hard job now."

In his early political years, Bridges was a progressive with a "liberal" outlook on life, but by the mid-1930s, he was walking the narrow line between liberalism and conservatism. He had not turned his back on the long-standing liberal goals of opportunity for all and social progress. His ideas of the means to achieve these goals, however, were changing. His self-description was simple: "I guess I really am a middle-of-the-roader." This varied labeling of Bridges' political convictions was to continue as his career unfolded.

As Bridges neared the end of his term, his son David, who had inherited many of his father's qualities, including his need for security, voiced a question that had been on Bridges' mind: "Daddy, what job are you going to have when you get through being governor?"

In early 1936, the answer was not yet clear. But whatever his job would be, it was certain that Bridges would continue his battle against the New Deal.

4

Little Boy Blue

"Never before or since has the Senate been more venerable for the array of celebrated statesmen . . . Calhoun, Webster, and Clay . . . And Franklin Pierce comes as the youngest member of the Senate."

Nathaniel Hawthorne, *The Life of Franklin Pierce*

WITH HIS SON'S question still echoing in his mind, Bridges reviewed his options. A second term as governor was a possibility, but he faced a stiff fight. Francis P. Murphy, who had bowed to Bridges in 1934, announced in April of 1935 that he would run for the Republican gubernatorial nomination, even if that meant he had to challenge the popular Bridges in the primary.

Murphy, the son of Irish-Catholic immigrants, had learned the shoe business from the ground up, starting as a teenager and eventually becoming part owner of the J.F. McElwain Company, the largest employer in New Hampshire. He served in the state legislature and on Governor Winant's executive council. He would make a formidable opponent. Bridges' supporters urged him to take on Murphy, but he refused to commit himself, beyond saying that he would run for "something" in 1936.

Another opportunity developed when Senator Henry W. Keyes, from Haverhill, contemplated a third term. He was not well known outside of New Hampshire, but his wife was the celebrated Frances Parkinson Keyes, author of a dozen best-selling novels.

Several problems made Keyes vulnerable. Because he had not made a floor speech since 1920, he had become known as the "Senate mute." He

Alf Landon, Governor of Kansas and 1936 Republican presidential nominee addresses a crowd of 4,000 from the observation car of the "Sunflower Special," in Nashua. Styles Bridges is at the extreme left and a sizeable portion of the G.O.P. elephant "Susanna" at the right.

was seventy-three years old and cautious to the point of being ineffective. The young and vigorous Governor Bridges, with his forward-looking stance, could probably defeat Keyes in a party primary and win the election over another popular young man, William Rogers, whom the Democrats were grooming for Keyes' seat.

To Run or Not to Run is the Question

One problem worried Bridges: Would voters think the jump to the Senate was too big to make after only one term as governor? Another possibility was to seek the Second District Congressional seat, then held by Charles Tobey, who had indicated that he might oppose Senator Keyes. Still another opportunity was in the wind—in the March 10 presidential primary, Bridges was one of sixteen candidates for seven delegate-at-large seats to the Republican convention. He finished first, ahead of both George Moses and Tobey. Even more gratifying, he topped the slate of delegates in 95 percent of the urban areas. This strong showing caught the attention of the party's national leadership.

Campaign memorabilia from Bridges short-lived consideration as a vice-presidential candidate in 1936 and his successful bid for the U.S. Senate the same year

Republicans needed a forceful national ticket in 1936, to oppose the immensely popular President Roosevelt. Those associated with Hoover's defeat could not present the kind of dynamic image necessary, so the party leadership looked to energetic young men with liberal voting records. Governor Alfred Landon of Kansas and Frank Knox, publisher of the *Chicago Daily News* and part owner of the *Manchester Union Leader*, were the leading favorites for the GOP presidential nomination.

Various state blocs touted their favorite sons for vice-president, especially those who had favorably impressed Young Republican clubs. Bridges' name began to pop up as a vice-presidential possibility. He eyed this entrance into the national scene carefully. His showing in the primary assured him domination of the Granite State delegation. He might be able to use this position as a base at the national convention to win the VP nomination. His friends in the party urged Bridges to make the bid for national office. Even the ultraconservative Moses backed the idea, but his suggestion became suspect when it was learned that he was flooding the state with letters seeking support for a run against Senator Keyes. Moses had lost his Senate seat to Fred Brown of Somerworth in the 1932 Democratic landslide.

Bridges received encouragement to run for Keyes' seat as well, even if it meant challenging either Moses or Tobey, or both. Governor Robert Perkins Bass was particularly enthusiastic about Styles' Senate run. A series of letters through the spring of 1936 between Bass and Bridges showed the older man's continuing confidence in the younger, whom he wanted to see succeed in public life. The problem of running for vice-president, as Bass viewed it, was not so much in getting the Republican nomination, as winning the election. Pessimistic about unseating Roosevelt, he wrote Bridges: "It seems to me a matter for serious consideration whether from an individual point of view you would not prefer a reasonably sure prospect of going to the Senate for six years, rather than the distinction of being a candidate for Vice President at a time when the status of the Republican ticket is definitely uncertain."

Bass felt sure that Bridges could be elected senator. "I stand ready to help financially and otherwise to that end," he promised, but a vice-presidential try was "too much of a gamble for me."

Bridges' deliberations focused on what Tobey intended to do. With Moses already an announced candidate against Keyes, Bridges made it known that he did not like the idea of becoming a fourth candidate, if Tobey was to give up his congressional seat for a Senate run. While Tobey weighed his decision, Bridges began building an organization for a Senate race. He was also preparing for the Republican presidential convention and the remote possibility of being drafted for the national ticket.

On June 6, 1936, Bridges declared his candidacy for Keyes' Senate seat, and Tobey announced that he would seek reelection to Congress.

The Republican convention delegation headed for Cleveland, where Bridges was elected chairman. The delegates agreed to support Knox for president because of his Granite State background. Governor Alf Landon arrived at the convention as the likely nominee. Giant Kansas sunflowers sprouted everywhere in the convention hall. The only speculation left was who would be his running mate. Landon had courted Senator Arthur Vandenberg of Michigan for that position, and when Vandenberg refused, the field opened up. Bridges was among those "boomed" to run with Landon. His candidacy gained support until Roy Roberts, then managing editor of *The Kansas City Star*, remarked that the party might be handing the Democrats a ready-made campaign slogan. Roberts was referring to the old English ditty, "London Bridge is falling down, falling down, falling down."

"How would 'Landon-Bridges falling down' sound?" Roberts asked.

Party officials quickly realized that a Landon-Bridges ticket might be ridiculed by the opposition. The possibility killed Bridges' candidacy.

Then there were practical considerations. New Hampshire, with only four electoral votes, was not considered a significant source of national strength, despite the popularity of its governor. And in the back of his mind, Bridges himself doubtless thought it was just as well he wasn't chosen. Roosevelt swamped the Republican ticket in the November elections, and Bridges would have gone down to a crushing defeat. His political career would have been abruptly curtailed.

In the interest of party unity, all the vice-presidential candidates withdrew their names from consideration. Knox bowed to Governor Landon, who was unanimously nominated for president, amid strains of "He's our sunflower, our one flower." (Which should have told someone something about their chances of winning the election.) Landon then threw the vice-presidential nomination to the convention, whereupon Bridges won a singular honor: He was chosen to nominate Knox for vice-president. Knox also won unanimous endorsement.

New Hampshire's delegates rejoiced as they headed for home that evening. Not only were they pleased with the Landon-Knox team, but they were also elated that Governor Bridges' role in the proceedings had catapulted the Granite State into national prominence.

Bridges had mixed emotions about his part in the convention. He wrote to his mother,

As I stood upon the platform, I realized that almost anyone I might nominate at that time would get the place on the ticket almost by acclamation. All the other candidates had abandoned their plans and had no nominating organizations on the floor. That included myself. As I stood there I wished for a split second that I were someone else so that I might put my own name in nomination. I quickly got over that dream.

In the Senate Race to Win!

Bridges assured the Granite State citizenry, "now that I am back, I want to tell you that I'm in that Senate race to win. But while I was in Cleveland, I certainly succumbed to the lure of that vice-president nomination. I guess I'm still a little young, and some of that convention excitement got into my blood." That confession won the hearts of his constituents.

In the three months between the Republican national convention and the September 15 primary, Bridges' prospect for victory appeared to improve. There was talk that he would benefit from the competition between Keyes and Moses for the conservative voters. A campaign swing through New Hampshire by Landon boosted his popularity. "I was very interested in seeing him elected," Landon later stated. "He had made a good Governor and would make a splendid senator."

In his campaign headquarters, manned by aides and volunteers, Bridges developed an efficient system of using campaign mailings. Some 350 to 400 letters went out daily.

One supporter absent from the Bridges campaign was Norris Cotton. While he continued to favor the governor, Cotton could not forget that it was Senator Moses who had sponsored a congressional job for him in the 1920s, so he could attend George Washington Law School and become an attorney. Cotton reportedly pleaded with Moses not to try and regain the Senate seat, insisting that he could not win over the youthful Bridges. When Moses refused to back out, Cotton gave him his support. Bridges understood. He later said, "One of the qualities I have always tried to live up to in my life is to remember and stand by my friends."

Moses formally announced his candidacy shortly after Bridges declared his intention. He had "been reluctant to enter the field against Senator Keyes, with whom I served for many years," he declared. "However, another contestant has appeared, and I can see no sound reason to permit him to occupy the field against Keyes alone."

Moses had substantial campaign funds at his command. A Bridges supporter reassured the governor, "Many of the rich and older folks are for Moses. Aren't you glad that most of us in New Hampshire are poor, common folks?"

Senator Keyes remained silent as the Bridges and Moses campaigns got rolling. Then, on August 4, he surprised everyone with the announcement that he would "retire from active participation in public office." His

H. STYLES BRIDGES

Candidate for the Republican Nomination

FOR

U. S. SENATOR

"I feel Governor Bridges is the candidate most experienced in the problems of Today." - - - - Former Governor Rolland H. Spaulding of Rochester.

BRIDGES FOR SENATOR COMMITTEE

Rolland H. Spaulding, Rochester, Chairman
Emile Lemelin, Manchester, Vice-Chairman
James C. MacLeod, Littleton, Treas. and Fin. Agent
Neil Tolman, Nashua, Secretary

Women's Division:
Mrs. Robert E. Walbridge, Peterborough, Chairman
Mrs. Glenn Wheeler, Bristol, Treasurer
Mrs. Gladstone Jordan, Groveton, Secretary

 I

Bridges campaign poster during the 1936 Republican primary

Modest Bridges banner in East Concord during the Republican primary campaign in 1936

departure left the nomination open to three candidates—Bridges, Moses, and State Representative William J. Callahan of Keene, a seventy-five-year-old State Fish and Game warden, then serving his twelfth biennial state house term. Callahan was never really in the running.

Clean Campaigns That Quickly Degenerated

Keyes remained strictly neutral during the campaign. Bridges and Moses pledged themselves to wage clean campaigns, but it soon became obvious that their standards differed. Each accused the other of underhanded tactics, and truth and rumor quickly became indistinguishable. Moses said Bridges was allowing his supporters to slander his reputation. Bridges, in turn, accused Moses and his organization of circulating stories that maligned his personal life and his family. Bridges wrote the Bass family, "I have never seen a more vicious campaign, nor have I heard such rumors, and it is the sort of last dying gasp of the Old Guard."

Moses accused Bridges of having aides on the state payroll and of having engaged in questionable dealings in the campaign. He also criticized the governor for publicizing his gubernatorial activities in Washington to curry public favor. Bridges repeatedly called for party unity, warning, "It cannot be accomplished if our ranks are to be divided by the machinations of wicked whispers, slimy slander and malicious lies. I am sorry this has happened in this campaign. I do not think it will affect the result, but a skunk is an unpleasant if not dangerous neighbor."

There was a marked difference in the two men's campaigns, springing largely from the disparate resources they had available. Moses' forces strung a huge banner across Concord's Main Street with his portrait. Bridges hoisted a small banner in East Concord that said simply, "Our neighbor, H. Styles Bridges, for U.S. Senator." Moses used expensive full-and half-page newspaper advertisements, reproducing letters of support from well-known individuals; Bridges could afford only small ads in which he cited his gubernatorial achievements.

The candidates' public records became a major issue. Bridges stressed his experience in the state house, whereas Moses said little about his two senatorial terms in Washington. Bridges listed specific measures and legislation to illustrate Moses' inconsistencies. Moses, in rebuttal, emphasized his ability to match wits with other senators. Bridges countered this self-praise: "The best campaigner against Moses is George Higgins Moses himself, because . . . [he] would so much rather be very witty and very clever, than be very bright and very discrete."

Moses sarcastically nicknamed Bridges "Little Boy Blue" because of his youth and because from his socks to his tie, the nattily dressed governor always chose clothes to complement his blue eyes. In later years, Styles' taste in clothing became a subject of comment among his Washington staff, as the always dapper Senator displayed his well-known "Yankee frugality." Gerry Zeiller, a legislative assistant in Bridges' office, recalled, "He had hundreds of suits and I don't think one cost more than thirty-five dollars, which was cheap in those days. He used to get three for a hundred dollars from a warehouse guy in Baltimore. And when the style changed from double-breasted suits, to single-breasted, he had his suits sent out to be re-tailored, rather than buy new ones." Tom Shannon, another legislative assistant in the 1950s, recalled with some amusement a comment he overheard at the dedication of the Pease Air Base: "This is the only time in history that a multi-million air base has been dedicated by a man in a twenty-two dollar suit."

The Moses epithet also implied that Bridges blew his own horn, an implication that Bridges was quick to turn to advantage. "I plead guilty to blowing my own horn as many times, in as many places, in a way to be heard by as many men and women of New Hampshire as possible," he declared. "In all this blowing I do not think I have ever blown one sour note. One thing I can assure you, I won't be found under a haystack fast asleep. I have tried to make everything I have said contribute not only to my advantage, but also to the benefit of the whole Republican ticket in the state of New Hampshire in November."

Bridges' principal weapon was to question the quality of Moses' Senate service. Moses was defeated in 1932 at the peak of his career, he pointed out, an indication of the voters' lack of regard for his Washington record. Moses' record was indeed controversial. Never a friend of labor, he favored "yellow dog" contracts, which prohibited workers from joining labor unions. He had voted against the women's suffrage movement and the World Court, which was part of Woodrow Wilson's plan to ensure world peace after World War I. Moreover, Bridges accused, Moses had reneged on public promises. In 1920, he promised war veterans his support for a bonus bill, but when he was elected, Moses opposed such a measure on several occasions. Moses' friendliness with power trusts and big business in general prompted William Green, president of the American Federation of Labor, to dub him "the errand boy of Wall Street."

Governor Robert Bass helped Bridges expose Moses' reactionary record. Bass had unsuccessfully run against Moses a decade earlier in 1926, when Bridges managed his campaign, and he was eager for Moses' defeat. "Many antagonisms which George Moses has aroused make him a more vulnerable candidate," observed Bass. Although Moses boasted of his influential contacts in Washington, he pointed out, of the forty-six senators who endorsed him in the 1926 campaign, only six remained in the Senate in 1936.

Each side scrambled for newspaper endorsements. Moses had many friends in the media, and Bridges failed to win such support. When the influential *Manchester Union Leader* endorsed Moses, the Bridges forces swung into action. Ted Johnston and other friends of the governor purchased time on local radio stations so supporters could explain why Bridges would make a good Senator. The most valuable speaker was Robert Bass—not only was he articulate, but he spoke fluent French and so reached that substantial portion of the Queen City's population.

Some endorsements were controversial. When presidental candidate Landon campaigned through northern New England, he stopped briefly in New Hampshire. Although Landon had a policy of remaining neutral in state primaries, Johnston maneuvered a photograph of Landon shaking hands with a smiling Bridges, as one governor to another. It was no official endorsement, but the picture was reprinted in newspapers across the state.

Moses came up with a bona fide endorsement from former president Herbert Hoover, still a powerful figure among Republicans. In a paid advertisement the day before the primary, the *Union Leader* printed a copy of a letter from Hoover to former governor Huntley Spaulding, endorsing Moses. Bridges was shocked because Hoover had praised having young people in the Republican ranks; also, Bridges and Hoover had been

*Elephant supporting "bridge" on the stage of Keene's Grange Hall during the 1936
U.S. Senate campaign*

friendly for years. The incident upset Bridges so much that he ordered
his campaign staff to contact every town chairman to assess the damage.

Then he called Hoover, who confirmed the letter. Bridges expressed
his dismay, and questioned the ethics of a national leader taking sides in
a state primary. Several months later, while speaking at a dinner in New
Jersey, Hoover explained that Moses had been a staunch supporter of his
administration and his endorsement had been in appreciation.

Victory Within Sight!

In the end, the Hoover endorsement did not matter. Bridges won a
smashing victory, polling the largest vote in New Hampshire primary
history, beating Moses by more than 13,000 votes—45,463 to 32,108—
while Callahan tallied just 3,547. When the jubilation subsided, Bridges
admitted, "I am a little weary, but it is a rather 'happy weary.'" He took
a three-day holiday before embarking on his final stretch run toward the
U.S. Senate.

Congressman William N. Rogers of Wakefield, in his fourth term, was
Bridges' Democratic opponent in the November election. Rogers was a
strong contender and received financial support from the national Demo-

Governor Bridges was the featured speaker at a reception for Col. Frank Knox, Republican candidate for president, in Manchester in February of 1936. From left are: Congressman Charles Tobey, George Moses, Styles Bridges, Louis Wyman, Sr., and Col. Knox.

cratic party. The Democratic ticket had another attraction in Amos N. Blandin, a sturdy Bath lumberman, who won statewide attention as House Speaker of the 1935 Republican-dominated legislature. He was the Democratic nominee for governor against shoeman Murphy, whose Catholicism was not expected to appeal to the north country's traditional Yankee Protestants.

Democrats stressed Rogers' close affiliation with Roosevelt's policies as reason for electing him to the Senate. Bridges' outspoken attacks on New Deal programs would render him ineffective in Washington, they said. Democrats also lashed Bridges for increasing the state tax on municipal properties.

Moses refused to help Bridges, and even tried to stand in his way. In a letter to Bass, Bridges commented: "Moses himself is apparently sour. Most everybody is in line, but some of his oldest friends and closest supporters are talking Rogers."

Bridges had clashed with Rogers earlier over the Merrimack River Valley Authority. The governor had successfully insisted upon state supervision of the project, while Rogers favored giving the Washington bureaucracy complete control. In discussing this dispute during the campaign, Bridges called Rogers "the administration's rubber stamp." He declared himself better equipped to represent New Hampshire's interests in the Senate: "I have acquired a more intimate knowledge of the New Deal projects than the average Congressman could possibly get in Washington, because I have seen them not merely as schemes on paper, but in their actual working. My practical knowledge of their working will be of the greatest value to me in making the changes which will be necessary."

Bridges and the Republican forces doggedly rolled up their collective sleeves to push their election slate to victory. The party's four major candidates—Bridges for senator, Murphy for governor, Tobey and Arthur B. Jenks of Manchester for Congress—traversed the state together, holding organizational meetings in each of the ten counties. Bridges averaged three speeches each weekday, and sometimes more, while continuing to tend to his gubernatorial chores. Near the end of the campaign, while making a series of speeches one evening in Manchester, an undisputed Democratic stronghold, Bridges appeared at a Franco-American Club. Arriving late, he hurriedly asked the chairman if he could speak immediately, as he had to rush on to other engagements. His request granted, Bridges began to berate "the horrible mess the Democrats have made in Washington." As he elaborated on that theme, Bridges sensed that something was wrong. Instead of applause, his words were greeted with a deadly silence. Midway through his speech, the governor noticed Rogers glowering in the rear of the hall. Upon leaving the rostrum, Bridges learned that there were *two* Franco-American clubs in Manchester. He had just addressed a Democratic rally!

The campaign swung to its grueling end, and the Republican state slate swept to victory in the November 3rd election, even though President Roosevelt won New Hampshire by nearly 4,000 votes. Winning the great majority of states, Roosevelt coasted to a second term. The state totals showed that Bridges defeated Rogers by fewer than 9,000 votes—107,923 to 99,195. Murphy became the Granite State's first Catholic governor. Jenks and Tobey also triumphed. The GOP strategy paid off.

Bridges and Henry Cabot Lodge, Jr., of Massachusetts, were the only new Republicans elected to the Senate in 1936. Congress would be thoroughly Democratic for the next two years. The number of Republican Senate seats dropped from twenty-five to sixteen, and there were a mere eighty-nine Republicans in the 435-member House. Not since the Civil War had the fortunes of a national political party fallen so low.

Revival of the stricken Republican party seemed an overwhelming task, but Bridges was not only to reinvigorate it, but to do battle against the mighty New Deal, using every resource at his disposal.

5

Middle-of-the-Roader

*"A Senator's wife . . . can learn more of prac-
tical politics and civil government [in the
Senate gallery] in one week than she can from
any book written on those subjects in a year."*

Frances Parkinson Keyes,
Letters from a Senator's Wife

BRIDGES WAS NEWS from the moment
he stepped off the train on his first
visit to Washington after the elec-
tion. Newspaper reporters greeted his arrival with one question: "How did
you do it?" As one of only two new Republicans elected to the Senate, he
was the center of attention. The media portrayed him as swimming successfully upstream against a raging Democratic current.

"Everybody knows I have been more liberal than the party leaders,"
he replied. "That is the only way I have been able to survive the repeated
Democratic landslides." Other Republican leaders should become more
forward-looking and less obstructionist if they wanted to regain national
standing, Styles suggested. In later years he was to repeat that theme time
and again.

As soon as he could, Senator-elect Bridges visited Charles L. McNary of
Oregon, the Senate minority leader. They conferred at length, discussing up-
coming committee assignments and Republican tactics for coping with the
huge Democratic majority. McNary stated he was impressed with the young
senator, and speculation about possible committee assignments for Bridges
rolled through New Hampshire. During one of his Washington visits, Bridges
was introduced to crusty John Nance Garner, Roosevelt's vice-president

65

A cigar-smoking newly elected U.S. Senator Bridges informally polishes his shoes before taking the oath of office in the Senate Chamber January 4, 1937.

and the Senate's president. He suggested to Bridges, "Stick to your work, stay in Washington and don't go chasing around the country." But soon after taking office, Bridges ignored that advice.

The Bridges family spent some time in Washington, while they considered moving to the national capital. Styles and Sally were concerned over the effects such a drastic change might have on their three sons. As they looked around for a suitable house that would accommodate three lively youths, the boys became enamored with Washington. Eight-year-old David, especially, enjoyed riding the senatorial subway to the Capitol. But living in Washington proved too costly, and Bridges kept the family based in its East Concord home.

Back in New Hampshire, and still in the honeymoon glow from his reception in Washington, Bridges announced that he would support any New Deal legislation that he considered sound; but he quickly resumed the role of one of Roosevelt's most consistent and harshest critics.

Early in December, Bridges announced the selection of his Senate staff. He named Elmer V. Cartledge of Warner as his executive secretary and chief aide. Gladys Gustafson and Margaret Abbot, his gubernatorial secretaries, were to serve in similar roles in Washington. Other staff appointees were Neil Tolman of Nelson, G. Barnum Redding, and George E. French. They traveled to Washington at once to begin operations in a three-room suite on the first floor of the Senate Office Building.

Bridges had problems to resolve at home before he moved to Washington. The 1937 state legislature was scheduled to convene on January 5. By custom, a retiring governor swears in the new lawmakers and delivers an exaugural address, but the U.S. Congress was scheduled to convene on the same day. After deliberation, Bridges followed the example of earlier governors in a similar dilemma, and resigned as governor in his final week in office, turning the inaugural functions over to Senate president Charles M. Dale, the acting governor.

On January 4, the day before Congress formally convened, New Hampshire's senior senator, Fred Brown, escorted Bridges, garbed in a traditional frock coat, into the Senate chamber. There he was turned over to the custody of Arthur H. Vandenberg of Michigan, the senior Republican senator, and escorted to the Senate secretary's desk, where he was administered the oath of office.

Each state has two senators, to ensure balanced represention in the legislative process. At the present time there are one hundred members of the United States Senate. The House of Representatives, on the other hand, is assigned members according to population. In 2000, the House has 435 members, with the more populous states having the majority of representatives. The Senate and the House are jointly responsible for declaring war, maintaining the armed services, assessing taxes, borrowing money, minting currency, regulating commerce, and creating all laws necessary for the operation of the government. The Senate holds exclusive authority over the approval of treaties and nominations to government positions.

A senator must be at least thirty years of age, a citizen of the U.S. for nine years, and a resident of the state he or she is representing at the time of election. Senate terms are for six years, as opposed to two years for the House, and one-third of the Senate members stand for reelection every other year.

Because of the limited number of members, and the length of their six-year term, United States senators wield a great deal of power in Washington. Styles Bridges would soon become one of the most powerful of them all.

Freshman Senator

Senator Bridges kept a low profile during his first weeks. It was a month before he filed his first bill, and almost two months before he took the floor to deliver his maiden speech. But he won substantial attention upon appointment to the powerful Senate Appropriations Committee, a distinct honor for a first-termer. The appointment was likely a tribute to his achievements as governor and as a spokesman for the Republican party. It also indicated how badly Republicans needed fresh leadership.

The 1936 election ousted most of the older anti-New Deal Republican senators, including Daniel O. Hastings of Delaware, W. Warren Barbour of New Jersey, Jesse H. Metcalf of Rhode Island, and Lester J. Dickinson of Iowa. William E. Borah of Idaho and Arthur Vandenberg had been forced into tacit support of Roosevelt's programs to avoid defeat, while a few other Republican senators, like Arthur Capper of Kansas, had become New Deal adherents.

Freshman Senator Bridges did not linger long in the shadows. He quickly won national attention through his frequent confrontations with New Deal legislation. January of 1937 marked the zenith of President Roosevelt's popularity. Federal programs and agencies introduced in his first term to cope with the nation's economic collapse were beginning to show results. Productivity and employment rose throughout the nation. People again had enough money to go to Gary Cooper's latest movie, or buy a copy of the best-selling *Gone With the Wind*, or take in a Big Band concert, or watch Joe DiMaggio hit a homer at Yankee Stadium. The Democratic party's theme song, "Happy Days Are Here Again," was slowly becoming a reality.

Rare photo of the U.S. Senate in session during confirmation hearing of Harry Hopkins as WPA Administrator in 1939. Styles Bridges is in the second row from the bottom just left of center.

Roosevelt initially induced America to accept his New Deal policies by the force of his personality. His political power became entrenched in the 1934 elections, when Congress became even more Democratic, and even this majority was topped in the 1936 landslide.

Roosevelt Tries to Pack the Supreme Court

As Roosevelt launched his second term on January 20, 1937, the only branch of the federal government yet to bow to the New Deal was the Supreme Court. The court had generally opposed any expansion of the government's role into individual lives; time and again, the tribunal struck down Roosevelt's reforms as unconstitutional. The overconfident Roosevelt decided to act in early February. He sent a message to Congress calling for reorganization of several agencies, placing them under control of his cabinet. He also proposed a reorganization of the federal judiciary system, adding judges at all levels to improve its efficiency. At the highest level, the Supreme Court, a judge would be added for each justice over the age of seventy who refused to retire. The heart of the proposal was immediately evident—the Supreme Court could increase its membership by as many as six, and all six would be appointed by Roosevelt.

As justices aged they were inclined to become less efficient, FDR reasoned, and this delayed vital court actions. Judges were not compelled to retire, and at that time there were several "old men" on the bench. New Dealers were slow to hail this proviso as beneficial to the tribunal's efficiency, however, while Bridges and other opponents accused the president of court packing. By adding so many judges to the high court, Roosevelt could effectively influence its decisions to his liking.

Roosevelt's effort to control the Supreme Court was a serious blunder. Constitutionally, it is a third branch of the government, not subject to domination by either the executive or the legislative branch. Critics immediately attacked the proposal, pointing out that Supreme Court decisions were then in the making on such important reforms as the Wagner Labor Relations Act and the Social Security program. It certainly looked as if the president was trying to ensure a favorable judgment from the court.

Granite State residents strongly supported Bridges' stand against court packing. During the debates on the controversy, his office had been so deluged with protests that the staff could hardly reply to them all. Only a few back-home letters favored the Roosevelt assault upon the Supreme Court. One in particular, from the Concord Central Labor Union, drew a sharp reply. Bridges responded to the union's show of support for the Roosevelt sortie, reminding the Central Labor leaders that any judicial changes should be made by constitutional amendment, rather than by Congress:

> The real issue is whether we are going to change our American form of government thereby destroying the independence of the Supreme Court. If the President's proposal is enacted into law, it will automatically make the Supreme Court subservient to the Executive Branch. That would mean that the Court would be bent to the Chief Executive's will.

In a Boston interview in February, Bridges observed, "No dictator is able to gain a foot-hold as long as our doctrines of separation of powers is preserved." A few days later, he told a group of Republican women, "The Supreme Court is the best umpire we can choose to preserve the game as we play it."

The chief argument Bridges used, which he repeated time and again, was stressed in a Lincoln's birthday speech in New York:

> The President's recent message relative to the reorganization of the judicial branch of the government was amazing. Every thoughtful citizen will object stren-

uously to the use of alleged inefficiency to throttle or change the viewpoint or makeup of the federal Judiciary. This move attempts to tear down the very foundations upon which American freedoms have been built.

The court-reform plan was more than a party or an ideological issue, Bridges insisted. Preservation of American democracy was at stake, he declared, citing the wave of dictatorships in other nations. At that time Hitler had invaded the Rhineland, Mussolini was imposing his will in Ethiopia, and the Soviet Union was expanding into Armenia. Americans were especially alert to the threat of dictatorship abroad and determined that "it won't happen here."

Bridges was such a forceful critic of Roosevelt's proposal that the Republican leadership drafted him to speak to a national radio audience on April 26, 1937. Calling his address "Will Real Democracy Survive?" he hammered away at the dictatorial aspects of the court dispute. To those who viewed Roosevelt's New Deal as having rescued the nation from economic disaster, rather than a move toward autocracy, Bridges retorted, "No dictator ever ran on a platform calling for dictatorship."

Summing up his position, he said, "The time has come for some plain, honest, vigorous, backyard talk. True liberals, as opposed to noisy, self-proclaimed liberals, are warning the American people against an encroaching, personal government. The public can repel the attack on the Supreme Court, but of what benefit would the victory be, if at the same time the people permit reckless spending and inflation to destroy the foundation of the government which they sought to protect? All financial security depends on a secure government."

His all-out attack on the Roosevelt court plan won Bridges dozens of speaking engagements. He developed a public identity as a fighter, opposing any and all threats to American democracy and favoring federal programs on a pay-as-you-go basis.

On February 25, 1937, the Senate passed the first part of the court-reform program, the Summers bill, 76 to 4. This allowed, but did not compel, a federal justice to retire at seventy with full pay. Bridges sponsored an amendment that would have delayed the effective date of the bill until after Roosevelt left office, but it did not pass.

The Senate devoted several months to consideration of the rest of Roosevelt's court plan, while public opinion continued to build against it. The Senate finally killed it on July 22, 1937, by referring it back to a committee and effectively barring it from further consideration. "Nothing of a more wholesome nature, nothing to give us greater confidence in the future of this country in my generation, has happened than the action of the Senate today," Bridges crowed.

The Hugo Black Nomination

Although Roosevelt went down to defeat, historians have noted, his efforts at control impressed the Supreme Court. Justices became more cooperative and less obstructionist on New Deal issues. The resignation of one of the court's most conservative members, Justice Willis Van Devanter, then seventy-eight, gave Roosevelt a lift as well, and he promptly nominated one of his greatest supporters, Senator Hugo Black of Alabama, to fill the vacancy.

The Black nomination came only a month after the defeat of the court bill. For almost fifty years, nominees for the Supreme Court had been automatically accepted by the Senate. Now, with several senators expressing negative feelings about the Black appointment, the Senate voted to deliberate and weigh the merits of the nomination. Bridges and Senator Hiram Johnson of California, an old-line progressive, questioned the nomination, citing evidence that Black had been a member of the Ku Klux Klan. The senators wondered how much the avowedly racist organization had supported him through the years.

On August 14, 1937, Bridges took the Senate floor and demanded that the Senate Judiciary Committee probe the KKK charges, and make its findings public. The hearings were held in secret, however, and on August 17, Black was confirmed for the high court by a vote of 63 to 16. It was somewhat ironic that, despite these charges, Justice Hugo Black became one of the most liberal Justices, particularly in the area of race relations.

Labor Unrest

As the national economy continued to improve in 1937, labor unrest spread across the nation. Labor unions had traditionally organized along craft lines—carpenters, plumbers, machinists, and so forth. The new Congress of Industrial Organizations (CIO), established by coal miner John L. Lewis, launched a drive to organize workers in various industries, focusing on such established organizations as the United Automotive Workers and the United Mine Workers. The CIO was more militant and radical than the older, craft-orientated American Federation of Labor (AFL).

The CIO began its expanded organizational efforts in the steel and motor vehicle industries, with the argument that all workers had a right to collective bargaining with employers on wages and working conditions. Henry Ford vowed to hire six hundred armed union-breakers to keep the CIO out of his automotive plants. In an attempt to cope with the growing hostility on both sides, the government created the National Labor Relations Board (NLRB). The Department of Labor, headed by Frances Perkins, first woman cabinet member, also tried to bring peaceful solutions to labor-management disputes.

Bridges, ever distrustful of big government, charged that officials of federal agencies tended to favor unions against management. While he had supported the fair settlement of labor disputes as governor, he insisted that government officials should aim for compromise labor agreements, rather than appearing to take pro-labor stands.

Other labor-related issues came before Congress. In June of 1937, Senator Hugo Black had joined with Congressman William P. Connery of Massachusetts to sponsor yet another federal board, this one to deal with the minimum wage. Senator Bridges was joined by senators Walter F. George and William Borah in making such a law more specific. They called for a 40-cents-an-hour minimum wage, along with time-and-a-half pay for more than forty hours worked in the course of one week. But the Black-Connery bill, which set the minimum wage at 25 cents per hour, banned "oppressive" child labor, and set the maximum work week at forty-four hours, prevailed and became law a month later. Constraints and exceptions to the final bill, however, reduced its implementation to only about one-fifth of the labor force.

As labor continued to flex its muscle, the CIO called for wildcat strikes (which occur without warning) and "sit-downs," a new phenomenon in American labor-management relationships. In a sit-down, workers physically occupied a plant and merely sat down, stopping work and effectively ending all operations. Bridges and others denounced this practice as a violation of property owners' rights, and joined in blaming federal labor agencies for not taking a stand against sit-downs. Unions countered that sit-downs were no worse than the management tactic of using lockouts, which prevented employees from working.

Bridges continued to berate the government for failing to use its agencies to curb the labor disputes, or at least outlaw sit-down demonstrations. While workers had the right to form unions for collective bargaining with employers, he insisted, they did not have the right to take over company plants. On April 14, 1937, by a vote of 48 to 36, the Senate rejected a resolution condemning sit-downs. Bridges had a minor victory a few days later, when the Senate passed a resolution censuring workers for striking, and employers for failing to deal with unions.

The Postal Investigation

Steelworkers instigated a particularly bitter and violent strike in the spring of 1937 against the Republic Steel Company, which refused to recognize a CIO union. As strikers picketed outside Republic plants in the

Midwest, nonunion workers labored inside. Some workers felt safer living at the plant during the strike, rather than face the wrath of picketers. Their families supplied them with food and clothing by mail, but at the Republic plants in Ohio, CIO pickets succeeded in blocking such shipments.

Using his position as a member of the relatively unimportant Senate Post Office Committee, Bridges proposed a possible illegal link between the CIO and the postal department. When Bridges learned that the CIO had curbed mail deliveries in Ohio, he demanded a Senate investigation, saying that the stopping of packages to nonunion workers was a violation of the postal laws. Bridges was quick to point out that the head of the Post Office Department was James Farley, who had been Roosevelt's campaign manager, and that the CIO had contributed nearly half a million dollars to the 1936 Democratic campaign.

Senator Kenneth D. McKellar of Tennessee, chairman of the Senate's Post Office Committee, called for an investigation. As the probe began, Bridges was invited to the White House for a session with President Roosevelt. He later told newsmen that the postal investigation was not discussed, but declined to elaborate further on the visit.

The first witness in the Senate probe was the postmaster of Niles, Ohio. He testified that he had been instructed by Washington postal authorities not to deliver "irregular" mail packages, and was told this was to include foodstuffs and packages of clothing sent to the nonunion workers within the strikebound plants.

A Washington postal official testified that the department had a right to refuse to handle mail that might be a threat to the carrier. Bridges stated that the CIO had sent intimidating letters and telegrams to local postmasters, demanding that questionable packages be returned to the senders. He also told the committee that a CIO official complained to the postmaster of Massillion, Ohio, for permitting the delivery of a pound of candy through the picket lines.

Bridges inveighed against Washington postal officials for failing to safeguard the mail when they knew a threat existed. He recalled that the Pony Express successfully operated against dangers in the pioneer years of the western states, and that President Grover Cleveland used federal troops to protect the mail during the long Pullman Company strike in 1894.

Bridges vainly demanded that Postmaster General Farley be questioned by the committee. The full committee voted 13 to 12 against that request, and the inquiry was terminated on June 27, 1937. Bridges then turned his evidence over to the Justice Department. The material eventually led to nine indictments for tampering with the mail.

Denunciations of the postal department drew national attention. *Time* magazine and several major newspapers, along with the media wire services, quoted Bridges' attacks at length, and photographs of the senator examining some of the undelivered packages were widely circulated. In its June 21, 1937, issue, *Time* magazine characterized him as "a man who rates even among Senate Democrats as no lightweight Republican heckler."

Challenging the TVA

Bridges also devoted much attention to the Tennessee Valley Authority, created in 1933 by the Roosevelt administration at the urging of Senator George Norris of Nebraska. The TVA had a dual purpose—to provide flood control in the Tennessee River Valley and to generate cheap electricity. (The project eventually turned to fertilizer production and became a much-copied model for economic soil conservation.)

Private power firms—especially Wendell Willkie's Commonwealth & Southern Company—opposed the TVA, but it had won substantial popular support through the years. On January 18, 1938, Senator Bridges rose in the Senate to accuse the agency of selling power to industrial users, to the detriment of the people the TVA was supposed to help.

The unfair rates had been set in secret, Bridges pointed out, with no public records by this public agency. He observed:

> The TVA was held out to the people down there as a great experiment in cost saving for the consumers. Yet, my investigation discloses that for every dollar's worth of current bought by the people in their homes, four dollars worth are sold to great corporations at reduced rates. . . . In short, this great humanitarian administration which poses as the protector of the ill-clad, ill-fed and the ill-housed . . . has now set a plate of cream at its back door for those whom the administration terms the fat cats of special privilege.

The charges fell on deaf ears at first. But then the three-man board that directed the TVA had a falling out, which became public. Chairman Dr. Arthur Morgan favored a showdown on the charges; his two associates refused to go along with him. Morgan began leaking information to Bridges and other Senate members.

On March 3, Bridges again took the offensive. He was joined by Senator William King of Utah in calling for a complete investigation of TVA operations. They charged both fraud and coercion. This drew a bitter response from Senator Norris, who had helped create the TVA. Norris opposed the probe and attacked Bridges as a lackey of the vested interests that promoted private power over public interest.

Bridges detailed his charges against the TVA in a radio speech on March 11, 1938, calling the agency "the worst scandal that has rocked our country since the days of the Teapot Dome." While its original goals had been worthwhile, he said, its operations had developed against the public interest. He cited the sale of phosphate land to the TVA at six times its value, claimed that 80 percent of TVA electricity was going to power companies, and slammed the agency's failure to submit its records for congressional review. Along with various other allegations of fraud, Bridges concluded by demanding that Congress revamp the TVA and improve its operations in the public interest.

His speech brought sharp rebukes from his associates. As Bridges continued to press for an investigation, Senator McKellar rose to accuse him of listening with an open mouth, rather than an open mind. "Newspapers are calling the Senator the new Coolidge and a candidate for President," McKellar charged. "The description has gone to the Senator's head so that he hasn't believed in anybody but himself since."

"Nothing has gone to my head," Bridges replied angrily.

McKellar shot back, "I think the Senator is right for a change, nothing has gone to his head."

Such floor disputes failed to dampen Bridges' ardor. As he rose at one point to embellish his claims, he said to the Senate, "I am going to tell you the story of a jackass."

"Not an autobiography, I hope," interjected Senator Alben Barkley of Kentucky.

Ignoring the remark, Bridges told of the TVA's purchase of a jackass as part of its agricultural improvement program. After searching most of the Midwest for the right animal, Bridges said, the TVA spent two thousand dollars getting the jackass to Tennessee, only to learn it could no longer breed. The beast was then sold for three hundred dollars.

"The TVA needn't have searched," jeered Senator Lewis B. Schwellenback. "They could have found plenty of [jackasses] in New Hampshire."

"As far as that goes," Bridges retorted, "they could have gotten one right off the emblem of the Democratic party!"

George Norris accused Bridges of attempting to discredit his pet agency. Norris stated that the burro had been purchased for two hundred and ninety dollars in 1934 and used for breeding for a year, then sold for three hundred and fifty dollars. Gleaning his information from the June 1937 *Congressional Record*, Bridges stuck by his story, stating on the record, "The Senator from New Hampshire still asserts that so far as he knows, based wholly upon the story in the *Congressional Record* at the time—which I assume to be accurate—that was the cost. . . . So far as the Senator from New Hampshire is concerned he is not at all impressed by the telegrams read by the Senator from Tennessee, because, for all I know, there may be many jackasses connected with the TVA."

A delighted press made much of these exchanges. Satires of a government agency searching for a perfect jackass appeared in most of the major newspapers, along with editorial cartoons.

In mid-March, Roosevelt called the three TVA directors together and ordered them to iron out their differences. Taking the offensive, chairman Morgan accused the president of attempted coercion. At that, senators began to think more seriously about the necessity of an investigation.

On March 15, Senator Norris withdrew his opposition to a TVA probe, provided that it be nonpartisan and made up of both Senate and House members. The Norris proposal was adopted a week later, and Roosevelt dismissed Morgan.

Bridges sought a seat on the nonpartisan committee, arguing that he had much information for its consideration. Norris opposed the idea, stressing that Bridges was far from nonpartisan on the issue. This precipitated more Senate floor argument, and on March 25, Bridges withdrew his request for a committee assignment. He was dealt a final insult when Senator Fred Brown of New Hampshire, an ardent Roosevelt supporter, was appointed to the committee. Both senators Borah and McNary resigned from the committee in protest of that appointment.

While Bridges had an impressive array of evidence against the TVA, most of it was lost when his office was mysteriously broken into late in May of 1938, in a curious burglary not unlike the Watergate break-in, some thirty-four years in the future.

The committee completed most of its investigating by December. Although it noted some wrongdoing by the TVA agency, it did not suggest any legislative action and ignored most of the criticisms Bridges leveled against it.

Yet in many ways, Bridges remained an "attack dog," often taking the negative approach to place his name before the public. Later in his Senate career he would develop his own secret files, to be used for political purposes and to his own advantage. His files are replete with "memos to the file" investigating a variety of individuals and issues. Bridges wanted to know everything that was going on in Washington, Concord, and elsewhere, and used this information to his political advantage. With only sixteen Republicans in the Senate, he had to find issues to be noticed and heard.

Moving the Republican Party Forward

As a vigorous spokesman, Bridges did much to revitalize the Republican party. In a 1937 speech in New York, he emphasized that the sagging image of the party was not necessarily fatal. He declared that Republicans should assume a role of being progressive constructionists, rather than simply obstructionists to the New Deal. Although the Republicans had been swamped in the 1936 election, "seventeen million votes had been cast for their national ticket, which resisted all the persuasions . . . of the greatest

Sally Bridges, whose tragic and untimely death in 1938 was a terrible blow to the Senator, his family, and the state.

political machine, the greatest spending machine, and the greatest propaganda machine in our history." To get back into the victory column, Bridges reiterated, Republicans should propose sound alternatives to the New Deal's centralization of power and its programs.

On another occasion he insisted that he was a liberal and New Dealers were radicals. "It isn't liberal to go bankrupt," he declared. "It isn't liberal to build up a crushing tax load. It isn't liberal to regiment people." The Republican party, he asserted, was the only alternative to one-man, one-party rule for the nation.

Back in New Hampshire, former governor Winant, who left the Social Security Administration in 1937, began having second thoughts about Bridges' political philosophy. Letters from Robert Bass to Bridges became less frequent. His one-time political ally, Congressman Tobey, also cooled toward him. Among his Granite State constituents, however, Bridges continued to be very popular. He and his staff responded consistently and quickly to their questions and appeals for consideration. By 1940, Bridges had developed his own party organization and a broad national image; the responses of his one-time friends like Winant and Bass meant little to him. "Going to Washington changes people," noted Sherman Adams. "You drop parochialism in a hurry and begin to see the big picture."

After only one year in the capital, the *Washington Times Herald* observed, "Senator H. Styles Bridges, serving his first term in Congress, has suddenly blossomed forth as the speaker of his party." Another paper commented, "It may be that the Moses who is to lead the Republicans out of the wilderness may be found in the person of Senator Bridges."

Tragedy in East Concord

In Concord, Sally Bridges was managing the family affairs. Perhaps concerned by her husband's slavish devotion to his political life, she purchased a set of golf clubs for Styles, in hopes that he would take up the game and learn to relax. When she failed to impress him, she turned to Ted Johnston and asked him to induce Bridges to take up golf. In deference to his wife, Styles did take up the sport, but he was never an avid golfer. In the words of some companions, he batted the ball around, playing only for the exercise.

Then, in May of 1938, a devastating and completely unexpected event took place; one that was to shake Bridges and his family to their core. Sally Bridges, at the age of thirty-five, was on her way to a dental appointment when she suffered a massive cerebral hemorrhage. She was rushed to Margaret Pillsbury Hospital, but there was little that could be done. Senator Bridges was flown from Washington in a Navy fighter plane, and arrived a few minutes after her death.

Shortly after his wife's death Bridges went briefly into semi-seclusion in Maine to try to recover from the shock of this incredible loss. This photograph suggests he found some solace in fishing and perhaps planning his next political move.

Nearly one thousand people attended Sally's funeral, which was held in the South Congregational Church in Concord. Neighbors and friends, as well as many important state and national figures were in attendance. The *Manchester Union Leader*, on May 30, 1938, reported that Sally was remembered as "a friendly, gracious woman, who had been a helpful wife and mother, rather than a person seeking official recognition because of the high offices her husband had gained." Norris Cotton, in an interview with the author, recalled that Styles was "heartbroken" by the tragedy.

After spending a few days with his family, Styles left the boys in the care of relatives and the Laurence Whittemore family, and departed on a Maine fishing trip, to ponder what was to follow. It was a strange occurrence. On May 30, the newspapers were filled with pictures of Sally's funeral; only a fortnight later, on June 13, Styles was photographed with a string of fish caught in upstate Maine—smoking his pipe, posing for the cameras. There is no record of Styles' thoughts, but he would quickly plunge back into his Senatorial duties and his political life.

The question has been raised: Should Styles have spent more time with his sons? Should he have attempted to fill the void in their lives, left by the loss of their mother? Probably. But the question of grief is a private one, even for a man who led such a public life as Styles Bridges. He was a complex, private man in his personal life. He was, from his earliest days, a loner, with few personal friends outside of his political circle. The loss, which must have been truly horrific, was a private affair for Bridges, and he dealt with it as such. How does one cope with the tragic sudden loss of a spouse? It is a question no one can answer.

Bridges emerged from the Maine woods determined to work harder than ever to ensure financial security for the raising of his three boys. This meant boarding schools and summer camps, seeing their father only on his infrequent visits to New Hampshire. John and Styles, Jr. adjusted to these circumstances, remembering their father with pride in later years. John, in particular, recalls his father as "an honorable, ethical, honest person." David, however, never seemed to recover, fighting bouts of depression and alcohol throughout his life. David was three years older than his brother John, and felt his mother's loss more acutely. He had long been the most difficult to manage, and after Sally's death, he became increasingly antisocial and aloof. Years later, when David died at forty-one, Jimmy Gaskell, who worked as an aide and a clerk in Washington during the Bridges years, remembered walking in the cemetery with Wes Powell, the senator's chief of staff: "Wes turned to me and said: 'You know what we are doing here today, Jimmy?' I said that we're at David's

The widowed Governor and his three sons, Henry Styles, Jr., David Clement Bridges, and John Fisher Bridges, at home in East Concord

funeral. Then Wes said to me, 'We're burying some of Styles Bridges' selfishness.'"

Return to Politics

Bridges turned to the 1938 campaign, the need for a stronger stance in the Congress, and a possible White House drive in 1940. It was clear that his family came second to his political ambitions.

Republicans had high hopes for the 1938 campaign, and Bridges began to work full time on party promotion. An abrupt economic downturn in 1938 made voters nervous. Bridges didn't hesitate to blame Roosevelt's policies for the recession. He wasted no words in berating the NLRB and the WPA, and he accused New Dealers of pork-barreling programs for their favorite spots while ignoring economic needs in other parts of the country.

Bridges spent considerable time in New Hampshire during the fall of 1938 to keep the state strongly Republican. His role was carefully planned: Rather than attack the Democratic nominees by name, he blasted "the Roosevelt New Deal." His strategy paid off handsomely. Charles Tobey was victorious against the Democrat Fred Brown in his second senatorial bid. Governor Murphy won a second term. Foster Stearns succeeded Tobey in the Second Congressional District, and Arthur Jenks was returned to his First Congressional District seat.

Republican success in New Hampshire was reflected throughout the nation. The party that was almost wiped out in 1936 increased its congressional representation by seventy-nine and gained six additional seats in the Senate.

Bridges was delighted. Never far from his mind was the Oval Office. He had been mentioned as a presidential contender in a poll taken by *Look* magazine in September of 1938. The list was long, but that didn't deter him. He wanted to see his name at the top.

6

War and Politics, Politics and War

"Then there is the Covenanter of strong religious faith, intransigent will, and a determination to trace one's own religious path, whatever opposition and criticism one might meet."

Gillian Gill, *Mary Baker Eddy*, 1998*

RESIDENTIAL POLITICS consumed Bridges in 1939. He hired an outstanding staff to help him achieve his goal. The brilliant and popular congressman Charles Hawks of Wisconsin was his campaign manager. His publicist was a handsome, mustachioed young Georgian named Charles Bargeron, who was considered one of the most effective of his breed in Washington. He hired Mollie Clinton, a former Barnard College teacher, and Richard Auerback, a young New Hampshire attorney, as researchers and speech writers.

Part of Bridges' strategy was to pay more attention to the Young Republicans. He urged them to help discard the old party leaders and vote in new ones. "In 1932, the Republican party went down for the count of ten," he said, "and in 1936 the corpse was supposed to be decently buried. But in 1938 it got up from the coffin, walked away from the funeral and now it has begun to scare the undertaker."

Presidential Aspirations

In early 1939, Michigan's Senator Vandenberg led the polls as a presidential candidate. He seemed reluctant to mount a serious campaign, however,

*Mary Baker Eddy was born in Bow, New Hampshire on July 16, 1821.

84

which encouraged other contenders to conclude they could top him. Bridges seemed to have made such a decision by the end of March.

Always frustrated by lack of money, Bridges faced the problem of financing a presidential drive. Edmund Converse of Bankers Trust and Palmer Beaudette, son of a wealthy Michigan automaker, took a liking to Bridges and contributed heavily to his campaign. Considerable financing came from small contributions solicited by a Bridges for President Club, which was organized in April of 1939 by George Conway, a Concord printer who had managed Foster Stearns' successful run for Congress.

On May 1, 1939, a mailing went out to party leaders urging them to back Bridges as the strongest Republican candidate for the 1940 presidential race. Bridges denied having anything to do with the pamphlet and said it was too early to announce his presidential plans, but he sent Conway a telegram thanking him for his efforts. That encouraged Conway to place newspaper ads spelling out the advantages of Bridges as president.

Response to the Bridges for President Club was encouraging. Former president Herbert Hoover gave a halfhearted endorsement when he observed, "This country has reached the stage again where it wants a New Englander President, not a New Yorker." The New Yorker was crimebuster Thomas E. Dewey, a district attorney who was rumored to be seeking the GOP nomination.

In June of 1940, the club released another pamphlet with a biography of Bridges, stressing his humble origin and his success as governor in sponsoring programs that had benefited the public. Two more pamphlets were issued by the BFPC in July and August. One spelled out his overall objectives by quoting from his speeches. The other sought to dispel any confusion between H. Styles Bridges and Harry Bridges, the longshoreman and leader of a 1934 Pacific Coast maritime strike. The text denounced Harry Bridges as a pro-Communist rabble-rouser, who was not even an American citizen. Senator Bridges was described as a man who believed in a fair deal for labor. From this time on the "H." disappeared from Senator Bridges' name in the national press. (The *New York Times* noted that this could be a good omen; presidents Cleveland, Grant, Wilson, and Coolidge had all dropped their first names in favor of their middle names.)

In late July of 1939, a series of articles about Bridges appeared in major newspapers around the nation, each including a photograph, a biography, and an appeal for support. The series proclaimed Bridges as the logical candidate for the Republican nomination in 1940, saying that his vigorous personality and proven record as a party leader outweighed the fact that he hailed from a small state.

On August 3, 1939, Senator Robert Taft of Ohio announced his candidacy, following in his father's footsteps. Bridges' announcement followed five days later. Meanwhile, Dewey also declared his candidacy. Bridges announced that he planned to campaign heavily in the western states, because of Taft's strength in the Midwest and Dewey's supposed appeal in the Northeast.

At the end of August, Bridges outlined details of his western campaign. Ironically, this gamble would end his presidential hopes. He called upon his supporters to sponsor unpledged delegates to the 1940 convention. "I believe that the election next year is important enough, and the conditions and issues are changing so that the Republican party should be free to choose the most logical candidate that can be picked under the circumstances present at that time," he explained.

While Taft and Dewey labored to win convention delegates pledged to them, Bridges hoped that neither would garner a majority. A deadlocked convention would then turn to a dark-horse nominee, even as the Democrats had in Baltimore in 1852, when they settled on Franklin Pierce as their candidate. Pierce went on to become the nation's fourteenth president in 1853, and New Hampshire's only elected representative to that high office. Through the same sort of maneuvering, Bridges hoped he could become its second. (In a bit of historic coincidences, it was in 1837 that Franklin Pierce served in the U.S. Senate, exactly one hundred years before Styles Bridges was sworn in for his first term. And both men would die in Concord, New Hampshire, Pierce at the age of sixty-four, Bridges at sixty-three.)

Before heading west, a confident and purposeful Bridges spent a few days at his East Concord home. He confided to a *Boston Globe* journalist, "It seems too bad to have to leave this delightful spot and spend forty-seven days on a speaking tour of forty states . . . but in these days a candidate for President cannot sit down and wait for the honor to come to him."

A few days later, on September 1, 1939, Hitler's forces invaded Poland. World War II in Europe was under way, although Americans still hoped they could stay out of the conflict. Congress was called into special session to deal with laws relating to U.S. neutrality. This delayed Bridges' campaign tour; and more important, it changed the entire complexion of the 1940 campaign.

Roosevelt addressed the special session of Congress, urging lawmakers to lift the embargo of arms sold to belligerents so the United States could help England and France. To keep the appearance of neutrality, the arms had to be transported in non-American vessels and sales were to be made strictly on a "cash-and-carry" basis.

Most senators responded favorably to Roosevelt's proposal as a way to help the Allies without becoming entangled in their war. But the isolationist block, led by Hiram Johnson of California and William Borah of Idaho, criticized the proposal as one that could lead the nation into war.

Bridges introduced a compromise, adding a preamble that pledged the United States to peace at all costs. While the Senate debated the issue, Americans flooded their congressional delegations with mail. Bridges received twenty-one thousand letters from New Hampshire, running 2-to-1 for Roosevelt's proposal. It eventually passed and went into effect in November.

Despite the military buildup in Europe and the Pacific, Bridges continued to think that domestic issues were more important than foreign affairs. While he hammered away at the poor economy, which he blamed on the New Deal, President Roosevelt focused on aiding the Allies against the Axis powers, without directly involving the American armed forces. Bridges claimed Roosevelt was using the European situation as a smokescreen to cover his domestic problems. However, Bridges' speeches primarily stuck to the same domestic issues he had emphasized since becoming a senator.

On December 18, 1939, Bridges returned home after a tour of eight thousand miles and thirty-four speeches. He told newsmen that the country seemed ready for a change in leadership, and that he had been impressed with the support he had encountered. Although new polls showed that Vandenberg, Dewey, and Taft were well ahead of him, Bridges continued to speak with an air of optimism. Using tactics that had worked in New Hampshire, he told farmers that New Deal bureaus were strangling agricultural initiative. He continued to harp on the need for a balanced budget and argued that economic recovery was hampered by the erratic behavior of New Deal agencies. He also contended that economic recovery was more important at that time than an enlarged national defense, and urged continued United States neutrality in the distant European war.

Dealing with the War Clouds

Americans in the 1930s were more concerned about surviving the devastating Depression than worrying about foreign affairs. The appalling casualty figures of World War I prompted most Americans to remain aloof from European struggles for power. Furthermore, the report of the Nye Committee, which met from 1934 through 1937, showed that war acted to make the rich richer, at the expense of average citizens. The result was a mood of isolationism—nothing beyond the nation's boundaries should require a sacrifice of either men or resources.

One of the first bills Bridges voted on as a new senator was a response to the Spanish Civil War. Americans were forbidden to sell arms to belligerents in a declared war, but the law did not cover civil strife, and shipping munitions to warring factions in Spain was in question. Senator Key Pittman of Nevada proposed a revision of the existing law to ban the sale of munitions for all types of warfare, including civil war. Bridges opposed the measure, saying it would be detrimental to weak nations that might be overrun by stronger neighbors. Isolationists were not impressed by Bridges' logic, and the Senate approved the bill, 66 to 6.

After that, Bridges began to question how well the nation was equipped to face an armed attack. He raised questions in 1937 and 1938 as to the wisdom of selling strategic materials to foreign countries, especially to potential enemies. He was also one of the first senators to demand an investigation into the sale of scrap iron and iron ore to Japan. John Warrington recalled that Bridges was fond of telling aides later in his senatorial career that he was one of the first to warn that iron sent to Japan would return in the bodies of dead American boys.

Although he sided with isolationists on some issues, Bridges maintained that the United States should protect its interests and deal fairly in international problems, not rushing in to take sides. As a member of the Senate Military Affairs Committee (later the Armed Services Committee), Bridges was invited to the White House for a briefing in the spring of 1939. He was shocked to learn details of the situation in Europe. Roosevelt had sworn the committee members to secrecy, but his remarks seemed so vital to the national interest that Bridges called on him to make this knowledge public, so the nation would know the dangers facing it. When the president refused, Bridges publicly accused him of establishing foreign alliances in secret.

In a debate with Senator Tom Connally of Texas on the "Town Meeting of the Air" radio program of March 20, 1939, Bridges defined his position more clearly, "I realize that we cannot stick our heads in the sand and pretend that occurrences in Europe and Asia are no concern of ours. I am not an isolationist in the sense of one who believes that the Atlantic and Pacific oceans are sure protection and that we can let the world explode around us," he stated.

In April of 1940, the America First Committee was formed by prominent isolationists like senators Borah and Wheeler. America First clubs quickly spread across the nation. In May, newspapermen William Allen White and Clark Eichelberger, director of the League of Nations Association, organized a rival group called the Committee to Defend America by Aiding the Allies. Membership was by invitation only. Senator Bridges was one of about six hundred Americans invited to join. He became active in the organization and frequently spoke on its behalf. Frank Knox, later named secretary of the navy, and Henry Stimson, soon to be secretary of war, were also active in the group.

Realizing that a cancellation of the project would favor Midwest ports over New England seaports, Bridges used the national-defense argument to attack the St. Lawrence Seaway project when it was first proposed in 1940. He argued that the seaway would provide an enemy navy with an easy invasion route to the central part of the nation.

Just before the nation's first primary in 1940, in New Hampshire, Bridges made a bid for another untapped block of voters. On February 8, as the armed forces waged recruitment drives, Bridges rose in the Senate and demanded an investigation of reports that the Army Air Corps had a "whites only" policy for its pilot training program. His charge forced the army to investigate. Bridges received substantial recognition in black newspapers across the nation, and is credited with leading the effort to begin training African-American pilots at the famous Tuskegee Air Base.

The 1940 Presidential Primary

February also saw Bridges on the road again in the West to address several Lincoln's Birthday rallies. By mid-March, he had delivered another thirty-five speeches in nine states, but polls showed him continuing to slip in popularity as the Vandenberg, Dewey, and Taft camps gained momentum.

In New Hampshire's primary on March 12, 1940, Bridges clung to his appeal for unpledged delegates and worked for a large vote to get the attention of the national party leaders. As Bridges had instructed them, Governor Murphy and other top party leaders filed as unpledged delegates. Bridges suffered a major disappointment when Dewey announced he would not contest for convention delegates in any primary in which a favorite son was a candidate. It was a smart political move, as his announcement deprived Bridges of his hope to trounce a major opponent in this first test of his vote-getting ability.

As expected, Bridges swept to victory in the New Hampshire primary, and captured his "uncommitted" slate of delegates. But two disturbing incidents occurred. One was that the Democrats elected a delegation pledged to Roosevelt for a third term, even though the president had not yet declared he would run again. The other was the surprise defeat of Governor Murphy as a Bridges delegate. This was regarded as a rebuff to Murphy's administration, and led to a rift that eventually caused problems for the Republican party in New Hampshire and for Bridges personally.

Bridges needed to face one or more of his opponents in a state primary to gauge his strength, but he chose to continue campaigning primarily in the West, instead of concentrating on the states with primaries and fighting for

A beaming Senator Bridges symbolically throws his hat in the ring as a presidential candidate in 1940 with the help of the Hat Style Council, which presented him with this twelve-hat wardrobe

unpledged delegates. Although he insisted that he was not waiting for the presidency to come to him, his tactics amounted to the same thing. The net result was that while he continued to gain national attention with his speeches, he failed to actively seek the support of convention delegates—those who had the power to give him the nomination.

After New Hampshire, primaries sprang up all across the nation. A pro-Bridges uncommitted slate of delegates won in Maine, but Dewey easily crushed Bridges and Taft forces in Wisconsin. By May of 1940, Dewey and Taft each had more than one hundred pledged delegates. In the Connecticut and Illinois primaries, the Bridges forces tried to dump Dewey, but failed. By mid-May, Dewey had collected 181 delegates; Taft had 110. Senator Vandenberg, whose quiet "front-porch" campaign had failed dismally, held only 38, although he remained the favorite of many party leaders. At about this time, Bridges slipped from fourth place to seventh in a Gallup poll.

Bridges drew cheers as he entered Philadelphia's Convention Hall on June 24, but he must have realized by then that his cause was hopeless. The convention seemed likely to nominate either Taft or Dewey, and if it became deadlocked, Wendell Willkie, the darkest of dark horses, would be the choice. President of a utility company, Willkie had never held public office. His campaign was so quiet and lackluster as to be almost invisible. He came to the convention without a single delegate pledged in his favor, but he was a new face and had a personal magnetism that inspired trust. The delegates fell in love with him.

The candidates—including publisher Frank Gannett and three favorite sons, in addition to Bridges—divided their time between the Convention Hall and their campaign headquarters at the Walton, Benjamin Franklin, and Adelphia hotels. Deals were made and unmade; favors promised and withdrawn. Rumor and speculation were as common as candidates giveaways. (Twelve tons of trash were collected at Convention Hall after only one day, *Newsweek* reported.)

As Willkie forces canvassed delegates for support, it was rumored that Bridges might be tapped as the vice-presidential nominee. Another report, that Governor Murphy—who was not even a delegate—was a VP possibility, seemed without foundation. It was, however, sufficient to increase friction between Bridges and Murphy.

As time for the balloting neared and groundswell support for the popular Hoosier grew, party professionals launched a massive "stop Willkie" campaign. It appeared that neither Taft nor Dewey would win on the first ballot, and Vandenberg was too weak to be a compromise nominee. In desperation, party organizers turned to Herbert Hoover to block the Willkie nomination, but he declined to even consider such action.

Bridges, his son John, and a GOP elephant were featured on the cover of the May 1940 issue of "The Republican."

On the first ballot, Dewey gained 360 votes out of the 501 needed to win the nomination. Taft placed second, followed by Willkie and Vandenberg. New Hampshire, Maine, and other unpledged delegates gave Bridges a first-ballot vote of 28.

Dewey and Taft held their leads on the second ballot, but Willkie gained sixty-six votes, and the gallery started the hypnotic chant: "We want Willkie! We Want Willkie!" A third, fourth, and fifth ballot were taken without a winner. Most of the favorite sons had released their delegations from any commitments, and support for Dewey and Taft eroded with each vote. On the sixth ballot, the tension in the hall was palpable. The vote totals could hardly be heard over the noise of the stomping, shouting crowd. When Vandenberg released his Michigan delegation, Willkie was over the top. The crowd went wild, buckets of confetti poured down on the delegates. They were jubilant—they had gotten what they wanted. Unfortunately, what they got was an untried, untested businessman with no political experience.

Willkie gained the support of party professionals, however, by choosing Senator McNary, the minority Senate leader, as his vice-presidential running mate. Bridges was turned down for the second slot, not because of a lack of national recognition, but because he was unacceptable to the party leadership. Forgotten were his efforts to revive the party in the dark days of 1937. Despite the confidence the party leaders had shown in him then as their fair-haired boy, he was no longer needed.

Bridges managed to dust himself off in a hurry. Always a party man, he campaigned enthusiastically for Willkie, which pleased the nominee, who recognized and appreciated Bridges' talents as a party leader. Bridges was important to Willkie's New England campaign, and Willkie chose him to respond to Interior Secretary Harold Ickes, who had announced that Roosevelt would refuse to debate Willkie publicly. Ickes accused Willkie of being a tool of the power trusts, and declared, "The president cannot call off the Battle of Britain in order to ride the circuit with Mr. Willkie."

The Democrats spent $7,500 disseminating the announcement, while Bridges' retort only cost the Republicans $4,000. The Democrats could spend more than the Republicans, Bridges asserted, because Democrat funds were collected from "New Deal business victims." He rapped Roosevelt for not speaking for himself before the American people and using the "Keeper of the White House Umbrella" as his spokesman. Bridges also labeled Ickes as "a Hitler in short pants" and a "common scold puffed up by high office." He accused the president of inaction while Hitler built up his forces, and then keeping foreign policy details from the American people.

Although Bridges traveled throughout the nation boosting the Willkie-McNary campaign in the fall of 1940, he still found time to work in New

Campaign memorabilia from Bridges 1940 presidential bid

Hampshire for the Republican slate of nominees, after having once again remained clear of the primary contests. Governor Murphy's proposed third term had met with great opposition, so Dr. Robert O. Blood of Concord, president of the State Senate, became the Republican candidate for governor. After considerable infighting, Murphy bitterly announced his retirement.

In November, Blood was elected governor, and Stearns and Jenks were returned to Congress. Bridges' support for Willkie helped the Republican candidate carry New Hampshire, but Willkie did not fare well nationally. FDR, who was perceived as being in control of America's role in the unfolding world turmoil, became the nation's first and only three-term president. Prosperity had returned to the nation, due in large part for orders from the Allies for war materials. However, Roosevelt's coattails were not as long in this election as they had been in the past. Republicans gained five more Senate seats, and lost only one House seat.

After the election, Bridges again blasted the president for failing to inform the American people on how involved the nation had become in the conflicts overseas. He voiced concern that disloyal Americans might hamper the war effort, pointing out that German troops had been aided by "fifth columnists" in some European countries. The existence of such organizations as the German-American Bund gave credence to Bridges' warnings.

He also denounced the waves of strikes that spread through various industries in 1940-41, as defense production boomed. Strikes were a form of sabotage, he declared. "A small handful of racketeering labor leaders, many of whom are aliens and a large percentage of whom are Communists, with some Nazis, are calling and continuing strikes at will," he asserted. To combat these elements, Bridges suggested in February of 1941 that all schools be required to teach American values to expose Nazi and Communist propaganda. He continued to echo this theme throughout his career.

By the fall of 1941, most Americans had conceded the need for preparedness. In October, when a German submarine attacked the U.S.S *Kearney*, an American destroyer operating off the coast of Iceland, Bridges became one of the first to call for the complete repeal of the neutrality laws, in order to permit the arming of all American vessels.

In December, Bridges embarked upon a speaking tour of the Granite State. On December 6, addressing a session of the New Hampshire Truck Owners Association in Manchester, he stressed that the nation was in a critical period, as the United States and Japan were negotiating over the withdrawal of Japanese troops from China. "This situation remains acute," he said prophetically, "and something may happen within twenty-four hours."

Senator Bridges receiving telephone confirmation from Washington at approximately 3:15 PM of the authenticity of the Pearl Harbor bombing reports on December 7, 1941. The scene is the Lebanon Town Hall following a Preparedness Meeting.

World War II Begins

The next day, as Bridges prepared to address a civil defense town meeting in Lebanon with his friend Judge Norris Cotton acting as chairman, he was suddenly called to the telephone. The Japanese had just attacked Pearl Harbor. Bridges relayed the shocking information to his audience, berating isolationists for delaying war preparations, then hurried back to Washington.

At a special session of Congress on December 8, Bridges joined the unanimous Senate vote for a declaration of war. He later told his constituents, "We are going into battle in the defense of our homes and the only way of life the people of New Hampshire and all Americans care to live."

Washington was immediately plunged into a flurry of activity. Despite the year-long "preparedness" campaign, America was far from ready for war. Behind blackout curtains, agency bureaucrats worked late, devising the elaborate system that would ration America's resources "for the duration." At the War Department, officials planned a Selective Service call, which would come in the form of a lottery. Streams of volunteers appeared at Red Cross and Civil Defense offices, eager to do their part. The Japanese attack on United States soil swept away the isolationist movement and "awakened the Sleeping Giant" of American industrial might. It would prove to be one of the greatest blunders in the history of warfare.

On December 31, 1941, Bridges slipped on an icy sidewalk and fractured his hip. Despite being hospitalized, he signed up for the draft, although he was not required to do so. His son, H. Styles Bridges, Jr., left his job with the New England Telephone Company to join the navy. Father and son signed their respective papers together in Bridges' hospital room.

Bridges continued to be in good spirits, despite the fact that his fracture did not readily heal. It was not until June of 1942, that he was able to return to the Senate. He was at once appointed to a wartime committee to monitor war productions and ensure that the government was not being overcharged by contractors. The group, known as the Truman Committee—its chairman was Senator Harry Truman of Missouri—became the watchdog of the defense industry.

Toward a Second Term

Bridges' first six-year Senate term was to end in 1942. Because of his chronic ill health, there was speculation in New Hampshire about whether or not he would seek reelection. On June 26, he announced he would seek a second term, with the following terse message:

> For six years I have had the privilege and honor of serving the people of New Hampshire in the United States Senate. I told you six years ago that if chosen to represent you in the Senate, my approach to each issue would be from one angle only and that is what is best for the people of New Hampshire and the country. Over the years, I have kept faith with you and in announcing my candidacy for the Republican nomination for reelection, I repeat that solemn pledge.

Bridges had taken to the Senate the same pay-as-you-go philosophy that endeared him to his constituents as governor. Senator Tom Connally, in his book *My Name is Tom Connally* (Thomas Y. Crowell, New York, 1954), observed that Styles "particularly enjoyed going through appropriation bills and pouncing upon little items, as if he had discovered criminal acts in the executive branch." Such behavior drew attention to Bridges from both sides of the aisle and in the national press, securing his old reputation as a Republican attack dog. He entered his second senatorial campaign after a busy term that had drawn much attention to himself and New Hampshire.

Although Bridges appeared assured of renomination by his own party, he faced a surprise opponent. A few days after his announcement, former governor Murphy announced that he was switching to the Democratic party. He denounced the Republican leadership as synthetic and unresponsive to the public needs. A month later, after negotiating with William J. Neal of Meredith, a prominent Democrat and agricultural leader, to run for governor, he declared his candidacy for the Senate.

Murphy had a substantial Republican following from his two terms as governor, and Bridges considered him a solid threat. Added to the Democratic endorsement, Murphy's appeal seemed far reaching. To make matters worse, Bridges' chief of staff, Elmer Cartledge, suddenly resigned in protest against the appointment of Ernest Martin Hopkins of Hanover, the president of Dartmouth College, as Styles' campaign director, an assignment Cartledge had wanted.

Seeking a new chief of staff, Bridges picked attorney Wesley Powell of Hampton Falls to run his office. Powell, who would later become governor of New Hampshire, performed his new duties with great success. With his staff once again intact, Bridges next turned to the Bass family for financial help. He got it, and Mrs. Bass agreed to head up a Women's Division for the campaign.

Bridges easily won renomination in the Republican primary, by an impressive margin of more than 10 to 1, against Arthur J. Gruenler of Hillsborough, a political unknown. Governor Blood and Congressman Stearns were also handily renominated. Congressman Jenks, however, lost out in the First District, as Chester Merrow of Ossipee squeezed out that nomination by a tight 10,988 to 10,140 vote tally.

Despite travel restrictions due to wartime gasoline rationing, Bridges devoted much time during his campaign to making contacts with local party committees and town party leaders. He called upon workers in critical industries to increase production to back the war effort, and criticized President Roosevelt's home-front strategy. Republicans, he promised, could be counted upon to produce "more gun barrels and fewer pork barrels."

Murphy spent most of his time attempting to raise issues against Bridges. He failed to get financial support or personal endorsement from Democratic national leaders. Attacking Bridges for his criticisms of the TVA, Murphy charged that his opponent was a friend of the big utilities. But this issue failed to draw much attention, as the war effort claimed virtually all public interest. Murphy then turned to personal attacks upon Bridges. He purchased newspaper space and radio time to rap Bridges' integrity and alleged lack of service to his constituents.

By mid-October, Bridges took issue with Murphy's attacks. He demanded an investigation by the Federal Communication Commission. Murphy owned a radio station, and refused to give Bridges equal time to respond to the charges his opponent was leveling at him. Bridges also demanded that the Senate Elections Committee check the sources of Murphy's extensive spending. A wealthy shoe manufacturer, Murphy was admittedly spending heavily, but there was little doubt that it was his own money. Bridges was probably not serious about pursuing an investigation. By this time, he had become committed to a policy of never taking anything for granted in a political campaign, and utilizing every opportunity to benefit his own candidacy.

Bridges led the Republican slate to a substantial victory in the November 3 election, topping Murphy by a vote of 88,601 to 73,656. Happy with his reelection, he probably no longer entertained higher ambitions. He was also less lonely in the Senate, as the 1942 election gave him thirty-six Senate colleagues instead of the fifteen from the 1937 election. Republicans boosted their membership to just nine votes short of a majority, and Styles Bridges, who had gotten in on the Republican recovery when the party was literally on the bottom floor, was rapidly gaining seniority.

Now he had to help the nation win the war.

7

Yankee Ingenuity

"Live Free or Die."

General John Stark
New Hampshire State Motto

AFTER PEARL HARBOR the nation's mood changed almost overnight. The enemy attack immediately unified the country and isolationism vanished. Americans were confident they would win the war. The question was: How?

Time was what America needed most. The Axis powers—Germany, Italy, and Japan—had been preparing for war for almost ten years. The U.S. tried to catch up in a few months, and amazed the world by actually doing just that. Within weeks of Pearl Harbor, millions of men headed for military training camps, and millions of women joined the workforce. Yankee ingenuity was the nation's most valuable asset in converting manufacturing plants into defense plants. Automobile manufacturers began to build airplanes and tanks; dress manufacturers turned out uniforms; food-processing plants produced GI rations. Life went into high gear. Shifts worked around the clock, enlistees jammed railroad stations, and the "blues" of the Depression swung into the jumpin', jivin' jitterbug.

The nation's darkest hours came in the spring of 1942, when the battle in the Pacific seemed hopeless. Americans got out their atlases to locate the tiny islands that were in the news. Wake Island was the first to fall to the Japanese forces. When the defense of Manila collapsed, General Douglas MacArthur retreated to Australia, promising to return and liberate the Philippines. In April, more than one thousand soldiers died on the Bataan death march, under conditions that horrified Americans. The battle of the Coral Sea ended in defeat for the U.S. Navy, and Corregidor fell directly after.

Then, when things seemed most grim, there was a victory. In June, the triumph of U.S. forces in the Battle of Midway sent a new surge of hope across America—a turnabout was on its way. Within a month, the U.S. Army Air Force began to bomb Nazi strongholds in France, and by fall the North African campaign had begun. The Allies were on the offensive at last.

Congress responded to wartime measures as quickly as possible. Dozens of new agencies cropped up for the war effort, including the Office of Price Administration, which was in charge of rationing—rubber, gasoline, food, even shoes. Hopeful office-seekers flooded Washington and business executives were drafted to work in government jobs as "dollar-a-year men," expecting to return to their regular jobs when the war was over.

Bridges' new chief of staff, Wesley Powell, resigned to join his three brothers in the armed forces. He was replaced by Hamilton S. Putnam, a Wilton publicist, who also resigned to join the navy.

The Manhattan Project

Bridges most important role in the war was a secret one: He emerged from the meeting with Roosevelt as one of only four senators entrusted with the secret of the Manhattan Project. As a leading opposition senator on the Senate Appropriations Committee, it was necessary for him to know the details of the project. The funding for this massive, risky undertaking was hidden in other appropriation bills, which had to be approved by the Senate without question or investigation. Bridges did his job. Funding for the Manhattan Project (named for the Manhattan district of the U.S. Army Corps of Engineers, where the idea for an atomic weapon originated) slipped through congressional appropriations, without suspicion or objection.

As early as 1939, physicists, including the pacifist Albert Einstein, had written to President Roosevelt urging him to begin a research program in the use of atomic fission as a military weapon. Military information hinted that the Germans were involved in their own "heavy-water" experiments—the first step in producing atomic-grade uranium—so time was of the essence. In May of 1941, six months before Pearl Harbor, forty tons of graphite and eight tons of uranium oxide were ordered for government experiments. Working at the University of Chicago, in a makeshift laboratory set up in an unused underground squash court, Enrico Fermi and his team of researchers achieved the world's first self-sustaining fission reaction, on December 2, 1942.

As funding became available, construction of the first plant for separating the large amount of uranium 235 (U-235) necessary to produce an explosive device, was begun two months later. The plant became functional on January 27, 1944. Construction of a second massive plant was begun in September of 1943, and was in production by February 20, 1945. It was, as historians were later to speculate, "the greatest scientific gamble in history" (*Delivered From Evil*; Robert Lechie, Harper & Row, 1987).

Certainly the cost of the project, more than $2 billion, was an astounding figure at the time. Years later, in 1961, shortly before his death, Bridges appeared on the CBS News program "*Washington Conversation*." The fiscally conservative senator recalled funding the experiment:

> I was one of only four senators who knew about the bomb, and we did spend two and a half billion dollars on it, funding it in secret through the Appropriations Committee. I've often wondered if the atomic bomb had not been a success, and it was found afterward that we had spent over two billion, which all of our colleagues except the four of us were unaware of, whether we would have been indicted, instead of praised, as we were when it was a success.

And what was it that Yankee ingenuity, with the help of Congressional funding, would bring into the world? Without question, a frightening new kind of devastation; but it would also bring about the end of the war in the Pacific.

In Japan in early 1943, the Imperial Army Aeronautic Technology Research Institute sent a report to the Japanese High Command, stating that development of an atomic bomb was feasible. Prime Minister Tojo gave the Nishina Laboratories in Tokyo unlimited resources for the development of such a weapon. Nishina Laboratories began to set up for the experiments, ordering two tons of uranium ore from a mine in German-controlled Czechoslovakia. The shipment, however, never reached Japan, and on April 13, 1945, the incendiary bombing of Tokyo destroyed Nishina's main research laboratory.

In Germany, the Nazi search for a successful chain reaction was being frustrated by a lack of "heavy water," essential to the success of their project, as American bombing raids and a daring sabotage operation of the Norsk-Hydro plant at Vermork in neutral Norway slowed research to a halt. But in America the experiments continued. In 1945 all the various facets of the program, spread out across the country, were moved to a single facility in Los Alamos, New Mexico, beginning a final push to bring mankind into the Atomic Age.

Fighting the Flynn Nomination

As Bridges started his second term in January of 1943, he was a veteran of dozens of legislative battles. He had been dogging Roosevelt for six years, and war or no war, he wasn't going to stop now.

The first dispute of 1943 was over an ambassadorship appointment. In early January, Edward J. Flynn, national chairman of the Democratic party, announced that he had just been appointed as ambassador to Australia and the Southwest Pacific. The fact that Flynn, not the president, made the announcement was a serious breach of protocol, and many senators were outraged. Talk of scandals involving Flynn's earlier career became public and a cause for concern, even among Democrats. While he was the head of the Democratic party machine in New York City, it was alleged, Flynn had had the courtyard of his Long Island estate covered with granite paving blocks, paid for by the city. A grand jury subsequently cleared "Paving-block Flynn," but now Senator McNary, the Republican minority leader, called for an investigation.

Bridges was quick to join the opposition to the appointment. He charged that while Flynn was sheriff of Bronx County he appointed the notorious gangster Dutch Shultz as a deputy. "In my judgement, the naming of Mr. Flynn as Ambassador or Minister to Australia or any other country on the face of the earth is an insult to the people of America and to the people of the country to which he is named," declared Bridges, the self-appointed Republican watchdog.

While the Senate's Republican leadership maneuvered to force public hearings, Bridges kept the issue alive in the national press, using every opportunity to embarrass the Democrats. In one speech he charged that Flynn had solicited the ambassadorship to gain immunity from prosecution. "I don't blame the Democrats for wanting to get rid of him after the way he bungled the last campaign," Bridges declared.

Under Bridges' needling, Democrats began to give serious attention to Flynn's qualifications. While only one Democrat, Patrick A. McCarran of Nevada, openly opposed the appointment, the Democratic majority voted for public hearings before the Senate Foreign Relations Committee.

To Bridges' surprise, the committee agreed to hear his charges, even though he was not a committee member. As he rose to excoriate the Flynn nomination, a group of Democrats walked out. Undaunted, Bridges observed, "Mr. President, it is my observation in looking about the chamber today that the stench of the Flynn appointment has become so nauseating to the majority members of the Senate that when it is known that the senator from New Hampshire would make further remarks, the majority of them beat it to the cloakroom."

Flynn later responded: "I do not expect Bridges to be among the class of just men capable of weighing plain evidence as against malicious detraction, because of his violent dislike of the administration."

On January 14, 1943, the hearings began and Senator Bridges got his day in court. He charged that Flynn's law firm was connected with a company that had paid bribes to "large Japanese interests" before the war. Further, he charged, as chamberlain (treasurer) of New York, Flynn had influenced the city to invest over $1 million in a shaky company that eventually collapsed, and criticized Flynn for appointing Dutch Shultz as a deputy sheriff of Bronx County, even though Shultz was wanted on fugitive charges. Finally, Bridges accused Flynn of rigging the jury that cleared him in the paving-blocks scandal, even procuring a federal job for the jury foreman. Witnesses gave evidence in support of these charges, and Bridges was pleased with the press coverage. He was disappointed, however, when New York mayor Fiorello LaGuardia, a long-time Flynn political enemy, and a potential star witness, declined to testify.

Flynn firmly denied all of Bridges' charges. No one could prove that he had failed to properly carry out any of the public offices he had held over the years, he declared. He reminded the committee that he had been exonerated of the paving-blocks charge. As for the Schultz appointment, the notorious gangster had used an alias; how was Flynn to have known who the man actually was?

After weeks of deliberations, the committee voted 13 to 10 to confirm Flynn's appointment; but the investigation had done him significant damage and it was clear a tough floor fight lay ahead. Flynn, a shrewd enough politician to foresee probable defeat, asked President Roosevelt to withdraw his nomination.

Styles Bridges—the Watchdog

With an eye out for government inefficiency, Bridges insisted upon being left free to criticize any of the wartime agencies that exceeded their authority or favored one group of citizens against another. He attacked the National Labor Relations Board for arbitrarily settling a contract dispute between the CIO and the Kaiser Shipbuilding Company, which produced the famous Liberty ships. Kaiser had drawn up a previous agreement with the AFL unions, and the NLRB invalidated them in favor of the CIO.

Bridges also attacked the War Production Board for setting up a federal salvage agency in New Hampshire to reclaim scrap metal, when one operated by volunteers was already in place—the only such facility in the nation not under federal control. The work of the volunteer salvage unit proved so successful that the WPB bowed to Bridges and disbanded its New Hampshire agency.

Campaigning for various war bond drives, Bridges asked New Hampshire workers to "make every home and work bench a battleground."

Oil for the military took top priority, and the war created an instant severe domestic shortage. Bridges fought for increased allotments for oil-poor New England and rapped government agencies for telling New Englanders to convert their furnaces from coal to oil, in order to save coal, and then reducing the area's oil allotment. He called for a pipeline to go from New Jersey terminals into New England, permitting summer storage of oil to prepare for winter demands, and he wanted more coastal and barge canals to expedite shipments as well. His advocacy won some relief for New England, and the gratitude of its citizenry.

Bridges frequently toured training camps to check conditions and called for a ban on slot machines, which he said enticed soldiers to waste their pay. He campaigned for bills to aid the families of servicemen, including some measures that eventually became part of the G.I. Bill of Rights. He intervened for families with several draft-eligible sons, so that not all would have to go to war, and arranged a transfer from the battle zone for the son of one family that had already lost two boys in the fighting. He also opposed the drafting of fathers into the armed forces.

Looking ahead, Bridges advocated an active role for the United States in postwar world affairs. The United States could not isolate itself once peace was restored, Styles knew, and when the idea of an international organization to deal with potential threats to world peace was first proposed in 1943 he supported it. He objected to Roosevelt's personal handling of foreign affairs without consulting the Senate and declared his support for American participation in postwar reconstruction.

Bridges Weds Doloris Thauwald

Sometime during his second term, Senator Bridges met Doloris Thauwald, who worked in the visa office of the State Department. As a senator in his early forties with seniority and power, Bridges was one of the most eligible bachelors in Washington. The casual acquaintance slowly grew into a more serious relationship, and on February 11, 1944, they were married in Doloris' hometown of St. Paul, Minnesota.

Doloris Bridges was almost immediately a controversial character in Styles' life. She seemed to inspire either intense admiration or open dislike. Those who shared her strong conservative beliefs considered her a good influence on the senator's public life. Unlike the modest Sally Bridges, who was more than content with her role out of the limelight, the new Mrs. Bridges considered herself an integral part of her husband's political career, and enthusiastically participated in Washington's social life and its political intrigue. Doloris was so outspoken

Doloris Thauwald, third wife of Styles Bridges

that on occasion she embarrassed her husband. She once called John F. Kennedy, running for president against Richard Nixon in 1960, "soft on communism." (Kennedy would later attempt to invade Cuba, using CIA-backed Cuban nationalists, in the ill-advised Bay of Pigs fiasco; and he ordered a naval blockade of Castro's island during the Cuban Missile Crisis.) An ardent feminist, she frequently berated Hollywood movie studios for portrayal of women in films. And in the *St. Paul Pioneer Press*, on January 14, 1952, Doloris expressed her views on U.S. foreign aid:

> It is all very nice to be charitable to the world, and concerned about its welfare, but I was really shocked recently when my next-door neighbor in Concord, N.H., told me she had not had meat on her table for four months. . . . Many people in the United States today are just not earning enough to cope with the fantastic food prices. They are respectable, proud, hard-working Americans who do not want help from anyone. They should be our first consideration. . . . We need to be careful, so that our money is not sent down the drain all over the world.

Doloris' extreme conservatism and her love for Washington's social life had a great impact on Bridges. While the senator occasionally found himself back-peddling from his wife's remarks, one can clearly hear his own positions reflected by his outspoken spouse.

Doloris was described as "a tall, stately, slender blonde . . . with large blue eyes, fair skin, and a heart-shaped face." She was known to be "a talented pianist, a good amateur photographer, and a fair golfer." Doloris became an active leader in New Hampshire and national Republican circles, and her politics, combined with her sometimes abrasive personality, finally severed what was left of Bridges' ties to the old progressive faction. This did not bother Bridges, because he had continued faith in his appeal to New Hampshire voters. Feelings among the old progressive faction in New Hampshire were that Bridges would have taken a far different path if Sally, the antithesis of Doloris, had survived.

Bridges was frustrated, however, by Doloris' unwillingness to accept that she herself was not the senator. "She oftentimes felt overshadowed by Dad and was frustrated by this," recalled John Bridges. She viewed Styles' senatorial staff as at her disposal, and had a reputation for using nearly everyone around her. Mrs. Scott McLeod (now of Concord, New Hampshire), whose husband had been a chief aide to Senator Bridges, felt that Doloris was a clear social climber on Washington scene. Certainly, Doloris' love of the capital's social life placed severe financial demands on Bridges' salary. He would return home after a long day at the office, only to be whisked away to parties or receptions each night—some of them crawling with "slimy characters" eager to gain the ear of a young senator quickly ascending his party's power hierarchy.

At the beginning of 1944, Senator McNary, the veteran minority leader, underwent surgery for a brain tumor. Republicans were unable to agree upon a replacement. Bridges was mentioned as a compromise, but leadership was settled upon Taft, Vandenberg, and Wallace H. White, Jr., of Maine. This created a fluid leadership, which enabled men like Bridges to rise to positions of more responsibility, and proved very valuable when the Senate returned to Republican control.

The Fourth Term Issue

Both political parties wondered whether President Roosevelt would seek a fourth term. No American president had left office during wartime, and Roosevelt was still popular enough to win reelection, although opponents grumbled that he had become a dictator. There were no term limits on the presidency; the two-term limit was carried on as a tradition, dating back to George Washington, rather than a legal requirement. Bridges joined with Wherry, his "twin,"* in sponsoring a bill prohibiting more than two terms for any president, which in 1951, became the 22nd Amendment to the Constitution. But for now, Roosevelt was free to run again, if he chose to do so.

On April 30, 1943, Bridges and Wherry addressed the fourth-term issue in a debate on the radio program *Town Meeting of the Air*. Opposing them were Governor Matthew M. Neely of West Virginia and Professor Max Lerner of Brandeis University. Neely praised the president and said he hoped that he would be drafted for a fourth term.

Bridges took exception. "Four more years of Roosevelt means four more years of Harry Hopkins, four more years of government by lame ducks repudiated at the polls and given higher offices in exchange for political slavery," he declared. "It means four more years of the New Deal wasters, four more years of crucifying small business, four more years of planned agricultural mismanagement which has led us to the brink of starvation."

The statement led to a heated exchange between the debate participants and the audience joined in, booing and cheering. Bridges lost his temper with Lerner, and shouted: "Is it any wonder that our young people do not

*Senator Kenneth Wherry of Nebraska, a newcomer to Washington, was often mistaken for Bridges because they looked so much alike. Even reporters got them mixed up at times, and pictures of the "twins" appeared in the newspapers. Wherry liked to recount the story of a woman who ended a conversation with him by praising New Hampshire's beautiful mountains; whereupon Wherry asked innocently if she had ever seen his Nebraska.

Senator Kenneth Wherry of Nebraska and Styles Bridges were at times mistaken for each other and were often referred to as "the twins."

know their history, with men like you teaching in our schools?" The moderator jumped in to cool the situation before it led to a fistfight.

The 1944 Presidential Election

While acknowledging that it would be difficult to defeat any president in the middle of a war, many Republicans believed Roosevelt was vulnerable. Bridges received a great deal of mail praising his stand against a fourth term, and there was again some speculation that he might run for president. In February of 1943, he asked that the New Hampshire delegates to the 1944 Republican convention be unpledged, further fueling the speculations. His running days for the nation's highest office were over, how-

William Loeb, publisher of the Manchester Union Leader, *and Styles Bridges at a meeting in New York City in 1944 urging Republican presidential candidate Thomas E. Dewey to loosen up a bit on the campaign trail.*

ever, as he made clear in several statements in late 1943 and early 1944. In the interest of party unity, he even withdrew his name from consideration as a convention delegate, and other prominent New Hampshire Republicans followed suit. Styles seemed to accept that his limited financial resources and the relative insignificance of New Hampshire's four electoral votes eliminated him as a serious presidential candidate. His political future would have to lie in the Senate.

The 1944 Republican convention met in Chicago, but it was a much more subdued meeting than the one in 1940, with little campaigning. Governor Thomas E. Dewey of New York was the front runner, although he had run into trouble in the early primaries. Dewey, a Harvard graduate and a former New York City prosecutor with an impressive record of combatting organized crime, appeared stiff and uncomfortable on the campaign trail. In *Thomas E. Dewey and His Times* (Simon & Schuster, 1982), Richard Norton Smith recorded:

> In 1944, finding himself trailing Stassen in the key primary state of Oregon, Dewey debated abandoning the contest. . . . Styles Bridges and William Loeb [publisher, *Manchester Union Leader*] came to the Hotel Roosevelt [in New York] from New Hampshire, practically begging the Governor to loosen up, to go out and show Oregonians some of the vinegary dynamism that private associates see every day. . . . Always careful to heed the best minds he can assemble, Dewey reluctant-

ly went along with the idea, barnstorming the town and cities, often without a coat or tie. He left his homburgs in New York, was photographed with outdoorsmen, inspected lumber mills, and smiled benignly at small children. . . . He went on to win the primary and establish himself as the man to beat at the convention in June. . . . A few days after his victory, Dewey was back in New York, where he found Bridges offering congratulations. Instead of thanks for the winning advice, the Governor had only regret in his voice. "Styles," he muttered, "You know, everytime I saw one of those God-awful pictures of myself I wondered whether I was messy enough to please Bill Loeb." But he'd won, hadn't he? Bridges retorted. And Dewey sat back with a different smile on his face: "Indeed I did."

Dewey, however, soon went back to his buttoned-down, prim-and-proper style; looking, some observers thought, like the figure at the top of a wedding cake. He eventually lost what many, including Senator Bridges, believed to be a winnable election.

In Chicago, Dewey was drafted as the presidential nominee on the first ballot, with only one dissenting vote. He chose Governor John Bricker of Ohio as his running mate. The key campaign issue was a promise that they would furnish a new national leadership to rebuild the nation, once peace was achieved. Bridges later toured the country for the Dewey-Bricker ticket.

Bridges' leadership once again swept New Hampshire into the Republican victory column. In the Congress, Republicans gained another Senate seat and lost only a few House seats. The White House remained Democratic, as Roosevelt easily won an unprecedented fourth term. He brought with him as vice-president Harry Truman of Missouri. Party officials thought Truman would do better in negotiating postwar programs with the Senate than Henry Wallace, who seemed to have lost touch with what Americans were thinking.

By the end of 1944, the war was going well for the Allies. Allied troops had landed in France on June 6 in the D-Day invasion and steadily advanced, liberating Paris in late August. In September, they entered Germany, but the Nazis were months away from surrender. In the Pacific, Marines had retaken Guam, and MacArthur triumphantly returned to the Philippines in October. Victory seemed close, but wasn't quite at hand.

To paraphrase New Hampshire poet Robert Frost, There were miles to go before Americans could sleep.

8

The Best-Kept Secret

*"On the morn of the atomic age . . . we will
assuredly plunge ourselves into mutual destruction, and turn our backs on the living
possibility of a Golden Age."*

John Gilbert Winant,
Governor of New Hampshire
Letter from Grosvenor Square

WHEN CONGRESS convened in January of 1945, the war in Europe
was close to its end. In the Pacif-
ic, the Japanese had been driven toward their homeland and would soon
face the Allies there—or so it was thought. The invasion of Japan seemed
inevitable, but no one wanted to think about the number of American
casualties it would bring.

On April 12, Harry Truman abruptly became president. Although Roosevelt had long been in ill health, his sudden death from a cerebral hemorrhage
rocked the nation and the world. Truman immediately asked for the help
of Congress in handling the difficult times ahead. Congress complied, and
Bridges' criticism of the administration became somewhat muted during
the next few months.

All spring, American and Russian troops marched toward Berlin, liberating Nazi death camps along the way. The horror of Hitler's "final solution"
staggered Americans—untold millions of people, most of them Jews, had
been tortured and exterminated. Bridges was one of the first senators to
urge the United States to back efforts to establish a Jewish state in Palestine,
in spite of British objections. (When Britain withdrew from Palestine, the UN

Harry S. Truman became president at the death of FDR on April 12, 1945. It is inscribed "Best wishes to my friend and colleague, Styles Bridges."

General Assembly voted to partition it into separate Jewish and Arab states. The United States recognized Israel on May 15, 1948.)

As the Allies closed in on Germany's capital, Hitler committed suicide, and what was left of Germany surrendered on May 8, 1945. V-E Day (Victory in Europe) brought an outpouring of joy and relief throughout Europe and the United States. The war in the Pacific was not yet over, however, and military leaders decided it was time to bring out America's secret weapon.

The A-Bomb Demonstration

In late May of 1945, as the A-bomb was close to becoming a reality, several of the scientists involved in the project urged a demonstration of the weapon's incredible destructive power. Such a demonstration, it was argued, would surely convince the Japanese of the folly of continuing the war. The idea was rejected by the military on several grounds, the first being, as Senator Bridges himself emphasized, there was no real proof the device would work, and if the bomb failed to perform as advertised, it would only encourage Japanese resistance. The military was also concerned over questions of safety—the bomber carrying the device could be shot down or intercepted, or an unexploded A-bomb could be recovered by the enemy and its secrets exploited. Furthermore, it was considered doubtful that any contrived demonstration would sufficiently impress the Japanese war leaders to "surrender unconditionally," as the Potsdam Declaration would demand.

Meanwhile, more than seven hundred thousand American soldiers were gathering off Japan for the anticipated bloody invasion.

On July 16, 1945, at the Alamogordo Air Base in the New Mexican desert, the world's first atomic explosion took place. It was an event that impressed and shook those scientists and military men who had gathered to watch. Brigadier General Thomas F. Farrell reported what he saw:

> The whole country was lighted by a searing light with the intensity many times that of the midday sun. It was golden, purple, violet, grey and blue. It lighted every peak, crevasse and ridge of the nearby mountain range with a clarity and beauty . . . the great poets dream about but describe most poorly and inadequately. Thirty seconds after, the explosion came first, then the air blast . . . followed almost immediately by the strong, sustained, awesome roar which warned of doomsday and made us feel that we puny things were blasphemous to dare tamper with the forces heretofore reserved to The Almighty.

(Richard B. Frank, *Downfall*; Random House, 1999)

Professor George B. Kistiakowsky of Harvard was also present. He observed: "It was the nearest thing to doomsday that one could possibly imagine. I am sure, that at the end of the world—in the last millisecond of the earth's existence—the last man will see what we have seen." (Robert Leckie, *Delivered from Evil*; Harper & Row, 1987)

But perhaps the most ominous statement came from Dr. J. Robert Oppenheimer, the scientist who would come to be most closely associated with the development of this fearsome weapon. "I am become Death, the shatterer of worlds," Oppenheimer said, quoting from the Bhagavad-Gita, the sacred text of Hinduism.

The world's second atomic explosion was only a few weeks away, and this one would not be for demonstration purposes.

With the estimated casualty figures for the invasion of Japan running anywhere from a quarter of a million to one million American soldiers, President Truman made what many felt was an inevitable decision. He issued orders for the atomic bombing of Japan.

Destruction of Hiroshima

Hiroshima was the seventh largest city in Japan. It had a population of 250,000 civilians, augmented by another 150,000 soldiers of the Imperial Army. The city had important aircraft-manufacturing facilities, as well as an Army Ordinance Depot, food and clothing distribution centers, and also shipyards and ship-building companies. It was home to the Japan Steel Company and contained a railroad hub and other industrial concerns. And it had not yet suffered any damage in the ongoing Allied bombardment campaign, which was a plus in the eyes of U.S. military men when it came to assessing the damage an atomic attack would produce. All of these factors placed Hiroshima at the top of the A-bomb target list.

On August 6, 1945, the U.S. bomber *Enola Gay*, a B-29 piloted by veteran flyer Colonel Paul Tibbets, took off from the island of Tinian, near Guam for the six-and-a-half-hour-flight to Japan. The *Enola Gay*, accompanied by three other B-29s, entered Japan air space on schedule, and in the early morning hours passed over the city of Hiroshima, where the crew released their cargo. Death, the shatterer of worlds, then visited itself upon Japan:

Suddenly an unearthly light of a whitish-pinkish cast engulfed the city, followed by an awful blast like a hundred simultaneous thunderclaps. A horrible, howling wind arose, succeeded by a wave of suffocating heat. Within a few seconds the center of the city vanished. Thousands of people on the streets or in the parks and gardens were instantly killed. Thousands more lay writhing in their death throes. Everything standing in the path of the explosion—walls, houses, apartment buildings, temples, stores, everything—was swept away and annihilated. Trains loaded with commuters were hurled from the tracks. Trolley cars were flung from the streets like gigantic toys. For three quarters of a mile from the center of the blast nothing was left erect or alive. What had been living beings—animals as well as humans— were frozen in attitudes of indescribable agony. Trees were uprooted and flung into the air like flaming spears. Green rice plants turned tan and the grass became straw. . . . Beyond the central circle of death even the most solidly built structures collapsed in simultaneous rows, and falling debris of beams and bricks, glass and girders, were seized by the wind and hurled about the city like missiles, killing and wounding many thousands more. Other homes built of wood and straw simply flamed and fell. Almost everyone inside these buildings died or was wounded. Those who escaped perished two or three weeks later from the delayed effects of deadly gamma rays. . . . Reservoirs and rivers were stuffed with corpses. People unable to bear that awful heat rushed into them hoping to cool their bodies, only to be boiled to death. Everywhere were dead and dying soldiers. They must have had their coats off before the explosion because they were burned from the hips up. Beneath the burned-off skin the flesh was wet and mushy. . . . Their faces were hideous. Their features had been burned off and their ears melted off. It was not possible to tell which way some were facing. Some were left with only their white teeth protruding, as though bared like those of a horse. Everywhere among those still living there arose a piteous crying for water.

(Robert Lechie, *Delivered from Evil*)

President Truman went on the radio that day to announce the bombing, and demanded the immediate surrender of Japan's armed forces:

We are now prepared to obliterate rapidly and completely every productive enterprise the Japanese have above ground in any city. We shall destroy their docks, their factories and their communications. Let there be no mistake; we shall completely destroy Japan's power to make war. . . . It was to spare the Japanese from utter destruction that the ultimatum of July 26 was issued at Potsdam. Their leaders promptly rejected that ultimatum. If they do not now accept our terms they may expect a rain of ruin from the air, the like of which has never been seen on earth.

The Japanese High Command seemed confused by this almost unbelievable attack. They were also the victims of much misinformation regarding the true extent of the devastation. Many of the Japanese war leaders fought vigorously among themselves against the acceptance of the "unconditional surrender" which the Potsdam Declaration demanded. Their delay proved catastrophic.

The U.S. military, believing that a strong show of force and determination was required to convince the Japanese of their untenable situation, ordered the second—and last—available atomic bomb to be used. On August 8, that device was dropped on Nagasaki, leaving that city, too, in ruins. In the span of just three days, two bombs had killed approximately two hundred thousand people, with untold others to die over the ensuing weeks and years from the effects of radiation. The devastation in these areas was beyond the ability of most people to comprehend. The Japanese had no option but to surrender, which they formally did on September 2, 1945, aboard the battleship *Missouri* in Tokyo Bay. The Second World War, which had claimed more than fifty million lives, was officially over.

Unlike the celebration at the end of the campaign in the European theater, V-J Day was subdued, jubilation tempered by the awful knowledge of the power of nuclear weapons.

Senator Bridges would later comment:

Back in the dark days of 1942, when our enemies were sweeping forward on all fronts, I was one of the two Republicans in the United States Senate who participated in what was perhaps one of the most secret conferences in world history—the planning of the Atomic Bomb. . . . I believe that our secret then and later was *the best kept secret of all time*. . . . Our country developed these bombs from necessity. In my opinion, our use of the Atomic Bomb in World War II saved many thousands of American soldiers from death or crippling injuries. . . . Advances in scientific research have brought much that is good to the world. These same advances, however, have placed in the hands of men the power to bring total destruction upon this planet. It is hardly necessary for me to state again that our greatest hope is for peace. All that we wish for ourselves is to live as free Americans—free of the oppression and fear which covers so much of the world today. We have learned, however, that we must be strong in order to be free.

Attorney Wesley Powell rejoined Bridges' staff in 1945 and later became chief of staff. Very able, he became governor of New Hampshire in 1959.

Post-War Adjustment

By the fall of 1945, millions of American GIs were headed home, counting the minutes until they would be civilians again. Bridges shifted his concerns to returning servicemen. He wrote a series of articles in New Hampshire papers detailing what the vets could expect on their return, and his office helped them understand the benefits available in various programs collectively labeled the G.I. Bill of Rights.

Wesley Powell rejoined Bridges' staff with a permanently injured arm. Powell, who could have written his own ticket, with a commission and an assignment to the Pentagon, enlisted in the Army Air Force after Pearl Harbor, hoping to become a pilot. He rose from buck private to sergeant and was assigned to the 15th Air Force in Italy. On his fifth mission, serving as a radio operator in a B-24 bomber, Powell was wounded by anti-aircraft fire, as 20mm cannon fire ripped through the plane. Bullets passed through his personal oxygen tank and deflected to his left arm and his side. He had emergency surgery in an Italian Field Hospital and was shipped back to the states, where he spent the next year in military hospitals, receiving the Purple Heart, before returning to Senator Bridges' staff. Over the next few years, Powell, who was an excellent public orator, toured the Granite State speaking to veterans' groups, helping with their readjustment to civilian life.

Bridges added several other veterans to his Washington staff: Bert Teague of Newport, Louis C. Wyman of Manchester, and James C. Cleveland of New London. All except Teague were young lawyers, who later became prominent New Hampshire state officials.

The adjustment to peace was just as difficult as the adjustment to war, if not more so. Americans wanted to forget the ordeal they had just come through; they wanted safety, security, and comfort. To many, this meant owning a house in the suburbs, with a patio, a deep freezer and a television set. They wanted to create a family—the Baby Boom was under way. The GI Bill made this "life of Riley" possible by financing college and arranging for low-interest mortgage loans for millions of veterans.

To meet the needs of this new family-oriented society, a massive building boom began. New housing developments, schools, shopping centers, and highways were built. As the standard of living rose, so did the cost of living. Truman felt that his most important job was to keep the economy stable in the face of such rapid growth, and he held on to price controls as long as he could, while Bridges and other Republicans spoke out for a free economy.

Truman also had to placate union workers whose wages had been frozen for years, and who now wanted a part of the general prosperity. In the spring of 1946, more than four and a half million workers went on strike, crippling the steel, railroad, electrical, automotive, and mining industries.

Bridges Involvement in the Coal Miners' Strike

Bridges became personally involved in one strike. Coal miners left their jobs, demanding that payments be increased for retired mine workers. Mine owners refused to finance the increases. The miners' pension fund was controlled by three trustees—one from the union, one from the coal producers, and the third an impartial disinterested individual. UMW president John L. Lewis, head of the miners' union and a pension trustee, vainly sought the support of his longtime New Deal friends to induce the operators to agree to the pension increases. In frustration, Lewis turned to the Republican congressional leadership, and learned from House Speaker Joe Martin that Senator Bridges would make an excellent mediator in the pension dispute. Lewis took the speaker's advice and approached Bridges, who accepted the role. After listening to both sides of the dispute, the Senator ruled in favor of the union. The mine operators protested and took their case to court, where the pension increases were confirmed.

Observers expressed surprise that Bridges' participation had resolved the dispute so quickly. Lewis enjoyed Bridges' blunt style and asked him to remain as a member of the pension of board in 1948, which included a yearly salary of thirty-five thousand dollars a year. Bridges accepted—a decision he was later to regret.

National Security Problems

In July of 1946, the Senate considered a new National Security Act, which would create a Department of Defense, by combining the departments of war, the navy, and the army. The act also elevated the air force into a third major military branch, separate from the army. The NSA also created the Joint Chiefs of Staff to coordinate military activities, set up the National Security Council to coordinate the activities of the departments of state and defense, and established the Central Intelligence Agency for both departments. The act spelled out that the CIA was to operate abroad only; the FBI would continue to gather information domestically.

The measure quickly ran into opposition from traditionalists. Bridges tried to work out a compromise with a Defense Council composed of executives of the armed forces, and the creation of a Department of Air for developing the air force. His version of the bill got little support, and Truman's bill became law. James Forestall, former secretary of the navy, became the first secretary of defense.

The Atomic Energy Commission was created in August of 1946 to explore peaceful uses for atomic fission. President Truman nominated David Lilienthal to head the new commission. Lilienthal had figured in the TVA scandal that Bridges had investigated in the late 1930s, and Styles challenged the appointment. He did not question Lilienthal's loyalty directly, but argued that his past record indicated that he would foster policies detrimental to American efforts to cope with Soviet aggression. Bridges' precedent would be used later in the McCarthy era. This time the Senate ignored Bridges' challenge and confirmed Lilienthal, 50 to 26.

Reelection in 1946

In September 1946, Bridges was again hospitalized. His second term had been plagued with illnesses, including appendicitis. The frequent hospitalization led friends and the press to speculate that he might resign in midterm, or retire when his second term expired in 1948. Bridges relished the battles ahead of him, however, and let it be known through Powell that he had no intention of either resigning or retiring.

As the 1946 election approached, Republican unity in New Hampshire was once again threatened. Sherman Adams announced that he wanted to run for governor against Charles Dale, who was seeking a second term. A number of candidates looked toward the Second District seat Adams would vacate. After some behind-the-scenes maneuvering with Bridges, Adams withdrew his challenge with the announcement that he would run for governor in 1948, and no one would be able to change his mind on that score. House Speaker Norris Cotton handily won the nomination to the Second Congressional District seat, and both Governor Dale and Congressman Merrow won renomination.

Bridges joined Tobey, Adams, Dale, and other candidates in waging an all-out campaign to elect Republicans, and recruited his staff to help in the campaign. Powell was appointed to arrange for rallies around the state. Because of his impressive war record, he was singled out to address veterans' groups.

Doloris Bridges spoke out as well, winning both friends and enemies. In a 1946 speech before the Manchester Business and Professional Women's Club, she urged women to take a more active role in business and politics, and to strive for equality with men. She again attacked Hollywood for producing films that "showed women as stupid" and promulgating the myth that women were not capable of political careers.

The November 1946 election gave Bridges a sweet victory, with the Republican state ticket burying the Democratic opposition. Possibly even more pleasing to Bridges were the national election returns. The underdog Republicans had ousted Democrats in so many states that they captured control of both houses of the Congress for the first time since 1930. Bridges hailed the returns. When interviewed by newsmen in his Washington office, Bridges pointed to his collection of elephants and said, "They're the same elephants, but their trunks are higher."

The Bilbo Challenge

Bridges was the senior minority member of a special committee appointed to investigate campaign expenditures. The committee's first job was to look into charges against Senator Theodore Bilbo of Mississippi, a Democrat. The NAACP had formally challenged the seating of Bilbo on grounds that he had coerced black votes in Mississippi and therefore had not been fairly elected.

Since the Bilbo challenge had to be acted upon before the 1947 Senate convened, hearings opened in Mississippi on December 2, 1946, with senators Bridges, Burke B. Hickenlooper of Iowa, and Allen J. Ellender of Louisiana. More than 150 witnesses charged that Bilbo's campaign had intimidated blacks, sometimes with threats of violence. Some black veterans had been denied the right to vote, despite their war records. Witnesses testified that court clerks had denied them the right to register; others testified that they had been beaten for their efforts. Court clerks admitted denying blacks the right to vote but swore they had acted in accordance with Mississippi custom, not because of anything Senator Bilbo had said or done.

Republicans wanted to refuse Bilbo a Senate seat, but to do so would require a floor fight. The subcommittee report never led to a showdown action, but the incident exposed an un-American voting system that a following generation would seek to correct through civil rights legislation.

A Blueprint for Waste

Bridges now had seniority over most other Senate Republicans, and looked forward to important committee assignments. Vandenberg became the Senate president pro tem, and Taft won the leadership of a Policy and Steering Committee, which was to handle the Senate Republicans' strategy on legislation. Although Bridges appeared likely to become the Senate majority leader, the assignment went to Senator Wallace H. White, Jr., of Maine. Instead, Bridges moved up to the choice position of chairman of the Senate Appropriations Committee, giving him control over the government's fiscal affairs, which he had long criticized. Now he could directly influence laws and work for his goal of a balanced budget. Still committed to "pay as you go," he labeled the Truman budget "squandermania."

Bridges was quick to let Truman know what his committee had in mind—a reduction in taxes, with a reduction in the national debt to make that possible. Bridges promised that all necessary government functions would continue, while "all fluff" would be weeded out.

One of his first acts as chairman was to make the appropriations hearings public. Bridges called the proposed Truman budget "a blueprint for waste" and promised to trim it substantially. By February, the Bridges committee reduced the armed forces section of the budget by several billion dollars. Next, the committee turned its attention toward trimming other departments and agencies, many of New Deal origin, leading to a deluge of mail from self-identified "concerned citizens." Smelling a rat, Bridges discovered that much of the mail was coming from government employees, nervous about losing their jobs.

As the Senate moved along on its budget deliberations, the House stalled on demands for a tax cut. Bridges maintained that a tax reduction could only be realized after a debt reduction. By June, only one major appropriation measure had cleared both branches, and the fiscal year was to end by July 1. Some compromises were needed and Bridges labored closely with his House counterpart to win final budget approval, with an overall $6 billion reduction from Truman's original budget.

The Cold War

During the war years, the United States had moved from an isolationist stance to a position as a world "superpower." Now, in the postwar years, the country found itself involved in the fate of almost every nation on the globe. The British Empire was disintegrating and communism was emerging as a potent force, not only in the Soviet Union but wherever there was instability.

The Cold War actually began before the "hot war" had ended, when it became apparent that Stalin intended the Soviet Union to occupy Eastern Europe and perhaps expand into Asia as well. The war was ideological, plus a ferocious competition for weaponry. Beyond the differences in economic systems, political thought, and religion lay a clash of national character as well. Two cornerstones of the American character are fairness and openness. Secrecy and intrigue had been an integral part of the Russian government from the days of the tsars. Any sense of justice or "fair play" meant nothing to a totalitarian society, and democracy seemed more sinister than inviting.

The Cold War, which began as an intense arms race between the Soviets and the United States, ended in much the same way. The undeclared conflict between the world's two superpowers, continued for more than forty years, until Republican Ronald Reagan instituted the so-called Star Wars Program in the early 1980s. This experimental program, designed to provide a blanket of security across America against incoming enemy missiles, proposed to use a new advanced technology that didn't exist at the time. The price tag for this venture was conservatively put in the tens of billions of dollars. The Soviet Union, however, believed that American scientists might actually be able to produce this new technology from the ground up, just as they had in the Manhattan Project, and thereby throw off the delicate balance of power that characterized the Cold War. In a desperate attempt to match this incredible expenditure, the Soviet Union actually bankrupted itself, causing the Russian Empire to split apart into separate entities.

Hunting Communists

Bridges was emphatically anti-Communist. In 1945, he called Russia "the great roadblock to the people of the world." In late 1945, an issue before the Senate Foreign Relations Committee alerted him to the danger of a weak America.

General Patrick Hurley, former ambassador to China, surprised the committee with testimony about the State Department and its relationship to China. Hurley had been dismissed from his post because he "had little or no understanding of the increasing confrontations between the Chinese

Nationalist government and the Communist forces against it and had failed to hold the confidence of the government leaders." Hurley's view was that he had failed in his mission because his authority had been undermined by State Department officials, and especially career diplomats stationed in China.

Hurley, a shoot-from-the-hip Oklahoma lawyer, claimed that State Department officials and diplomats favored Mao Tse-tung's Communists over Chiang Kai Shek's Nationalist government. The State Department denied the allegation, and the issue of the subversion of American policy was shelved for a while, but Hurley's charges struck Bridges and a few other senators as disturbingly serious.

Some Americans suspected that a pro-Communist conspiracy was developing in the United States. Bridges took note of this possibility and began requesting dossiers from FBI director J. Edgar Hoover, who kept tabs on thousands of Americans. When a spy ring was discovered in Canada in February 1946, Bridges demanded to know if the State Department was cooperating with the FBI to find links with alleged spy rings in the United States. In August Bridges sent a letter to Secretary of State James F. Byrnes with a list of people who worked in the State Department and were suspected of having Communist leanings. Bridges asked Byrnes what he intended to do about it, but received no reply.

The issue remained dormant for a few months. Then, in the spring of 1947, Winston Churchill declared to an American audience that the Kremlin had rung down an "Iron Curtain" across Europe, behind which the Soviets had imposed a brutal and totalitarian rule.

It seemed to Westerners that the Soviet Union was seeking to dominate the world through subversion and coups d'etat, rather than by outright conquest. Communism, said William C. Bullitt, former American ambassador to Russia, grows like an amoeba, putting out pseudopodia—if it met no obstacle, the Soviet Union would flow on. Agreeing with this assessment, the Truman administration began to think in terms of containment rather than confrontation. They would cultivate nations bordering on Soviet territory to act as a barrier to the spread of communism.

The Problem of Foreign Aid

When Great Britain announced that it was withdrawing from Greece and Turkey in March of 1947, the United States feared that the Soviets—or communism—would flow in. On March 12, the Truman Doctrine was born: "It must be U.S. policy to support free peoples who are resisting attempted subjugation by armed minorities or by outside pressure." The Senate voted immediate aid for the threatened countries.

Senator Bridges discusses produce from a German farm outside Weisbaden with the farmer's wife during the Appropriations Committee inspection tour through Europe in 1947.

Following up on the idea of strengthening friendly nations, the Marshall Plan was announced on June 5. It was to consist solely of humanitarian, not military, aid. Secretary of State George C. Marshall, who had replaced Byrnes, made these important points when he outlined the plan: The U.S. was not directing its efforts against any nation or ideology, but against "hunger, poverty, desperation and chaos." And the purpose of the plan was to revive "a working economy in the world so as to permit the emergence of political and social conditions in which free institutions can exist." The Soviet Union was invited to participate, but refused, calling the plan an imperialist plot to enslave Europe.

Questions about foreign aid disturbed Senator Bridges. He was concerned about goods, especially food, leaving the United States to the detriment of the American economy. In 1947, he decided to travel to Europe to witness firsthand what foreign aid was doing. The trip took him to most European countries, including Yugoslavia and Hungary. Because of his anti-Soviet remarks the USSR refused to grant Bridges an entry visa.

Bridges noted the destruction caused by the war and the efforts at rebuilding. He was especially impressed by the farmers in France and Germany. As a result of his trip, he began to favor international aid programs, but wanted closer supervision over the destinations of money and goods because of the corruption that existed, especially in the black markets. Bridges also believed that aid programs should be aimed at helping the Europeans recovering from the war to become self-sufficient, and not creating a dependence on the United States.

In the spring of 1948, the Soviet Union abruptly cut off rail travel to Berlin, thus cutting off all aid from the United States. The American response was immediate: "If we can't use the rails, we'll use the skies." The Berlin Airlift began and continued until May 1949. During the airlift, the German Democratic Republic (East Germany) formed and barricaded itself from the West. Soon afterward, the Western nations signed the Brussels Pact, which stated that if one of the signatories was attacked, the other members would render all military and other assistance needed. This pact led to the establishment of the North Atlantic Treaty Organization (NATO).

As the 1948 election neared, President Truman reconvened Congress to act on foreign aid bills relating to China. Communist forces had routed the Nationalists in Manchuria and were bearing down upon northern China. In this instance, Bridges charged, aid was being held up by the State Department. Why? he demanded. The administration had been quick to aid Greece and Turkey, so why not China? Truman didn't want to state the reason publicly, but he felt the Nationalist government was too corrupt to support. Bridges continued to challenge him on the issue.

Notes on the Bridges Family

Back in New Hampshire, the Bridges family moved into an historic house in East Concord, which they furnished with antiques to give it an authentic early New England atmosphere. To head off speculation that he might try again for the presidency, Bridges announced his third term bid early in 1947. He also withdrew his name as a favorite-son possibility.

The senator was now a grandfather. Styles, Jr. and his wife, Marion, announced the birth of a son. And in 1947, Alina Bridges was chosen "Mother of the Year" in Maine. In a newspaper article in *The Quincy Patriot Ledger*, Styles' mother is described as "extremely quick-witted, modest, almost frighteningly honest, and altogether wonderful."

When asked what it was like to have a son in the Senate, Mrs. Bridges reportedly smiled and said, "Oh, I'm used to it now."

Doris Bridges, an English teacher in nearby Milton High School, who lived with Alina at the time, chimed in: "I'll tell you when Mother was

*Alina Fisher Bridges was chosen Mother of the Year for the State of Maine in 1947.
This regal photograph reflects her strength and pride in the accomplishments of
her three children.*

thrilled. . . . it was when Styles became governor of New Hampshire." To which Alina responded, with what the article called "an amused, far-away look in her eyes," recalling a time that obviously pleased her, "He was very young when he was elected governor—only thirty-six. He was the nation's youngest governor at the time. And you know, for a long time, he never told people how old he was; he wanted to be older! I was very proud of him. He did it all by himself. . . . had no money, no influential family. . . . I stayed up all night long listening to the election returns on the radio. It was very exciting."

She had been widowed when Styles was only nine, Mrs. Bridges went on, and her son had taken on the role of becoming "the man of the house" after his father's death, as she supported the family by teaching. Doris commented, "You asked a minute ago what it is like having a son, or in my case a brother, who is a United States senator. I'd say a more important fact is that he is a son and a brother who is always thoughtful and considerate of his family. As busy as he is, he always calls right after an election. . . . And he never forgets Mother's Day or our birthdays."

Not surprisingly, political discussions dominated the Bridges household when Styles came to visit, Doris commented, and the family often stayed up late into the night discussing the issues of the day. But more important to Alina was the fact that she saw the senator relaxing on his visits home with the family, away from the hectic pace of Washington life.

She described Styles as always being politically minded, even as a young child. "In our house in Maine, we had engravings of both Lincoln and Washington," Mrs Bridges said. "From the time he was a tiny child, he was interested in them and used to get up very close to study them."

"Styles must get some of his flair for politics from my mother," Doris commented. "There is nothing she loves so much as listening to the election returns, especially when Styles is running for office."

In 1947, despite his long list of successes, Styles Bridges' career had only begun.

The Democratic party was splintering in 1948. Former New Dealers were convinced that Truman, who was now calling for a "Fair Deal," had abandoned the Roosevelt vision. Many of them rallied behind former vice-president Henry Wallace. At the Democratic convention, the young Minneapolis mayor, Hubert Humphrey, proposed a commitment to civil rights, which was adopted by the convention, although not without opposition. Southern delegates walked out in protest and formed their own party, the Dixiecrats. They nominated Strom Thurmond, governor of South Carolina, for president. This was a serious blow to President Truman; while a Democrat presidential nominee

Senator Bridges shows off some of his collection of more than 250 elephants in his Washington office

could possibly win without left-wing support, no Democratic nominee had ever won without the support of the southern states.

Truman's dilemma cheered Republicans and they looked forward to electing the first Republican president since 1928. Governor Thomas E. Dewey of New York grabbed an early lead in the 1948 primaries, but he faced a strong challenge from Governor Harold Stassen of Minnesota. In addition, there was the dark-horse possibility of Senator Taft. The Dewey and Stassen forces battled right up to the Republican convention in Philadelphia. Bridges, one of the few party leaders trusted by both camps, initiated some compromises in the interest of party unity, which gave the nomination to Dewey. Governor Earl Warren of California was chosen as the vice-presidential candidate.

President Truman's main campaign issue was the "do-nothing" Republican-controlled Congress. He called the Republicans' claim of a budget surplus "juggles and scrambles of figures." Bridges belittled Truman's claim, saying the president was trying to make a campaign issue out of nothing.

Back in New Hampshire, Adams announced for governor and Dale retired after a second term, as agreed upon two years earlier. Congressmen Merrow and Cotton stood for reelection. Bridges won renomination without opposition, and the Democrats chose Alfred Fortin of Manchester as his opponent.

Bridges' supporters in Hillsborough, N.H. during his 1948 reelection campaign

The Republican campaign began with a visit by Governor Earl Warren to Concord. Bridges then began touring the state, assigning his wife, Doloris, and Wes Powell to handle rallies he could not reach. Then a problem developed that was similar to one he had encountered as governor.

The 1948 Election

On September 18, Textron, Inc. announced the closing of its huge textile mill in Nashua, throwing three thousand residents out of jobs. Senators Tobey and Bridges stepped in to try and avoid the type of economic chaos that had erupted a decade earlier upon the closing of Manchester's Amoskeag mills, when Styles had been governor in the early 1930s. Tobey tried vainly to induce the company to rescind its decision, whereupon Bridges joined him in getting all available federal agencies to help Nashua cope with the sudden loss of jobs. As a result of the Tobey-Bridges efforts, the closing produced only temporary problems. Bridges won reelection endorsements from several newspapers across the state, including the *Union Leader*, which had just been taken over by William Loeb, soon to become one of the most important opinion-makers in the state.

The New Hampshire Democrats groped for issues. Fortin charged Bridges with being too friendly to utility companies and other pressure groups, just as Murphy had done six years earlier. Bridges stressed his accomplishments as appropriations chairman—the Senate had approved budget reductions, despite pressures from federal agencies. He also stressed his opposition to communism, calling the Soviet Union "a red spider spinning its web." The United States should work to keep other nations free of that web, he said.

The November 2 election gave Granite State Republicans another sweeping victory. Bridges toppled Fortin, 129,600 to 91,760, for his greatest plurality to date. Dewey also carried New Hampshire, as expected. But on the national scene, Truman scored an upset, becoming president in his own right. Democrats also regained control of both branches of the Congress, as the Republicans lost nine Senate seats and seventy-five seats in the House.

In August 1948, *Time* editor Whittaker Chambers declared that several of the New Deal's officials were members of the Communist party. He named several, including Alger Hiss. Even more startling, a few days before, a Connecticut woman named Elizabeth Bently had revealed that she had been a spy for the Soviet Union, and that she had worked with other government employees, among them former Roosevelt aide Lauchlin Currie.

These sensational announcements raised a furor that would continue for several years. They helped elect Congressman Richard Nixon and Senator Joseph McCarthy in 1948, who both rode the anti-Communist wave to victory. Bridges, too, would be at the forefront of the Red Hunt.

9

Who Lost China?

"So many people have tried to rule themselves, and are still trying, that one begins to believe that the time is not far distant when the United States, one of the most radical, will become the most conservative of nations."

Winston Churchill, New Hampshire novelist and candidate for governor of New Hampshire

BRIDGES WAS both disappointed and puzzled by the Democratic sweep of 1948. He had thought that the people welcomed the Republican budget reductions of the 80th Congress, yet they returned President Truman and the Democrats to power.

As the 81st Congress prepared to convene, Republicans reorganized to confront the Democratic majority once again and to devise a plan of action for the 1950 election. Bridges was now the second-ranking Republican, and sat on the Republican Policy Committee. He was also the top-ranking Republican on the Senate Appropriations Committee. At the age of fifty, he had become an elder statesman and a Republican force in the nation.

Circumstances forced Bridges to take time away from politics. In late November of 1948, he had a gall bladder operation and went to Arizona to recuperate in the warm winter sun until Congress convened. Back in Washington in January, he found the election of a Senate minority leader was the first priority. Persistent conflict between the left and right wings of the party had been handled in the 1946 session by the appointment of three men to make policy decisions, but this arrangement could not continue. Senator Taft, the conservative leader, was unacceptable to the moderate wing. He agreed to the election of Senator Wherry as minority leader. Wherry had earned a reputation as a fair man, and was uncompromising in his opposition to the Truman administration.

Bridges surveyed the freshmen members of the 1948 Senate. Maine had elected Republican Margaret Chase Smith, the first woman to sit in the Senate in her own right. Minnesota sent young Hubert Humphrey, who had stirred the Democratic convention with a demand for a civil rights plank in the platform. Texas Democrats had narrowly elected Lyndon Baines Johnson, and such future leaders as Paul Douglas (D-Illinois), Clinton Anderson (D-New Mexico), Karl Mundt (R-South Dakota), Joseph McCarthy (R-Wisconsin), and Estes Kefauver (D-Tennessee) also joined the Senate.

The China Crisis

For the first few months of 1949, major foreign problems took up the Senate's time. The escalating China crisis was the focus of Bridges' attention for much of that year. The American government had been giving military, economic, and political aid to the Chinese government since the 1930s, only to see most of the money squandered by the Nationalists. The Communists, on the other hand, offered an attractive program of land reform and egalitarian rule to China's millions of peasants. Despite continued assurances to U.S. officials that he would rid the army of corruption and inefficiency, Chiang Kai-shek, head of the Nationalist government, failed to do so.

The end of World War II found Chiang so isolated in Western China, so far removed from the industrial and commercial centers, that he had to be airlifted to accept the Japanese surrender. The growing, dynamic Communist party easily took control in North China. Seeking to help Chiang and his Nationalists, the United States worked out coexistence agreements between the two forces in 1945 and 1946, but they quickly broke down and a civil war erupted.

If Chiang might had been able to expand control over the Chinese countryside, he might have won. His army, better equipped than the People's Liberation Army and outnumbering its forces 3 to 1, still could not hold the Communists back. Further, failure of the Nationalist government to stimulate the economy and rebuild key industries ruined the Chinese middle class, and they, too, turned to the Communists.

By 1948, when Chiang launched his forces into the battle of Hsuchow-Pangpu against the Communists, he was desperate. By the end of January 1949, his army had lost sixty-six divisions, and the war. The Nationalist regime and the remnants of its defeated armed forces retreated farther south, and eventually evacuated to the island of Taiwan (Formosa).

The American public was staggered by the defeat of the Chinese government. What had been dismissed as a ragged band of peasant reformers, led by revolutionary Mao Tse Tung, had toppled what was thought to have been a strong ally. It was as if an insignificant Communist movement had taken over Britain or France—or, as some pointed out, as if a ragged group of patriots had managed to seize control of British colonies in North America. The surprise was all the greater because wartime controls on information had kept most Americans from learning of their government's futile attempts to bolster China's weak and corrupt regime.

Even the State Department had not expected Chiang to collapse so quickly. His failure so exasperated the department's Far East section that it washed its hands of him and of the Nationalists; a decision that was to come back to haunt the United States.

As Americans learned about the events at Hsuchow, they demanded that something be done to halt the march of Communism. There was a general feeling that if the United States had curbed Communist expansion in Turkey and Greece, it should do the same in China.

In a Des Moines, Iowa speech on November 12, 1948, Senator Bridges had called for an immediate airlift of supplies to aid the stricken Chinese Nationalist army. "These Communist forces now spreading over North China are no simple group of indigent patriots, but are controlled by Moscow as part of the world Communist movement," he declared. He demanded that General Douglas MacArthur, the American proconsul in Japan, be sent to assist the Nationalists.

The U.S. government's response was that China had already been lost to the Communists, and Chiang could not be saved. Truman, on the advice of the State Department, stopped shipments to China because the goods were expected to fall into Communist hands. The Democratic-controlled Senate refused to call an investigation, as Bridges and other Republicans demanded. Elbert Thomas (D-Utah), chairman of the Senate Foreign Relations Committee, concurred with the State Department's decision and said that China had fallen because of corruption and incompetency.

While the Truman administration looked upon the Communists as eventual victors, the Republicans called this position inexcusable. They sent William C. Bullitt, former ambassador to the Soviet Union, to China to review conditions. If they received American supplies, he reported back, especially aircraft, the Nationalists at Taiwan felt they could still reverse the war. The State Department rejected Bullitt's findings, but Republicans used his report to demand a reversal of the Truman administration's policy.

Acheson Appointment Disturbing to Bridges

The president had given the Republicans another, tangential issue to oppose in January. Secretary of State George C. Marshall resigned, and Truman
appointed Dean Acheson to replace him. Acheson had long worked in the
State Department, and rose to become undersecretary. He was well known
on Capitol Hill, with strong New Deal ties, and his appointment drew the
fire of conservative Republicans. One of Acheson's main drawbacks, they
claimed, was that he had worked with Alger Hiss, whom Chambers had
accused of spying for the Soviets. Hiss was then under indictment for perjury in connection with those charges. When it was pointed out that both
Hiss and Acheson had worked with President Roosevelt at the Yalta peace
conference, where apparent concessions had been given to Stalin, this
drew more fire. As undersecretary at the State Department, Acheson was
associated with China's collapse as well.

Bridges told the Senate he wanted the State Department guided by
men who would be firm on foreign policies, and who would not permit
men like Hiss to hold government jobs. Truman's influence and Acheson's
political connections were greater than Bridges', however, and the Senate
confirmed the appointment. When asked why he had waged an obviously futile fight against Acheson, Bridges, declared, "This vote should be interpreted as a vote against the policy of the State Department that has lost
us China."

The question of "who lost China?" became a long-lasting political issue.
Bridges decided to use his power on the Senate Appropriations Committee
to force State Department action. In March, he joined with other senators
in backing a bill to send $1.5 billion in aid to China. Acheson retorted that
such aid would be a waste, since the Chinese government had already collapsed. In April, Bridges made Acheson's statement public and demanded
an investigation, declaring, "Mr. Acheson's letter is one more utterance
consistent with the blindness of top officials of the United States government
towards the friendly nation of China, and towards China as one of the vital
weak spots in the tremendous effort of free peoples to stop the spread of
Communism. By what quirk does the Secretary of State and his associates
work for the defeat of Communism in one part of the world, and condone
it in another area?"

This demand for a probe gained little support among fellow senators,
but it helped Republicans keep the issue alive, particularly in the face of
White House inaction. Truman's foreign policy, however, created a dispute
within the Republican party. Truman had based his foreign-affairs activities
on a bipartisan approach, which Roosevelt had used to good advantage, but
there was nothing bipartisan about the criticisms of Bridges and Wherry.

One of the supporters of the bipartisan philosophy was Arthur Vandenberg, the Senate's senior Republican and a ranking member of its Foreign Relations Committee. He called for a showdown with Bridges and Wherry. In a party policy committee session on April 26, Vandenberg accused Bridges of sniping at an essentially sound policy. Bridges chided Vandenberg for defending a bipartisan policy that he said did not exist. The rancor raised by this confrontation deepened the division between Republican moderates and conservatives.

On April 29, 1949, Truman summoned Bridges and Wherry to the White House, where he and Acheson documented why the State Department had given up on China. The lack of morale and the corruption of the Nationalist government were revealed. Bridges left the meeting shaken, and declined any comment to the press, which was unusual for him. Wherry said only, "I learned some things today I didn't know before."

By May, the People's Liberation Army occupied Shanghai and was preparing to attack south China. Former Flying Tiger commander Claire Chennault asked Congress to rush aid to the Nationalists, but his appeal was in vain. On May 13, despite Truman's briefing, Bridges once again demanded an investigation to force the State Department to publicly explain its China actions.

In August of 1949, as the Communist army neared Canton and Chungking, the State Department issued a formal announcement that the United States had done its best to save China, but the Nationalists had defeated themselves by failing to broaden their political base. Most of this State Department "white paper" was based on a secret 1947 report made by General Albert Wedemeyer, suggesting that American aid be given only if the Chinese agreed to governmental and land reforms and submitted to American supervision of its aid. In response, Bridges stated, "It is clear to me that the Chinese war was lost in Washington and not in China."

Back to Domestic Problems

Much of the domestic work of 1949 was routine. President Truman's budget drew the usual criticism from Republicans. Bridges charged that it increased federal spending without increasing taxes. The Democrats said the budget was in balance without added taxes, and the Senate Republicans formed an anti-tax bloc to keep them to their word.

More alarming to Bridges was Truman's proposal on February 23, 1949, calling for a National Health Insurance Program. Bridges quickly labeled it a step toward socialized medicine, as had been adopted in Great Britain and later in Canada. He firmly opposed the NHIP and rallied the New Hampshire medical profession to oppose the measure, ensuring its support in future years.

Bridges issued his customary attacks against government waste. This time he rapped the Government Printing Office (GPO). He said it had become a gargantuan spending center, pointing out that the agency now comprised 256 printing plants, which turned out about twelve billion pamphlets yearly. He derided Uncle Sam's "book-a-minute club," but his complaints got little attention.

In July of 1949, Senator Bridges voted with the majority to retain the Taft-Hartley law, which had been initiated by the Republican-controlled 80th Congress. This statute, which bans the closed shop and allows employers to sue unions for breach of contract, had been challenged by labor as unfair because it allows companies to keep operating during a strike.

Bridges' Trusteeship in Mine Worker's Union Questioned

Late that summer, Bridges suddenly found himself the center of attention in another labor issue. He had won praise when he accepted the position of neutral trustee of the United Mine Workers Union, to solve the coal miners' strike over pension demands, but now it became known that he was being paid a stipend of $35,000 a year, plus expenses, as a trustee.

Bridges' trusteeship had continued through the spring of 1949, and he helped prevent the ongoing feud between union leader John L. Lewis and the mine owners' representative, Ezra Van Horn, from destroying the board. Bridges was instrumental in lowering the pension eligibility age from 62 to 60, and in keeping the fund solvent. All of this, however, was forgotten when his salary figure became public.

There was nothing illegal about Bridges receiving the salary, but many senators questioned the ethics of a $12,500-per-year senator taking such a large amount from a special—interest group. The Senate Banking Committee launched an investigation. Bridges was outraged that his honesty should be questioned. He insisted that the demands of the job earned him every penny, and that the $35,000 figure included money paid to a secretary and legal counsel. His critics, however, saw someone advocating economy to the government while taking money from a possible pressure group. As the furor increased, Bridges promised on August 13, that he would eventually resign the post, but would not quit under pressure. A few days later, the Banking Committee hearings uncovered the fact that Bridges received another $12,000 yearly for expenses. Bridges' own records showed that he netted about $26,000 annually for his efforts.

To complicate the matter further, Van Horn charged that Bridges and Lewis had misused the pension fund by raising benefits, threatening to bankrupt the operation. He demanded Bridges' immediate resignation. Bridges retorted that Van Horn was only seeking to reduce owner contribu-

Trustees of the United Mine Workers' pension fund in Washington, D.C. From left are Senator Bridges, Ezra Van Horn, who represented the mine operators, and John L. Lewis, president of the union.

tions to the fund. Hoping to quiet Congressional criticism, Bridges announced on September 4 that he would no longer accept the salary.

Bridges' peace offer was of no avail. The investigation continued, with the charges becoming uglier. Van Horn was correct in saying the fund was not designed for larger pension payments, nor was it supposed to assist widows and dependents of miners who were killed or maimed while working. By late September, as the fund neared bankruptcy, Bridges said the solution was to increase assessments from both miners and the operators. The companies rejected that proposal, and a strike followed.

To make Bridges' situation even worse, just as board action seemed necessary, Van Horn abruptly resigned. Groups of miners charged that ineligible workers had been given pensions, and filed suit for the removal of both Lewis and Bridges from the board. Some of the mining companies also sued for misuse of funds.

When the mine owners finally agreed to end the dispute by appointing a new trustee to represent them on the board, the pension fund had became a complicated tangle of lawsuits, countersuits, wildcat strikes, and vicious public charges. On November 11, 1949, Bridges resigned from the board in disgust, and demanded a public audit of the fund to clear him of any wrongdoing.

Embittered, Bridges asserted in a radio interview that he had well earned the salary—which totaled some $70,000 over a two-year period—as an administrator of a fund totaling over $100 million. He emphasized that he served the public by getting the miners back to work in 1948, when all other efforts to end that strike had failed. "The administration did not look with favor upon the fact that Republican efforts would solve the problem, with which they were unable to cope," he added pointedly.

Bridges Becomes Conservative

The pension-fund case was to return to haunt Bridges again and again through the rest of his career. For the time being, however, it was forgotten in the shuffle of far greater problems facing the nation. Fears that Bridges had voiced through his second term of a worldwide effort to subvert democracy in the United States—both from abroad and from within—came to life in 1949, as the threat of communism began to grip the nation. It was the beginning of a low point in American history, when citizens turned against each other in distrust, confused about what was the right thing to do.

It was up to the American people, rather than the government, to give new vigor and new strength to the preservation and improvement of the democratic way of life, Bridges declared. On June 29, 1949, in a commencement address at New England College in Henniker, accepting the first honorary degree ever given by the college, he concluded his remarks with the statement, "The American people have drifted to the point where they are accepting federal aid and federal controls as an easy way out of their difficulties." Bridges, who had been a leader of the old Progressive wing of the New Hampshire Republican party, was now labeled a conservative. Deservedly or not, he was to be identified with the conservative elements for the rest of his life. He certainly was not an ideological conservative like Senator Taft. Nor could he be classified as one of the liberals whom he constantly berated. He was definitely a pragmatist, and frequently a mediator between the opposite wings of his Republican party.

Security Problems

In May, an unsettling event occurred. Bridges had long been concerned over the security of atomic information—and with good reason. After the disappearance of some uranium from a Chicago factory, Bridges issued a stinging attack upon David Lilienthal and the Atomic Energy Commission.

He called for new regulations for the security of atomic secrets, and for tighter personnel security to keep the A-bomb out of the possession of the Soviet Union.

It appeared to be too late, however: On September 24, 1949, the Russians successfully detonated an atomic device. The event stunned Americans. Bridges was quick to declare that it was technologically impossible for the Soviets to have made the bomb without stealing some of America's secrets. Actually, the intricacies of atomic fission are not that difficult for a careful and patient physicist to understand, and the Soviets had been working on the project for years. Most Americans, however, believed that nuclear reaction was a deep secret that no one else was capable of deciphering.

Subsequent events confirmed Bridges' suspicions. In December, a former U.S. Air Force major charged that he had been ordered by Harry Hopkins to leak atomic information to the Russians. The charge seemed farfetched and was never proven, but was readily believed by some people. A month later came the sensational arrest of British scientist Klaus Fuchs, who admitted passing secrets to the Soviets from Britain's atomic program, which used information supplied by the American government.

In the wake of Fuch's arrest, the FBI accused David Greenglas, a former employee at the Los Alamos atomic-bomb project, of spying for the Soviets. Greenland and his wife agreed to testify for the prosecution in exchange for their lives, and named Ethel and Julius Rosenberg as the center of their spy ring. The Rosenbergs steadfastly maintained their innocence, and many believed that the political climate made a fair trial impossible; but in 1951 the pair were convicted and sentenced to die. They were executed in 1953, the first American citizens to suffer the death penalty for espionage.

These events fueled the anti-Communist hysteria of the time. Bridges insisted that the State Department should be purged not only of "reds" but "pinks," or "fellow travelers," as well. He called again for Acheson's resignation, saying that his policies were weakening America's reputation abroad, and Truman was weakening the country at home with "creeping socialism."

In a Nashua speech on January 26, 1950, Bridges charged that the United States was overrun with 19.5 million federal employees, and that the government was plotting to control the minds of students with federal aid to education. He concluded, "We are entering a decade of decision, and our greatest problem is that of socialism creeping into our way of life."

Earlier Bridges had asked on the floor of the Senate, "Are there any guts left in this country? Any in the State Department? Any in the administration? Any in the United States Senate? China asked us for a sword and we gave her a paring knife."

A few days later, he was joined by Senator William Knowland (R-California) in demanding Acheson's resignation. Bridges declared, "It is now time for the men responsible for the China policy to submit their resignations to the President. . . . It should be clear to Americans that the time is here when if responsible American officials cannot change our policy, it is time to change our officials."

At the same time, after failing to win formal recognition of their government from Washington, Communists seized the U.S. consulate in Peking and forced its American staff to flee the country. While Bridges rose to address this affront, the Democratic Senate leader, Scott Lucas of Illinois, proclaimed that the United States should remain calm and that American relations with the new Chinese government were simply undergoing a period of strain and adjustment. His argument prevailed and the furor subsided, but anger remained.

On January 24, a jury convicted Alger Hiss of perjury. The fact that Acheson had defended the man's service record gave Bridges another reason for demanding Acheson's resignation. "How many more termites are there in the State Department?" Bridges asked. "If Stalin himself had been our Secretary of State, he could scarcely have done a better job for Stalin in China than our State Department has done."

The McCarthy Charges

The fiasco in China, the possible selling of atomic secrets to the Soviets, and dissatisfaction with Secretary Acheson touched off one of the most bitter incidents in the nation's history. On February 9, 1950, Senator Joseph McCarthy of Wisconsin, little known until then, made a speech in Wheeling, West Virginia that became famous. The State Department was infested with Communist agents, he charged. Between 57 and 205 "card-carrying Communists" were working in policy-making jobs, with Acheson's knowledge and consent. In the normal course of events such an inflammatory statement might have been passed over as mere hyperbole. But given the Communist takeover of China and the new Soviet bomb threat, many took McCarthy's statements seriously, and the great "witch hunt" of the 1950s began.

Belonging to the Communist party had not been illegal during the 1930s, when many intellectuals explored the plausibility of Karl Marx's economic and social theories. But in 1940, with World War II looming on the horizon, the Smith Act made it a crime to belong to any organization calling for the violent overthrow of the U.S. government. This was generally interpreted to mean the Communist party. In 1950, the McCarran Act would add severe restrictions, widely called black-listing, against anyone sus-

FBI Director J. Edgar Hoover, Doloris Bridges, Attorney General William Rogers, and Senator Bridges share a light moment in Washington.

pected of having ties to Communist organizations.

McCarthy's charges aroused immediate public reaction. On the heels of his speech, charges of Communism in the American government fast became the most important issue in the nation. The House Un-American Activities Committee had been probing such charges since 1945, and President Truman had ordered all federal departments to check the backgrounds of their employees. Some Communist party members had been uncovered and were either dismissed or transferred, momentarily quelling the controversy. Truman had declared that the loyalty of federal employees was secure and what "few security risks had been found, had been weeded out."

Friendship with J. Edgar Hoover

For some time Bridges had been collecting files on possible subversives from the FBI and from a Senate Policy Committee researcher named Maurice Joyce. Now the senator stepped up his efforts. He investigated the few party members in New Hampshire, who had been based in Concord, along with their "fellow travelers," who had opposed him on key issues. Although it is a fact that Styles had developed a close working relationship with J. Edgar Hoover, director of the Federal Bureau of Investigation, however, there is no evidence that Bridges ever used any of this information against the persons or groups involved.

Hoover had been appointed as director of the bureau by Calvin Coolidge on May 10, 1924, after working for the Justice Department since 1917. From the beginning, Hoover understood that the activities of federal agencies, even those as powerful as the FBI, are driven in large part by public opinion. He made certain that the bureau received widespread and positive mention in the media and carefully cultivated friendships with powerful political figures, such as Senator Styles Bridges. When the Communist witch hunt of the 1950s began, Hoover threw his agency into the fray with all the fervor of a religious zealot.

Hoover shared with Bridges the propensity for file collecting, and gathered information on everyone for whom a dossier could conceivably be kept.* The working relationship between the senator and the FBI director grew from an understanding of the power and influence each man knew the other wielded. Bridges, with his position on the Senate Appropriations Committee, effectively controlled the government purse-strings; Hoover, as America's "top cop," had an information-gathering system second to none.

Memos and letters between the two reveal the extent of their alliance. In the paranoid atmosphere of the Communist-witch-hunt era, the Senator suspected that his office phones were tapped, and casually asked Hoover to "send someone over to see if there were any 'bugs' in the system." This Hoover apparently did several times, each time dutifully reporting back to Bridges with a personally signed message, "Phone lines were checked, nothing was found."

On several other occasions, when critical votes on FBI appropriations came before the Senate—one in particular when a much-disputed FBI pension reform package was pushed through the legislature—Bridges received personal letters of thanks from the director. Whenever Styles needed inside information on someone, he did not hesitate to ask Hoover directly. In one instance this included highly personal information on a Bridges campaign opponent, Eugene S. Daniell. A copy of the file was quickly sent to the senator's office.

Acheson on the Carpet Again

Secretary Acheson defended himself against the McCarthy attack. On March 1, he stated that he would not tolerate any disloyalty and would

---

*To this day, the Federal Bureau of Investigation continues to collect files on individual Americans. Unlike the days of the McCarthy witch hunt, however, American citizens have the right under the Freedom of Information Act, passed in 1966, to request any unclassified information the government may have collected about them. This can be done by contacting the U.S. State Department in Washington, D.C. Further information on this subject may be found by visiting the FOIA website at: www.elecreadroom@state.gov.

continue the policy of removing security risks from the State Department. Republicans sensed that a potent election year issue loomed, and they pushed McCarthy's call for an investigation until it was finally granted, over administration protests.

Before the State Department probe began, Senator Bridges brought Acheson before the Senate Appropriations Committee. Using the same tactics that he'd used in the TVA and Flynn investigations, Bridges pointedly asked Acheson if anyone convicted of a crime should be removed from government service. Acheson said yes. Bridges then asked if such a person's friends should also be investigated. Again Acheson replied in the affirmative. Whereupon Bridges concluded that Acheson himself should submit to a probe, because he had been friendly with Alger Hiss.

Bridges, McCarthy, and Wherry continued to demand Acheson's resignation. The trio claimed that a master spy like Klaus Fuchs existed inside the State Department, and that Acheson was protecting him. As headlines repeated the charge, Truman came to Acheson's defense. On March 31, the president issued a blistering attack upon the three senators and accused them of trying to sabotage the nation's foreign policy for political gain. He reported that security checks on three million government employees had produced only 126 potential security risks, and none of them had been a spy or a Communist party member. Calling McCarthy a great asset to the Soviet Union, Truman said that the Senate "has three saboteurs—Bridges, Wherry, and McCarthy."

Bridges and Wherry continued their push for an investigation into the State Department, confident that McCarthy could back up his charges. McCarthy, however, was able to name only four State Department people with Communist connections, and none of them proved to be "card-carrying Communists" as he claimed. So McCarthy, as he would do so often during his investigation, abandoned that charge and moved on to other agencies.

McCarthy Fails to Produce Communists

After the State Department investigation failed Senator Bridges began to have second thoughts about McCarthy. His misgivings about the Wisconsin senator had begun to surface earlier, when, as John Warrington recalled, "After one of McCarthy's more virulent speeches, in which he claimed to have in his possession a definitive list of 'card-carrying Communists' employed by the government, Senator Bridges along with Wherry went to McCarthy's apartment in the Carroll Arms in Washington. There they found McCarthy intoxicated, and when they demanded to see the so-called list of State Department Communists, McCarthy refused to produce it."

Senator Joe McCarthy and his aide Roy Cohn near the peak of the senator's power during the infamous Communist witch hunt of the 1950s

On April 16, Bridges stated in a Milwaukee speech that he believed McCarthy had gone too far in naming a specific number of Communists in the State Department. He continued to believe that the probe should continue, because the government needed tighter risk supervision than the Democrats were providing. This was to become the chief Republican apology for McCarthy—his methods were bad, but his investigation was needed.

In July, a special committee chaired by Senator Tydings (D-Maryland) looked into the specific charges brought by McCarthy, and found no evidence to substantiate them. While the Tydings Report might have finished McCarthy, it became only the beginning of his allegations. As each of his charges was disproved, McCarthy simply made more charges against different departments, triggering further investigations.

Bridges moved into his role of compromiser. Placing distance between himself and McCarthy, he met with Truman and told him that the entire affair might have been prevented had the president consulted the Senate before stopping aid to China. Truman promised cooperation and named two Republicans, John Foster Dulles of New York and John Sherman Cooper of Kentucky, to aid Acheson.

As McCarthy began to stumble, the moderates bore down on him. On June 2, six Republican senators, including Charles Tobey of New Hampshire and Margaret Chase Smith of Maine, signed a declaration of conscience in which they rapped McCarthy for an assault on basic American freedoms. They accused him of "selfish political exploitation of fear, bigotry, ignorance, and intolerance." At the same time, the sextet hit out at the Democratic government for not being more alert to Communist threats.

With the splitting over McCarthyism in an election year, Republican pressure was put on the Wisconsin senator to produce some tangible evidence. He thereupon announced that he could prove that one dedicated Communist was in a key policy-making role in the State Department. He declared his allegations would stand or fall on this one case—apparently forgetting his original claim of 57 to 205 Communists in that agency. McCarthy then launched an attack on Owen Lattimore, a professor at Johns Hopkins University who also worked as a consultant for the State Department.

McCarthy told the Senate he could prove that Lattimore was a Communist, and that he had been a principal planner of the American desertion of China. But McCarthy's key witness refused to say that Lattimore had been a Communist party member, and Acheson produced Lattimore's working file, which showed that he had never held a policy-making role or participated in the China decision.

If McCarthy had any information that Lattimore was a spy he should turn it over for official action, Attorney General J. Howard McGrath demanded, but the senator refused. In spite of ridicule and widespread questioning of his motives, McCarthy rose before the Senate and claimed that he had "new evidence" that Lattimore had spied, but he had no corroborative evidence. Thus the case upon which McCarthy said his allegations would rise or fall, abruptly fell.

The Lester C. Hunt, Jr. Affair

This should have ended McCarthy's investigations, but the witch hunt would continue for several more years, ruining many lives in the process. One victim of this politics-of-fear mentality was Senator Lester C. Hunt (D-Wyoming). Hunt had long detested McCarthy's tactics, believing that the Wisconsin senator's behavior demeaned the Senate itself. In the 1954 election, Hunt's senate seat became the target of Republican operatives, as the two parties fought for legislative control of the Senate.

On June 9, 1953, Hunt's son, Lester C. Hunt, Jr., a student at the Episcopal Theological School of Cambridge, Massachusetts, was arrested on a morals charge in a Washington, D.C. park. The young man had been picked up after agreeing to engage in a homosexual act with an undercover police officer. The offense was only a misdemeanor, and the youngster's first offense, so the police agreed not to prosecute. But Republican operatives got wind of the offense. It was alleged by columnist Drew Pearson and others that senators Herman Welker (R-Idaho) and Styles Bridges, who was then chairman of the Republican Campaign Committee, informed Senator Hunt that if he did not withdraw from the race, where the popular Wyoming legislator was predicted to win reelection, his son would be prosecuted. After much soul searching and assurances of support from the Democratic leadership, Senator Hunt decided to stay in the Wyoming senate race.

At the same time, according to Rick Ewig, in his article *"McCarthy Era Politics: The Ordeal of Senator Lester Hunt"* (Annals of Wyoming, Vol. 55, 1983), Welker and Bridges also contacted Inspector Roy Blick of the Morals Division of the Washington Police Department. According to Ewig, "The two Senators allegedly attempted to pressure Blick into having Hunt, Jr., prosecuted. Disregarding Blick's arguments that normal procedures had been followed in the Hunt case, Welker said he might be obligated to make a speech on the Senate floor on the matter." Ewig further alleged that either Bridges or Welker handed Blick an envelope, with the statement, "Inspector, this is your resignation. If you do not prosecute the Hunt boy, your resignation will be accepted immediately."

After Senator Hunt's refusal to withdraw his son was brought to trial, and found guilty of soliciting a plain-clothes officer for lewd and immoral purposes. He was fined one hundred dollars for the offense. The stigma attached to the proceedings affected Senator Hunt greatly. He withdrew from his colleagues, and took his meals alone in his office. He "told a number of [Drew] Pearson's staff that he could not bear to face his Senate colleagues and might not ever appear on the Senate floor again." Facing health issues and fearing that his son's ordeal would be relived in the Wyoming Senate race, the elder Hunt finally withdrew. The pressures, however, only increased. A campaign began calling for his resignation, so that the Republican governor of Wyoming could appoint a Republican to finish his term. The Democrats, still believing Senator Hunt's campaign to be viable, continued to try and persuade him to run.

Unable to face the mounting pressures, the senator locked himself in his Washington office on Saturday, June 19, 1954, and there shot himself in the head with a .22 caliber rifle, which he had concealed under his coat. He died a few hours later.

The resulting furor, driven by public outcry generated by Drew Pearson and Marquis Childs' articles on the "blackmail suicide," caused Welker and Bridges to attempt to refute the charges. On July 9, Inspector Blick signed an affidavit stating that Welker and Bridges did not attempt to coerce him into prosecuting Hunt, Jr., but the affidavit did little to explain why a relatively minor charge, which had supposedly been dropped, was suddenly reinstated and brought to trial. Stories continued to surface claiming that Senator Hunt had discussed the blackmail attempt with political friends and relatives. According to Ewig, William M. Spencer, a cousin of Sen. Hunt and Chairman of the Board of Directors of the North American Car Corporation in Chicago, wrote a scathing letter to Herman Welker after the Idaho Republican eulogized Hunt in the Senate:

> I was shocked when I read this. It recalled to my mind so vividly my conversation with Senator Hunt a few weeks before he died, wherein he recited in great detail the diabolical part you played following the unfortunate and widely publicized episode in which his son was involved. Senator Hunt, a close personal friend of mine, told me without reservation the details of the tactics you used in endeavoring to induce him to withdraw from the Senate, or at least not to be a candidate again. It seems apparent that you took every advantage of the misery which the poor fellow was suffering at the time in your endeavor to turn it to political advantage. Such procedure is as low a blow as could be conceived. I understood, too, from Senator Hunt, that Senator Bridges had been consulted by you and approved of your action in the matter.

Bridges and Welker denied all the charges, of course, pointing to the Blick affidavit as proof of their innocence. And in the end, Republicans lost the Wyoming Senate seat to Democrat Joseph O'Mahoney. The story endures as an ugly example of partisan politics during the McCarthy era.

The China Lobby

Some people wondered where McCarthy was getting the information for his accusations. Newspaper columnists, including Drew Pearson, and several national magazines, notably *The Reporter*, began writing about the influence of the so-called China Lobby, suggesting that this was McCarthy's source. In a curious ironic twist, Styles Bridges would find himself tainted by libelous allegations generated by Pearson's columns and *The Reporter* articles.

The China Lobby was a well-orchestrated effort to influence American legislators, carried out by a number of Chinese officials, especially H.H. Kung, who was Chiang Kai Shek's brother-in-law and minister of finance of the defeated Nationalist government. It was later discovered that Kung enriched himself in this enterprise, at the expense of his own government.

Throughout World War II, China maintained a large propaganda operation in this country. When peace came, the bulk of this apparatus fell into the hands of Kung and his family, who converted their connections in the United States and other countries into a commercial organization. As China began to collapse, the Kung group tried to get American support, including troops, to prop up their government. When that effort failed, the group turned to other enterprises, such as buying tin on the world market at depressed prices and selling it to the new Communist regime. Another Kung deal was to bid the price of soy bean futures down to its lowest point in years, and then, after almost cornering the market, selling out and driving the price substantially higher.

Over the years, the China Lobby rewarded various Americans with gifts or business deals for their support of the Nationalist cause. It also rewarded people for assisting them to consummate deals, subvert government regulations, and help raise money for congressional campaigns.

In June of 1950, Senator James B. McMahon (D-Connecticut) demanded an investigation to determine which senators were connected to the various China Lobby activities. Several had apparently received campaign support from American Alfred Kohlberg, who owned an import business specializing in Chinese linens until the Communists took over China. Most of those who received campaign funding were conservatives, and they included Senator Bridges. This raised the question: Would Bridges have so vehemently criticized the State Department for its China policy had he not received contributions from Kohlberg? Bridges was furious that someone would question his integrity. He admitted receiving $2,000 from Kohlberg in 1948, but declared he "was for China ten years before I ever heard of Kohlberg."

Charges were made that Bridges' China support was given for a contribution and that constituted nothing less than a bribe. But the Justice Department subsequently cleared Bridges of any wrongdoing.

William Loeb, publisher of the *Manchester Union Leader* and a friend of Bridges, belonged to what was known as the American China Policy Association, of which Kohlberg was chairman. (William Loeb also became chairman of the organization at a later date.) It was later said that this group was largely financed by the Kung Enterprises. It was also asserted that it was this group that supplied McCarthy with his names. Whether Bridges met Kohlberg through this group, or through his friendship with Loeb, is not clear. Regardless, the China Lobby, as it came to be called, may well have contributed substantially to the nation's anti-Communist hysteria of the early 1950's to cover the Nationalists' failure to keep communism out of Asia.

As the McMahon committee was completing its investigation, another catastrophe was in the making. On June 25, 1950, North Korean troops crossed the 38th Parallel into South Korea.

10

The Korean Conflict

"You have to grasp power properly. If you grasp it like a bird and hold it too tightly you'll crush it. If you hold it too loosely, it'll fly away."

Styles Bridges

A CIVIL WAR had been festering in Korea since the end of World War II. After the occupying Japanese army was defeated in 1945, the nation was divided into North Korea, under Kim Il Sung, and South Korea, under Syngman Rhee, as a compromise peace settlement between the Soviet and U.S. governments. American troops were stationed in South Korea to help keep the peace.

President Truman called the June 25 invasion an act of aggression. He promptly ordered American forces into action, and asked for a special meeting of the United Nations General Assembly. The UN responded by sponsoring an armed force under the command of General Douglas MacArthur.

By June 29, the North Korean Army had captured Seoul, the South's capital city. In August, the North Koreans were pushing toward Pusan, at the southernmost reaches of the peninsula. Then, on September 15, MacArthur outflanked the North Koreans with a surprise landing at Inchon. From there, UN troops broke through the Pusan perimeter, recaptured Seoul, and crossed the 38th Parallel on September 30.

The UN authorized its forces to pursue the retreating North Koreans deep into their own territory, but China warned that it would enter the war if the UN reached the Yalu River on its Manchurian border. By the time of the November 7 election, Americans felt confident that the Korean "war" had

149

been won and the spread of communism halted. Bridges lauded Truman's prompt action. He was pleased that an aggressor had been checked, and satisfied that his criticisms of the State Department had earned results.

Bridges had other concerns in the summer of 1950, as New Hampshire's Republican party seemed to be falling apart. As in 1944, Senator Tobey was the center of the dissension. There was no question that Governor Sherman Adams, along with congressmen Norris Cotton and Chester Merrow, would again get their party nominations, but Tobey was another matter.

The Tobey-Powell Fight

Unlike Bridges, Tobey never seemed to learn the art of the political game. He often attacked Republican party policy, and once observed, "Parties are nothing, but the people are everything." His position came from his conscience, rather than from the influence of his supporters. If an idea appealed to Tobey, he backed it, regardless of political consequences and without caution. So he continued to be controversial and seemingly politically vulnerable.

Tobey had joined the United World Federalists—called "One Worlders" by their detractors. The group wanted the United Nations to be strengthened into an organization capable of preventing aggression and enforcing peace. The Federalists also favored disarmament and an end to U.S.-Soviet competition, particularly in the burgeoning arms race. A vocal conservative minority in New Hampshire condemned these views as pro-Communist.

Tobey had also angered conservative Republicans by siding with Truman on a number of issues. In 1949, it was widely believed that he would retire the next year, and the state Republican leaders began considering a candidate to replace him. But Tobey refused to retire, regardless of party sentiments. With his characteristic fervent oratory, he announced that he would run for a third term.

He had attracted national attention as a member of the Kefauver Committee, which was investigating organized crime. The Senate hearings on this subject were televised and widely watched. On camera, Tobey questioned gamblers and gang members in his evangelical yet intellectual style, which appealed to large numbers of viewers. This, and his attacks on Senator McCarthy, assured him the support of moderate Republicans in his quest for a third term. On the other hand, the conservatives who opposed Tobey controlled the state Republican organization.

Unlike 1944, in the 1950 race there was no shortage of aspirants to run against Tobey. Merrow, Cotton, former governor Robert Blood, and Concord Attorney Robert W. Upton were all mentioned as early as 1948. The party leadership, however, wanted one man, not several, to oppose Tobey in the primary. As in 1944, Bridges maneuvered behind the scenes to reach consensus for a single acceptable candidate.

After much consideration, Bridges and William Loeb, then a rising influence in the party, asked Cotton to oppose Tobey. But remembering that Tobey had beaten Stearns in 1944 by seven thousand votes, Cotton declined. He wrote to Bridges and Loeb that he valued the continued support of the Second District voters and did not want to leave them. "Their confidence in me would be considerably shaken. When I ran for Congress three years ago, I proclaimed that if elected, I would stick to the job long enough to build up enough seniority to try to accomplish something for the Second District."

Other Republicans were considered, but they all seemed to have liabilities. Adams was in the moderate camp, and Merrow seemed colorless—and his election victories were by close margins. At this point, Wesley Powell offered himself. With his successful record as a Bridges spokesman, some of the party leadership liked the idea. On October 13, 1949, he resigned as Bridges' chief of staff and announced his candidacy against Tobey.

At first, Tobey's campaign staff may have felt relieved, as Powell had never before run for state office. He presented a favorable image on issues to conservatives, however, and had a strong following among veterans and young Republicans, as indicated by his choice of the youthful Hugh Gregg, mayor of Nashua, to head his campaign.

The party leadership, including Bridges, became so confident about Powell's campaign that it remained neutral in the primary. The result was one of the bitterest Republican primary battles in New Hampshire history, reminding observers of the Bridges-Moses contest of 1936.

No sooner had Powell announced his candidacy than Tobey began attacking him, and Powell retorted in kind.

Commenting on the Soviet atomic bomb, Tobey said a nuclear war was out of the question, because neither side could win, and the United States should concentrate on peaceful use of atomic energy. "The atomic bomb is here to stay. The question is, are we?" he asked.

Many Americans wondered the same thing, and were investing in the construction of backyard bomb shelters to protect their families in case of a Soviet attack. Schools were holding "atomic-bomb drills" as well as more traditional fire drills, and students were instructed in the dangers of radiation poisoning. Powell, however, recalled the panic after Pearl Harbor and called for a strong, prepared military, able to use whatever weapons were available.

Powell's campaign was carefully planned. In February of 1950, he began outlining his positions on public issues, comparing them to Tobey's.

1950 political cartoon in the Concord Monitor

He attacked Democrats for trying to bring socialism to the country, and big labor for supporting the excesses of the New Deal. He rapped deficit spending and called for a balanced budget. He labeled Tobey a "Truman Republican." This label became one of Powell's battle cries, as his research showed that Tobey had sided with Truman "more often than not."

At the same time, Tobey called on all Republicans to support the president's bipartisan foreign policy. The *New Hampshire Sunday News* commented, "Senator Tobey appears to take delight in providing his primary opponent . . . with ammunition for the charge that Tobey is a Truman Republican."

By June, Tobey began to realize that he was up against a strong opponent. Powell had set up an impressive campaign staff, which included many veterans who worked energetically for their candidate. In addition, Powell had mustered the support of most of the state's leading newspapers. The Loeb papers issued almost daily criticisms of Tobey. Even such moderate newspapers as the *Concord Monitor* and the *Portsmouth Herald*, along with the weekly *Peterborough Transcript*, occasionally attacked Tobey.

By July, political observers agreed that Tobey was in trouble. He apparently felt the same, for he began touring the state. His emotional podium pounding rallied the moderates somewhat, but campaigning kept him from his Washington chores. In a classic line, Powell commented on Tobey's travels: "He would not have to be up here mending his fences if he did not sit on them so much."

Tobey had often upset forecasters and won elections against strong opposition, observers recalled. He was the only man in Granite State history to have served as House speaker, Senate president, member of the executive council, and governor, followed by service in both houses of the U.S. Congress. In the 1950 campaign he used television and newspaper ads to ask for votes, along with direct appeals. His public exposure through the Kefauver hearings and appearances on *Meet the Press* was of inestimable value. To keep up with the times, he rebuilt his political organization under the direction of his son, Charles W. Tobey, Jr., and included a veterans' division that worked on his behalf.

By the middle of August, the charges became more personal. Tobey claimed that money was pouring into Powell's coffers and noted that Powell was offering free dinners throughout the state to attract voters. He charged that Bridges was responsible for the influx of Powell's financial support.

Bridges had personal affection for his young former chief of staff, and what relationship they may have had in the primary campaign is not on record. Although many of Bridges' known supporters had now become Powell backers, it could not be demonstrated that their support was solely because of loyalty to Bridges. Powell was not the creation of a political machine, in short, his campaign showing was due to his personal appeal and political capabilities.

Bridges may have given private encouragement, but financially and politically, he remained neutral in the Tobey-Powell contest. He had once before violated his policy of preprimary neutrality and lost; he was not about to chance another such occurrence. Above all, Bridges treasured the preservation of party unity.

Tobey charged in August that an Exeter banker was furnishing unlimited funds to Powell. The man denied the allegation, and Powell again accused Tobey of unfair tactics. As the September primary approached, Tobey lost the support of several party leaders, including former governor Huntley N. Spaulding. The final weeks of the campaign saw continued repetition of charges and countercharges by both candidates.

On September 12, Adams, Cotton, and Merrow were renominated without trouble, but the vote counting in the Tobey-Powell race went on into the night. Voting had been heavy, and Nashua came up with a surprise by casting twice the number of ballots as it had in the 1948 primary. The final count showed Tobey a victor by a slim margin, defeating Powell 39,203 to 37,893. Even though Nashua's Mayor Gregg ran Powell's campaign, Tobey carried that city 1,687 to 1,067.

It was later said that the CIO had put on a last-minute drive to induce Democrats to switch to the Republican column to help Tobey.

The primary defeat failed to curb Powell's senatorial drive. He considered calling for a recount, but dropped the idea. His staff wanted him to run as an independent in the November election. Even as Republican leadership issued a call for party unity, Powell's staff was checking the procedure for getting their candidate on the election ballot. Powell bided his time before taking formal action.

Powell aides began circulating petitions to place his name on the ballot against Tobey and the Democratic candidate, Emmet J. Kelley of Berlin, a veteran party warhorse. Powell conferred with Governor Adams and other party leaders about his plans, and it was hardly any surprise when a proposed Powell split met with a negative response. But Powell's staff was still determined to see him defeat Tobey. If he failed, the Powell votes might at least unseat Tobey, giving the election to the Democrats. On September 30, 1950, Powell went against party leaders and filed as an independent candidate for senator.

Bridges was perplexed by Powell's move. Tobey appealed to the Senator to talk Powell out of running, but still smarting from Tobey's attacks the previous summer, Bridges refused to intercede. His heart was with Powell, but to support him against Tobey would compromise his zeal for party unity. On the other hand, to support Tobey, even as a party nominee, would anger many of Powell's supporters, who were also Bridges followers. So Bridges chose to solve this problem by campaigning for the Republican party, without mentioning names.

Failing to gain Bridges' support, Tobey took legal steps. He challenged Powell's petitions, since they were signed by both Republicans and Democrats and not by voters calling themselves independents. While the lawyers wrangled, Tobey kept hounding the Republican state committee to give him all-out support.

Then Tobey's lawyers discovered that the state Ballot Law Commission had set a wrong date on his candidacy, and that Powell had filed too late. The commission confirmed the error and ruled Powell's candidacy invalid, much to the relief of Tobey and the state Republican committee.

Undaunted, Powell supporters next decided to mount a write-in campaign. Even if Powell lost, Bridges feared, he might draw sufficient Republican votes to allow Democrat Kelley to win. Styles felt pressured to campaign for the Republican ticket, including Tobey, although Loeb backed the Powell write-in drive.

Still trying to dodge the Tobey-Powell issue, Bridges denied that he "controlled" Powell, but that wasn't enough to satisfy the call for party unity.

On October 31, seven days before the election, Bridges endorsed Tobey by name, and warned that any write-in votes would only help the Democrats.

The election gave Tobey a third term, by the most impressive majority of his career. He beat Kelley 106,142 to 72,473, while Powell garnered only 11,958 votes.

Nationally, the 1950 election gave the Republicans fresh hope. The party came within two seats of capturing control of the Senate. Republicans in California sent Communist-hunter Richard Nixon to the Senate, and in Illinois, Democrat Majority Leader Scott Lucas was upset by young Everett M. Dirksen, who would become an outstanding Republican spokesman. When Bridges returned to Washington, he found Taft in complete control of party affairs, since Vandenberg had become seriously ill. That set of circumstances appeared to give Taft the party's presidential nomination in 1952.

MacArthur vs Truman

The Korean conflict was far from over, and dominated the congressional session. On November 26, Chinese forces crossed the Yalu River into Korea, and attacked the overconfident MacArthur army. UN forces began to retreat. For several months, it was feared that the Americans faced an utter rout, but they dug in and in January held a new front above Seoul.

Stung by having to retreat, MacArthur called for an attack on mainland China from Formosa, and heavy bombing of Chinese bases in the Manchurian region. Truman insisted upon restricting the fighting to the Korean peninsula and refused to heed MacArthur's demands. Instead of going through the chain of command, the general spoke out publicly to win support for his stand. He expanded his argument to include the use of atomic weapons, a position Bridges himself mirrored in a New Hampshire speech, stating, "Atomic weapons should be used, if necessary, to end the Korean war."

On April 5, Truman announced plans to negotiate a truce between the Koreas. MacArthur responded caustically, "There is no substitute for victory." Although numerous Americans agreed with him, many were coming to terms with the idea of "limited warfare." It was clear that nuclear weapons could not be used in every confrontation, and the dangers from radiation could not be confined within the borders of any one country, even one as large as China. Truman felt that the use of nuclear weapons would bring retaliation from the Soviet Union, and he did not want to be remembered as the president who started World War III.

MacArthur's open antagonism to Truman was a breach of military discipline, as the president of the United States is also the commander-in-chief of the nation's military forces. Charged with insubordination and violating

General Douglas McArthur arrives at the Capitol in Washington escorted by Senators Styles Bridges and Harry Byrd.

presidential orders, MacArthur was relieved of his command. Truman replaced him with General Matthew Ridgway. The decision to remove the popular MacArthur, who many Americans considered the hero of the Pacific Theater in World War II, buried the president under an avalanche of denunciations and impaired his political effectiveness.

MacArthur arrived in Washington to a hero's welcome on April 19. He addressed Congress, urging them to expand the war into China. His speech, which was broadcast to a huge audience on radio and television, closed with his oft-repeated line, "Old soldiers never die, they just fade away." Thunderous applause followed.

Bridges agreed with MacArthur's stand on Asia and demanded that the Americans either press for victory or quit Korea entirely. Republicans once again demanded the resignation of Secretary Acheson, who they thought was "soft on communism."

MacArthur testified in secret before the Senate Armed Services Committee, but his cause was inevitably public. Bridges debated the issue on NBC television with the prominent New York Democratic leader, W. Averill Harriman. MacArthur's plan could lead to lasting victory, Bridges contended. Harriman replied that he considered it strange that the United States should end one war by starting another.

Republicans, placing great hope in MacArthur's testimony, believed he would pave the way for Congress to take over the direction of the war, and win it. MacArthur failed to prove out the Republican hope, however, as he gave scant ammunition to Truman's detractors, and even admitted that Truman had been within his rights as commander-in-chief to dismiss him. With that, the old soldier truly began to fade away.

The committee's report exonerated Truman, but the Republican members, led by Bridges, filed a minority report. They denounced Truman for failing to press for victory, and demanded that Congress be given the opportunity to declare war as provided in the Constitution. Bridges charged that Truman had put political considerations above military goals. He told newsmen, "I can only conclude, as the hearings end, that our government had no positive policy to bring victory over the aggressors in Korea."

Bridges continued to reflect American uneasiness about the distant Korean conflict. By June of 1951, Seoul had been retaken by UN and American forces, and the North Koreans, with their Chinese allies, had been pushed back into a static position roughly corresponding to the 38th Parallel. At this point, the Communist forces agreed to negotiate a truce. When the truce parleys began in August of 1951, it was thought that the actual fighting would cease, but both sides continued to skirmish over their fronts as the negotiations dragged on for two long years. More than fifty thousand American soldiers died in the conflict. Some twenty years later, the Chinese threat would play an important role in another long-drawn-out conflict in Vietnam, as military strategists concluded that it was not possible to win a conventional land war against the massive Chinese army. The alternative, which was to use nuclear weapons, posed an even greater threat to world peace.

When it seemed as though no end was in sight, Bridges complained: "The Truman-Acheson administration claims this is a police action against aggression. Well, the United Nations has not defeated the aggressors. Instead, our people are talking truce with them. General MacArthur wanted to fight this war through to ultimate victory, but he was fired when he spoke out against needlessly killing American boys while fighting a war under special State Department rules."

Premier Shegaru Yoshida of Japan signing the Japanese-American Security Pact on September 8, 1951 in San Francisco. John Foster Dulles, Secretary of State Dean Acheson, and Senator Bridges look on.

On September 30, 1951, the Republican senators came up with an interesting document. Plainly aimed at the MacArthur ouster, it called for government protection of the constitutional right of free speech without redress. All the Republican senators signed the resolution, which stated in part:

> Within the framework of laws which safeguard the rights of individuals, it has been the historical privilege and the sacred duty of Americans to criticize our government. This power in the hands of a free people has prevented the accumulation of evil in government. . . . Any attempt to restrain the inherent right of an American to criticize his government must be resisted by all freedom-loving persons. . . . We, therefore, the undersigned members of the United States Senate pledge to the American people that we shall fight to guarantee that, in the difficult days ahead, no man's voice will be silenced.

While Bridges joined with McCarthy and others in sponsoring the right to criticize the government, they obviously did not want the principle applied to Americans with Communist ideas, or others who might favor different forms of government. McCarthy was continuing his anti-Communist crusade, in spite of his failure to produce evidence of such subversives in the government. Apparently no one noticed the hypocrisy of the McCarthy position.

Partly to offset these charges, the State Department hired a Bridges staff member, R.W. Scott McLeod, to act as a security officer and to guard the loyalty files. McLeod, however, failed to find any disloyal employees in the State Department, and he refused to go before McCarthy's committee for questioning until he actually found a Communist. McLeod never appeared before the committee.

In July, President Truman chose Bridges as a delegate to the signing of a permanent peace treaty with Japan. The senator also witnessed the signing of a mutual defense treaty with America's former enemy, which would cement an alliance that endures to this day. Bridges approved it as a permanent curb on the Chinese Communists.

Bridges Becomes Minority Leader

Both Wherry and Vandenberg died in 1951, leaving a vacuum in the Republican leadership. Bridges immediately announced that he did not want to be minority leader, which would mean giving up his other important committee assignments. The moderates proposed Senator Leverett Saltonstall of Massachusetts to fill the gap, but the Taft wing opposed that compromise.

Fearing a party split, Bridges and others attempted a compromise of their own, suggesting that several senators share the minority post, as

The Daniel Webster desk

had been done after Senator McNary's death. The Taft forces opposed that proposition as well. Conservatives begged Bridges to reconsider, because his long-time policy of compromise to avoid party infighting made him acceptable to the moderates. He finally agreed to become minority leader, but with the proviso that he fill the position only until after the 1952 election. On January 8, 1952, Bridges was elected over Saltonstall, 26 to 15. Later in January, he resigned as the Senate's Campaign Committee chairman to devote more attention to the minority leadership, as well as to his posts on the Appropriations Committee and the Armed Services Committee.

Bridges had mixed reactions to his new honor. It seemed like a reward for his party efforts, as he had joined the Senate in the politically gloomy 1937 period, and he was proud to have Daniel Webster's desk, with the initials "D.W." carved into the wood, moved to the front row of the Senate Chamber. During his second term, Bridges had had the century-old Webster desk removed from storage and refurbished for his use in the Senate, because of his admiration for the noted New Hampshire statesman of the early 1800s. When Bridges died, the desk was taken over by Senator Norris Cotton. Before his retirement, Cotton won unanimous approval to make the Webster desk the permanent seat of New Hampshire's senior senator.

Bridges' new job demanded much of his time, and he was not able to give his usual attention to the annual budget problems. Another scandal suddenly broke around him. Since 1949, various congressional committees had been investigating "influence peddlers"—people who courted congressional favors. (Because they could conduct business only outside the House or Senate chambers, they were also called "lobbyists.")

When Bridges assumed the minority leadership role, he was connected with one of Washington's most notorious influence peddlers, Henry Grunewald, a mysterious figure whose background was murky. A South African immigrant, Grunewald had been active in Washington political circles since 1930. After holding a variety of positions, he became the agent of Henry Marsh, another shady Washington character. This connection led to other introductions in various circles of power in the Congress and the federal bureaucracy.

Grunewald specialized in making contacts with powerful politicians, lobbying for companies or for individuals. For this service he received generous fees, stocks, or other gifts. Grunewald also helped funnel money to candidates in various states. It was charged that he was involved in shakedowns, wiretapping, and money laundering—preventing funds from being tracked back to their original source. One of Grunewald's clients was Harvey Klein, a Baltimore liquor dealer. When Klein sought a congressional contact, Grunewald sent him to Bridges, who was well known for having an open-door policy toward anyone who needed a favor.

Klein had parlayed a four thousand dollar investment in Canadian liquor into a $20 million deal during World War II. In 1949, the Internal Revenue Service charged that Klein owed $17 million in back taxes, seized his assets, and prepared to prosecute him. Klein sought out Bridges via Grunewald, and through his attorney, William Maloney, asked for assistance in calling off the IRS action. Bridges agreed to help and contacted Charles Oliphant, chief counsel for the IRS.

In testimony before the King Committee in the spring of 1952, Bridges insisted that he had received no money for his services, and that he was unaware that Klein was being charged with fraud in his tax returns. Bridges also explained that he considered his action on behalf of Klein as merely helping a citizen battle an insensitive bureaucracy, which he had done for many others. When the investigation concluded, Bridges was convinced that he had been exonerated, as the committee made no formal report against him. His honesty, or at least his judgment, had once again come under question, however.

Campaigning for Eisenhower

By late 1951, Truman's administration had become unpopular among the American people. As Lyndon Johnson, the thirty-sixth president and one of the most politically astute people to hold national office in the twentieth century, was later to discover, drawn-out conflicts, with no discernible goals or resolution in sight, do not play well with the U.S. electorate. The years of Democratic domination of the national government seemed to be near an end. Republicans, however, were not unified. Moderates and conservatives battled each other for control of the party. Governor Thomas Dewey had twice lost presidential bids, leaving the moderates without major leadership. For conservatives, the time seemed finally ripe for Taft to win the party's nomination, something he had tried to do since 1940.

By legislative vote in 1949, the Granite State's 1952 presidential primary became the first in which party members were given the opportunity to directly vote their preference for president. Prior to that time, the voting was only for delegates to the presidential convention.

Taft visited New Hampshire to test party sentiments in the summer of 1951. Bridges introduced him to a Hampton Beach gathering, but offered no help or endorsement, correctly assuming that the moderates might yet challenge his candidacy.

General Dwight David Eisenhower, the popular Allied Forces leader who remained in Europe to protect American interests after peace was restored in 1945, had been mentioned by both Democratic and Republican factions as a possible choice for president. MacArthur seemed too volatile, he too had supporters among Republicans.

New Hampshire's moderate Republicans, headed by Governor Sherman Adams, drafted Eisenhower late in 1951 to become a candidate for president in the 1952 primary. The general at first declined to permit having his name entered in the primary, but he later gave his tacit consent without personal participation.

Adams became chairman of the Eisenhower committee, and was joined by Senator Tobey, Congressman Cotton, former governor Blood, and House Speaker Lane Dwinell. While Eisenhower remained aloof from the campaign, Taft devoted much of his time to personal tours of the state, with Powell and Loeb heading up his supporters.

In spite of pressure by both Taft and Eisenhower forces, Bridges clung to his neutrality. He stated, "I have, still do, and shall continue to maintain my neutral position in this campaign. I believe by so doing, I can best serve my country and the Republican party, in view of my position as Republican leader in the Senate." At a Lincoln's Birthday dinner rally in Grand Rapids, Michigan for Congressman Gerald R. Ford, Bridges spoke of the need for

*Senator Bridges and Governor Sherman Adams greet
Senator Taft of Ohio on his entering the New Hampshire
primary in 1952.*

new federal programs and a reasonable foreign policy, with no mention of the Taft-Eisenhower contest.

The New Hampshire primary drew a record turnout. Eisenhower toppled Taft 46,661 to 35,838; MacArthur got only 3,227 votes. Bridges won a write-in nomination for vice-president with 6,535 votes, which was gratifying, but of no consequence. On the Democratic side, President Truman ran into a stunning defeat in his bid for another term, losing to Senator Estes Kefauver of Tennessee.

By the time the Republican convention met in Chicago in July, Eisenhower had eclipsed Taft. He won the nomination on the first ballot, despite a bitter floor fight that was masked by cascading balloons, showers of confetti, and shouts of "We Like Ike!" Richard Nixon was chosen as Eisenhower's running mate.

Adams, who had stumped the country for Eisenhower after the New Hampshire primary, was his floor manager during the convention. Afterward he crisscrossed the nation as a chief aide in Ike's campaign, while New Hampshire Senate president Blaylock Atherton of Nashua filled in as acting governor in the Granite State. When Eisenhower was elected president, he appointed Adams as his chief of staff.

Eight former governors of New Hampshire convened at the State House in Concord during Hugh Gregg's governorship. Seated from left: H. Styles Bridges, 1935-37; Robert P. Bass, 1911-13; Huntley N. Spaulding, 1927-29; Standing: Francis P. Murphy, 1937-41; Robert O. Blood, 1941-45; Charles M. Dale, 1945-49; Sherman Adams, 1949-53; Hugh Gregg, 1953-55.

Before the GOP convention adjourned, Senator Bridges called upon the delegates to unite behind their candidates, but Taft remained aloof. Bridges threw himself into the election campaign with his customary vigor and enthusiasm. He reiterated that Republicans could better run the government than Democrats, who had nominated Governor Adlai Stevenson of Illinois for president and Senator John Sparkman of Alabama for vice president. Bridges also hammered against price controls, and for firmer opposition to communism around the world.

In September alone, Bridges traveled more than ten thousand miles for Eisenhower and Nixon. Touring the southern and western states, his greatest success was in heavily Democratic Mississippi, where he drew sustained applause for his attacks on the Democratic party. After that tour, he welcomed Eisenhower to New Hampshire to endorse the party's nominees.

A glitch appeared in late September, however, when it was disclosed that Senator Nixon had benefitted from a secret fund established by a California businessman. While Eisenhower considered dropping him from the ticket, Nixon appeared on television in an emotional appeal, citing his wife's cloth coat as proof of his integrity and claiming that the only present he'd received was the "little dog Checkers" given to his daughters. The famous Checkers speech won Nixon immediate sympathy and support.

Compared to the 1950 imbroglio, the Republicans had little trouble in the state's 1952 election. Congressmen Chester Merrow and Norris Cotton were easily renominated, and Mayor Hugh Gregg of Nashua won the nomination for governor to succeed Adams.

New Hampshire's Democrats were so poorly organized that Eisenhower buried Stevenson, 166,287 to 106,663. Nationwide, the election returns yielded even better news for Republicans. Eisenhower swept the nation with a landslide victory. There would be a Republican Congress, too, with a one vote majority for the party in the Senate.

At last the GOP was in the driver's seat. After twenty years of promises, it was time to see what they could do.

11

Man and Senate

"The longer you stay in public office, the more distant the outside world becomes."

Warren B. Rudman,
Senator from New Hampshire

Dwight David Eisenhower took office as an exceptionally popular president. Times were good for most Americans, and they had confidence in this modest man with the wide grin who'd struggled with poverty as a boy on a Kansas farm. Like MacArthur and Patton, Ike was a war hero, but he had none of their flamboyant egotism. A cautious man, he knew better how to organize men and materials than to lead a battle charge. And that's how he approached the presidency —as an exercise in resource management, not a crusade. Never comfortable on a soapbox, he was distrustful of grandstanders like Joe McCarthy. It was said by many that Ike much preferred the game of golf to the game of politics—which may have been the secret to his success as president.

Eisenhower was clearly a moderate and conservatives did not trust him to overturn the policies put in place by Democrats during the New Deal. They demanded that the Senate be organized to prevent the new president from deviating too greatly from the concepts of what they thought should be done.

Because of his ability to pacify the party dissension and find workable compromises, Bridges was urged to remain as Senate majority leader, but he declined, insisting that he wanted to return to his committee work. He helped forge a compromise by which the conservative Taft became the majority leader, in effect yielding his seniority to Taft, while the moderate

166

President Harry Truman and his successor Dwight D. Eisenhower leaving the White House on January 20, 1953 en route to the Capitol for the inauguration. Senator Styles Bridges and House Speaker Joe Martin are in the front seat.

Leverett Saltonstall of Massachusetts became the Republican whip—the man who made sure senators were in place when a vote was called. McCarthy, meanwhile, was given a committee chairmanship with a mandate to expose the Communists he claimed were in the government.

Such future leaders as Barry M. Goldwater (R-Arizona) and John F. Kennedy (D-Massachusetts) joined the Senate in 1953. Lyndon B. Johnson (D-Texas) was elected to the post of minority leader, the youngest such leader in Senate history.

President Pro Tempore of the Senate

As party roles fell into place, the Republican majority proposed Bridges for Senate president pro tem. He accepted, the youngest senator to be elected to that office since 1891. This recognition of his leadership was gratifying after so many years of work for the party. President pro tempore of the United States Senate is a high honor usually, but not always, conferred upon the senior member of the majority party. (The Granite State has played an outstanding role in furnishing presidents pro tempore of the Senate. Senator Styles Bridges was the sixth N.H. senator to hold this high

Bridges and Vice President Nixon share a lighter moment at the Inaugural Ball.

A serious moment for Senator Styles Bridges and Prescott Bush of Connecticut at the Inaugural Ball in January, 1953

office, following such dignitaries as John Langdon of Portsmouth, Samuel Livermore of Stratham, Daniel Clark of Manchester, Dr. Jacob Gallinger, and George H. Moses, who was elected as president pro tem in 1925 and reelected in 1927, 1929, and 1931.) As president pro tem, Bridges would preside over the Senate when the vice-president was absent, an important post since Nixon rarely came to Capitol Hill. It also meant that Styles was third in line for the presidency, after the vice-president and the speaker of the house.

Although tension was already developing between some Republicans and President Eisenhower, they united to celebrate their triumph at the inaugural ceremony on January 20. Bridges led the congressional delegation, escorting the president to the Capitol to take the oath of office. Despite any differences, there was a general feeling of optimism for the nation's future.

Eisenhower's appointments raised little controversy. Sherman Adams began his iron-handed reign as the president's chief of staff. John Foster Dulles easily became secretary of state. Dulles, a lawyer and the son of a Presbyterian minister, brought a rigorous sense of morality to international relations, consistently seeing them in terms of good (the West) versus evil (the Soviet Union). He promised that no security risks would be tolerated in the State Department.

Only one appointment caused controversy—Eisenhower's choice of career diplomat Charles E. Bohlen as ambassador to the Soviet Union. McCarthy attacked him as undesirable because he had participated with Roosevelt in the Yalta Conference and had worked for Secretary of State Acheson. McCarthy's guilt-by-association tactic failed, however, as the president denounced his attack. Bridges sided with Eisenhower, which guaranteed confirmation of the Bohlen appointment.

McCarthy raised another challenge to the president. He proposed an amendment that would cut off foreign aid to any country that traded with a Communist country, including European nations friendly to the U.S., which needed American trade to strengthen their economies. Eisenhower personally appealed to Bridges to defeat the McCarthy proposal. It was voted down, but Bridges then sponsored a reduction in foreign aid appropriations, which was approved over the objections of the president.

The budget was Bridges' main concern. The senator announced that he would be no kinder to the Eisenhower budget than he had been to Democratic fiscal proposals. Cuts were made, and despite some opposition from the White House, the project neared completion early in 1953.

About this time, Congress launched an investigation of one of Bridges' old adversaries, the Kaiser Corporation. The company had won a bid to build a cargo plane for the air force, then built up cost overruns that doubled the bid price on each plane, while deliveries were only half made. Bridges was instrumental in exposing the details and forcing cancellation of the contract. (In the ensuing decades, however, cost overruns would plague government agencies, in particular the military.)

In the course of his campaign, Eisenhower had pledged firm action in the drawn-out Korean truce negotiations. He had visited Korea in December of 1952, as promised, bringing hope to the troops on the front line. On July 27, 1953, he announced that an armistice had been signed between North Korea and the United Nations, ending the conflict. Although a treaty was never achieved and American forces remained in South Korea, the shooting stopped. Bridges said of Eisenhower's achievement: "The signing of the truce will come as a great relief to many millions of Americans, particularly those anxious relatives and friends of young men on the battle front. It means an end to the unnecessary bloodshed and death that made this war one of America's worst."

The Senatorial Losses

Two deaths in late July tempered the Senate's celebration over the end of the Korean conflict. On July 24, New Hampshire's venerable senator,

In August of 1954 Robert Upton, a prominent Concord attorney, was appointed to fill the remaining term of the late Senator Tobey. From left are Senator Bridges, Vice President Nixon, former President Herbert Hoover, and the newly appointed Senator.

Charles W. Tobey, suffered a massive coronary thrombosis and died at Bethesda Naval Hospital two days after his seventy-third birthday. He had been active in public life for nearly forty years. A man of large vision, he had been an advisor to the UNESCO conference and a member of the U.S. delegation to the conference that established the International Monetary Fund, held in Bretton Woods, New Hampshire, July 1944. Bridges led the funeral delegation, which included all of the living New England senators, Vice-president Nixon, and others who had worked with Tobey on the Kefauver committee.

Governor Gregg had to appoint someone to replace Tobey, and there was no dearth of suggested names for the post. Wesley Powell, Norris Cotton, Bert Teague, Sherman Adams, and even Doloris Bridges were considered to fill out the time until 1954, when a senator could be elected to complete Tobey's final six-year term.

Gregg even considered himself for the temporary appointment, as other governors had done before him in a similar situation, but dismissed the idea. The post was vigorously coveted by several prominent politicians, as whoever Gregg appointed would naturally have an advantage in the 1954 election. He finally decided to appoint someone with no political ambitions, and on August 14, gave the appointment to prominent attorney Robert W. Upton of Concord, a veteran party leader and a close friend of Senator Bridges who had never run for public office and was not expected to run in the 1954 election to succeed himself.

Only a week after Tobey's death, the national party suffered another serious loss. Senator Robert Taft, known as "Mr. Republican," died suddenly. (Taft was probably best remembered for the Taft-Hartley Law, passed in 1947, which curtailed the power of labor unions.) His long-time relationship with Senator Bridges is reflected in a comment Taft made to his administrative assistant, Jack Martin, just before he went into the hospital for the last time: According to Julius Klein in the *Overseas Report* of December 8, 1961, Taft said: "Stand by Bridges, help him. He has the courage and integrity needed in these critical times to carry on."

These vacancies required a reshuffling of the power structure and touched off another clash between conservatives and moderates; the former rallied behind Knowland and the latter passed over Saltonstall in favor of the young Illinois senator Everett Dirksen.

Once again both sides asked Bridges to become the majority leader, but again he refused. He still felt his major committee assignments were more important to the public interest. Knowland won the post, and the dispute left Dirksen firmly established as the leader of the moderates.

As the 1953 session ended in August, Bridges felt that his budget-trimming had been successful and expressed the belief that the budget could be completely balanced in another two years, if the Republicans remained in control. Eisenhower did not agree that cutting the budget was a high priority. He sensed that the public and private differences among the congressional Republicans presented a threat to his administration's proposals. He was particularly unhappy with the Senate conservatives, and in December, he called a conference with the congressional Republicans to try to resolve the differences. Bridges and his fellow Republicans heard their president call for more foreign aid, more money for the Defense Department, and fewer anti-Communist investigations in the government.

The most important task facing the Republicans when the 1954 Congress convened, Eisenhower insisted, would be to produce legislation that could be presented to the voters before the fall election. This, he said, would show that the GOP had a successful program for the management of the government. Eisenhower criticized McCarthy at the meeting, and urged him to tone down his anti-Communist crusade, although he made no direct effort to stop the maverick senator.

As the 1954 session opened, the Republicans reflected outward harmony. Bridges praised the president's State of the Union address as forward-looking, but criticized the proposal to reopen the St. Lawrence Seaway project. The Seaway had been discussed for years, and some canals had opened, but no overall schedule existed for completion. A master plan had been approved in 1949, and dredging work was expected to begin in September. Bridges opposed the Seaway because it would shift shipping from New England ports into the Great Lakes area.

In the spring, Bridges, as chairman of the Appropriations Committee, and Stuart Symington (D-Missouri) toured Europe to evaluate uses of foreign aid there. They reported being impressed with the progress that had been made in supervising the funds, but expressed concern that France's efforts to defend her colonies against insurgents, such as in Algeria and Indochina, would drain the forces of NATO. Bridges suggested that the United States assume the defense of Indochina, but the State Department quietly dismissed that proposal. Still, the U.S. military kept advisors in those areas and monitored the situation closely in ensuing years.

The End of McCarthy

Upon his return to Washington, Bridges found that the harmony between the president and Congress had collapsed. Eisenhower made it known again that he wanted McCarthy to stop his hunt for Communists in government. But instead of heeding the president, McCarthy launched a new attack, this time against the Department of the Army. The main issue was to be the army's refusal to grant special treatment to a former McCarthy aide. Eisenhower ordered the army to refuse McCarthy's demands, and an investigation followed.

Network television decided to cover the April hearings, and millions of Americans watched as McCarthy played to the cameras, insisting that there were scores of Communists in the army. The army's skilled lawyer, Joseph Welch of Boston, finally demanded that McCarthy name the alleged Communists publicly, so they could be promptly removed.

As usual, McCarthy was bluffing; and now he was cornered. To cover his lack of specific information, he rose up and issued a new charge, calling an aide of Welch's a Communist—a completely unfounded allegation. In a dramatic moment, Welch stared at McCarthy and said: "Until this moment, Senator, I think I never really gauged your cruelty or your recklessness. . . . Have you left no sense of decency?"

This scene, in full view of the American public, finished McCarthy for good, although it was months before the Senate acted to censure him.

Fearing party damage from the McCarthy fiasco in an election year, and ever mindful of the change in public opinion toward McCarthy's witch hunt, Republicans moved to investigate the investigator. In December, Mc-

Carthy's career ended with a censure resolution, saying he had "acted contrary to senatorial ethics and tended to bring the Senate into dishonor and disrepute." Bridges continued to believe that there was basis to McCarthy's accusations, even though none of them bore fruit. But although Bridges never completely repudiated McCarthy, this did not affect his home-state popularity.

Helping the Folks at Home

Senator Bridges' third-term years marked the height of his political power and influence—and he never forgot how he got there. He opened his office door to his Granite State constituents and to all others who knocked or called, no matter how busy he might be with his other responsibilities. His files overflowed with letters asking for various kinds of help. Many were requests for help in understanding how to get federal contracts or how to use various federal aid programs. Veterans asked how to receive the benefits due them; families asked for help in clearing the name of a relative who'd gotten a black mark in the military; everyone wanted help in dealing with red tape, particularly in the IRS. When the Crotched Mountain Foundation, located in Francestown, New Hampshire, was threatened with loss of its tax exemption status because of a loophole in the law, Bridges sponsored a bill to correct the problem.

This help to his constituents worked both ways—reciprocity is the grease that keeps the wheels of government running smoothly. Voters told Bridges what was bothering them, he tried to fix it, and they returned him to Washington. Tom Shannon, a member of Bridges' staff, recalled, "He helped the little guy. That was his strength. If a man couldn't get into a VA hospital, Styles would call the administrator of the hospital, *personally*. And behind everything was the veiled threat that if the guy didn't produce, he would know about it. I remember one time when I was working for him— a member of the air force was trying to get home from Germany. His mother, who lived in Littleton, was dying and the boy naturally wanted to be with her. Styles put in a call, but the air force dragged its feet and the boy didn't get home in time. His mother died forty-eight hours before he arrived. Styles was so mad, he took a half million dollars out of the Air Force budget for the slight."

The Newington Air Force Base

In 1949, when the Defense Department closed Grenier Air Force Base in Manchester and reduced production at Portsmouth's naval shipyard to eliminate several hundred jobs, Bridges took action. He was unable to save the out-dated air base, but he induced the navy to increase construction and repair facilities for submarines at the shipyard. In 1955, Bridges won a commitment from the navy to maintain about eight thousand jobs at the Portsmouth shipyard, and he procured substantial federal aid for the Portsmouth school system and other nearby school districts because of the large number of federal employees with children in the area. With the shift to atomic-powered submarines, Bridges helped secure maintenance facilities for the new vessels at Portsmouth, which ensured that the base would not become obsolete.

The possible establishment of an air force base in Newington was announced in 1951. The project met with general enthusiasm statewide, but many Newington residents opposed the idea, fearing it would be an unwelcome imposition upon their modest town. A large part of the controversy centered on government land acquisition. The government purchased 3,027 acres for the project, paying an average of $406 an acre. Some people were paid in excess of $2,000 an acre for their land, while others received less than $50 per acre. Many citizens claimed that government assessors simply did not know the value of much of the wooded acreage, and were understandably upset.

The furor increased when the federal government applied the law of eminent domain against property owners who refused to sell or turned down the proposed payment for their land. Eminent domain, in essence, means that the government, be it state, local, or federal, has the right to bring condemnation proceedings against any property that stands in the way of a public project. Eighty-eight people and families lost all or part of their property as a result of government condemnation action in Newington. In addition, nine roads were seized, as well as a right-of-way along more private land for a water main which would lead to the air base. Among the casualties of these proceedings was the Gerrish Furber House, built in 1794, a homestead that had been farmed by the Hoyt family for several generations.

Naturally, the people who happened to be in the path of the project were outraged. But, as John Frink Rowe wrote in *Newington, New Hampshire* (Phoenix Publishing, 1987), "all the fighting, the hard feelings, the scorn, and the anxiety amounted to exactly nothing."

Such confrontations are part of every large-scale government project, and Bridges understood the importance of the air force base in terms of jobs to the area. It was, after all, the senator's obligation to "bring home the bacon" to his state, and the proposed air base, Bridges knew, would bring economic stability to the region for years to come. For strategic reasons, a new base was going to be built somewhere in New England, and Bridges

Senator and Mrs. Bridges arriving for the opening ceremonies at Pease Air Force Base in Newington in 1954.

was determined to see that it came to New Hampshire. With that in mind, he went on the offensive. Bridges charged the Newington citizens with being selfish and won endorsements for the project from around the state, including the influential William Loeb and his newspapers. The Loeb papers presented a series of articles praising the base and its benefits to New Hampshire, quieting many of the protesters' concerns. In the end, Rowe wrote, "the condemnation cases were duly heard and settled, many of the people were satisfied with the final payment, many were not; but the battle was over at last." Work on the base began in September 1951.

A year later, however, the air force stopped funding the project, stating that it was reevaluating all new programs because of spending cuts authorized by Congress. Bridges intervened, and construction was begun again in February 1953. But in May the air force once more announced it was canceling the project, as funding had again run out. The decision spurred demonstrations around the state, and legislative leaders joined with Governor Gregg to see what could be done.

Bridges was angry with the air force, which he had supported for years. He had advocated its creation after World War II and had supported appropriations that financed the new Air Force Academy in Colorado Springs. He pressured Defense Department officials to confer with Governor Gregg and explain their actions. Meanwhile, Newington's antibase forces renewed

President Eisenhower and Vice President Nixon with Styles Bridges and Henry Cabot Lodge, Jr., the only two new Republicans elected to the U.S. Senate in 1936

their opposition, and urged the air force to stick by the abandonment. After months of vacillating, the air force announced that no final decision would be made until after the new federal budget was enacted. This was plainly a blatant attempt to pressure the Senate Appropriations Committee. Bridges applied pressure of his own, and by September, the base project was reactivated. Newington was again the site of demonstrations for and against the project, and Bridges was both attacked and praised for his role in the decision.

On July 3, 1954, a formal groundbreaking ceremony was held and construction of the giant base was begun again. Bridges monitored the situation to make sure that the air force paid close attention to the needs of the community during construction and the subsequent arrival of military families.

Notes on New Hampshire Politics

The 1954 election marked changes in New Hampshire politics. The Democratic party had suffered so many defeats that its morale was at low ebb. Conflicts marred party unity and leadership shifted in 1954 from Manchester to Laconia, the chief community of the Lakes Region in central New

Bridges poster in his reelection campaign of 1954

*Norris Cotton taking the oath of office from Vice President Nixon as Governor Lane
Dwinell and Styles Bridges look on*

Hampshire. Laconia's young mayor, Gerard Morin, decided to run for the
Senate against Bridges, who was bidding for his fourth term. Eugene S.
Daniell, a prominent Franklin legislator, entered the Democratic primary
against Morin and waged a memorable campaign. Touring the state with two
hand puppets named Low and Mr. B. Ridges, he made the Bridges-Loeb
friendship an issue. The satire amused many Democrats, but didn't get
Daniell enough votes to beat Morin. Thomas McIntyre, former mayor of
Laconia, launched a campaign to unseat Chester Merrow, congressman from
the First District. McIntyre won the First District nomination over Alfred
Fortin, a veteran Manchester party leader.

On the Republican side, the 1954 election campaign at first seemed
that it would be without conflict, but that supposition proved wrong. Governor Gregg upset expectations by deciding to return to the family business
rather than seeking a second term. This led state senate president Lane Dwinell, an easygoing Lebanon manufacturer, to decide to run for governor. He
readily won the nomination over Elmer Bussey of Salem, a political unknown.
James C. Cleveland, who briefly worked for Bridges in Washington, ran
successfully for the state Senate, and he would later be elected to Congress.

Wesley Powell announced on October 4, 1953, that he would run for
the Tobey/Upton Senate seat. Congressman Norris Cotton also eyed this
nomination and repeatedly asked Upton whether or not he was going to retire, as originally anticipated. When Cotton failed to get a definite decision
from Upton he announced his candidacy against Powell—whereupon

Memorabilia of the 1954 campaign

Upton surprised everyone by announcing he would run for the post as well. Cotton won the nomination in the September 14 primary, with Upton finishing second and Powell at the bottom.

Cotton's bid for the Senate left the Second District congressional seat open. Eight candidates, led by former state Senate president Perkins Bass of Peterborough, scrambled for that nomination. Perkins, the son of former governor Robert P. Bass, had been close to Bridges during his teenage years. The two often exchanged letters at a time when Robert Bass was often away from home caring for Perkins' mother, who suffered from tuberculosis. The younger Bass nosed out former Bridges aide Bert Teague 14,591 to 13,855 in the primary, while the six other aspirants managed to accumulate about 4,000 votes among them.

Senator Bridges planned his usual "run hard" strategy for his fourth term, but he didn't need to. Now, as a senior statesman, he wielded more influence than ever and was seen as the major power broker in the state. His failure to censure McCarthy, however, combined with the air-base issue and some aspects of his conduct in Washington, raised the specter of opposition within the party. Several Republicans began evaluating their chances of upsetting Bridges, Perkins Bass among them. Bridges' increasing conservatism and his outspoken wife, Doloris, whom the Basses disliked, had created a widening breach, gradually costing Styles what had once been a warm friendship. Perkins Bass recalled, "I believe that Styles wanted to maintain the friendship. . . . but as far as my father's influence . . . it was gone. Doloris had taken over." Perkins believed that Senator Bridges "became much more conservative, largely because of Doloris—she was very conservative, almost radical. He was under her influence a great deal."

Perkins Bass did not openly challenge the powerful Bridges, but quietly canvassed the state for possible weaknesses in the senator's constituency. He even hired a professional pollster to measure public opinion, in an effort to measure Bridges' strength among the voters. It was a discreet move until the *Manchester Union Leader* learned of the survey. Loeb assumed that the Democratic National Committee was financing the poll, and ran several editorials demanding to know why the DNC was snooping around New Hampshire.

While the newspaper never learned of Bass' sponsorship of the poll, it reprinted the results, which showed that Bridges' constituency was as solid as ever. The voters were going to support their senior senator no matter what. Bass abandoned his fishing expedition to concentrate on the congressional seat, which he won.

12

Brushes With Scandal

"It was against the law, but everybody did it."
Political columnist and Pulitzer Prize Winner Jack Anderson

O N JULY 20, 1954 *The Reporter*, a Washington-based magazine, published an article intending to expose Bridges' misuse of power. "Senator Styles Bridges' Far-Flung Constituents" was a carefully researched presentation by Douglass Cater, Washington editor of the magazine, who had taken almost a year to assemble the information. Basically, the article was a recounting of the scandals that Styles had been involved in during his career. In addition to the China Lobby, the United Mine Workers' fees, and the Klein-Grunewald case, plus Styles' association with industrialist Armand Hammer, the article dealt with a number of other dubious connections.

British-born Arthur Rothwell was a China Lobby investor of questionable character with a half-dozen different enterprises, among them the Franconia Trading Corporation and Oriental Fine Arts. On February 26, 1951, Rothwell purchased property at Wolfeboro Neck, on Lake Winnipesaukee, from the estate of Frank Hopewell. A month later, a mortgage was taken out on the property, known as Spruce Acres, ostensibly to finance extensive renovations. The area was apparently to be used by China lobbyist Louis Kung, along with his friends and relatives, as a summer retreat. Kung never controlled the property, and Rothwell's name did not appear on any of the deeds until he sold the holdings in 1966, after Bridges' death. In fact, Kung's use of the property was based almost entirely on hearsay and the suspicions of neighbors. There were reports of "long black limousines"

182

with Chinese occupants, and Madame Chiang Kai-shek was believed to have visited the property personally. It was probably Bridges who recommended the estate to Kung, which suggested a friendly relationship between the parties. Bridges later got a part of the property.

Shortly before he died, Hopewell had surveyed a parcel of land within his estate, presumably with the intent to sell. Rothwell sold that piece of land to former Bridges' aide Louis C. Wyman, then state attorney general, for "the sum of one dollar, plus other considerations." The other considerations may have been Wyman's legal advice over a period of time, or Mrs. Wyman's service on the board of one of Rothwell's creations, the Franconia Trading Corporation.

How Bridges Worked

The Reporter article infuriated Bridges on two fronts. The first, and probably the most important, was that it appeared during an election year, and thus could cause damage not only to the senator personally but to his beloved Republican party. The timing was no accident, of course. Styles had become a full-fledged power broker, both in the Senate and in New Hampshire politics. Commonly known as "a man with no enemies," Bridges in fact had more than his share of political and personal opposition. While his friendly, outgoing manner perhaps precluded him from considering anyone a true enemy, he was nevertheless a powerful man, one who was not afraid to use his influence in the back rooms of the legislature, where deal making and polite arm twisting are the keys to success and longevity. The smoke-filled back rooms were, in truth, Styles Bridges' arena. It was here, in the close confines of what is commonly known as "the old boys' network," that the senator was able to bring his forceful personality and his talent for organization into full focus. Throughout his entire career, the personal touch in these back-room meetings were Bridges' forte, the key to his success as a politician. John Warrington, Bridges' executive secretary from 1958 to 1961, commented about Styles: "He was not a floor Senator. He was a committee tactician, he wanted to get things done."

Bert Teague, Bridges' legislative assistant, recalled, "If there was going to be a close vote on a particular piece of legislation, Bridges was the guy both sides came to see to get that extra vote—Democrats as well as Republicans. He had friends on both sides of the aisle."

The Reporter article was clearly directed at limiting Bridges' effectiveness in this critical arena. No one loses power and influence faster than a Washington politician draped in a cloud of scandal.

Rowland Evans, co-host of CNN's political interview program *Evans, Novak, Hunt & Shields*, covered the U.S. Congress in his early years in Wash-

"Oh, Pretty Good — How Are Things With You?"

Herblock cartoon from the Washington Post

ington for the *New York Herald-Tribune*. Much of this inside deal-making took place in a small, almost overlooked office in the Capitol designated P-47, where Styles Bridges held court. It was here, in an office that the *Los Angeles Times* (March 18, 1959) described as looking like a broom closet, that much of the principal legislation of the 1950s was given the final stamp of senatorial approval. Evans recalled, "Bridges was well liked, but feared and respected as well. He was a crafty, yet decent man, and I often looked to him for political information."

Another reason the article so angered Bridges was that the accusations, while largely speculative, held some kernels of truth. It was also common knowledge in Washington of the 1950s that if someone wanted something done in the world's most politically charged city, Styles Bridges was the man to see. And money wouldn't hurt, either.

As *The Reporter* article reiterated, Bridges had accepted a salary from John L. Lewis and the United Mine Workers to the tune of some $70,000 dollars, for his two-year stint as a trustee on the board of the UMW Welfare and Retirement Fund. While an investigation concluded that there was nothing illegal about accepting the money and the position, the senator's judgment was called into question, and he eventually resigned the trusteeship. He did not, however, offer to give back any of the money.

The senator also interceded in the well-publicized tax case, involving Baltimore liquor dealer Harvey Klein. A generally unscrupulous man, Klein ran afoul of the IRS while shipping whiskey from Canada to the United States. By running the transactions through several dummy corporations in Cuba and Panama, Klein and his partners parlayed a $4,000 investment into a $20 million windfall, and were eventually indicted by a grand jury. Bridges himself was called before a Congressional Investigation Committee on the matter. Representative Cecil King, chairman of the committee and a Democrat from California, rebuked Bridges, saying that the senator's friends had undoubtedly "taken advantage" of him. "All of us have had tricks played on us. You were probably selected to be taken advantage of because of your distinguished position as Chairman of the Appropriations Committee."

Senator Bridges listened to the remarks "with an expressionless face," reported the Associated Press. The *Washington Post* was a bit less kind, reporting on the same date: "Yesterday's hearings may have been in the best tradition of Congressional courtesy. But it did nothing to brighten Senator Bridges' tarnished reputation. Indeed, the Senator's vague, evasive and equivocal replies gave an impression of more concealment than of candor."

The fact of the matter is, while Bridges never publicly gave the reasons for his intersession on Klein's behalf other than to say he was merely trying to help a distressed citizen, Harvey Klein had a close association with Dr. Armand Hammer, owner of United Distillers, Inc. and its Canadian subdivision, United Distillers of Canada, of which Klein was a stockholder. Hammer's family sent young Armand to China in the early 1920s to collect a bad debt. He remained overseas to help establish a trading company, that later provided the new Soviet Republic with much-needed international trade. Hammer made a fortune out of this venture, building it into several companies, the largest of which was Occidental Petroleum. In the late 1940s, Hammer began buying distilleries for the purpose of producing industrial alcohol. One of these plants was located in Newmarket, New Hampshire, and inevitably he became acquainted with Senator Bridges.

The two men had a close association over the years. In one instance, Hammer sought Bridges' aid in securing the right to operate an army ordnance plant. Hammer had submitted a high bid for the project and it had been awarded to another company. Bridges tried to induce the army to reconsider the award, but after some discussion and an investigation, he dropped the case.

Hammer was a long-time Bridges supporter and campaign contributor. Styles and his wife were frequent guests on Hammer's yacht, and at least once accompanied the Hammers on a cruise to the Caribbean. Bridges frequently interceded on Hammer's behalf, supporting the wealthy industrialist's dealings with federal government contracts.

Bridges' association with Harry Grunewald, another Washington insider and money man who was himself later indicted by the government, also calls the senator's judgment into question. Grunewald's Washington ties ran deep. He was in the old FBI during World War I and was also a prohibition agent in the 1920s, as well as an investigator for Joseph McCarthy's Un-American activities committee. One of Grunewald's clients was John L. Lewis, of the United Mine Workers. Grunewald later claimed that it was Styles Bridges who helped him get his investigative job with the UMW.

Bridges also accepted political contributions from the highly suspect China Lobby, and fought tirelessly for the anti-Communist government of Chiang Kai-shek's nationalistic forces, now in exile on Taiwan. Styles' close ties to the Kung family, relatives of Chiang Kai-shek and the operators of the United States branch of the powerful Bank of China, are also suspect. Arthur Rothwell, another close associate of the Kungs, was also a frequent contributor to the Bridges' campaign funds. And it is a fact, as *The Reporter* article stated, that soon after prominent members of the China Lobby purchased a large tract of property on Lake Winnipesaukee in Wolfeboro, a portion of that land was deeded to Styles' wife, Doloris, and became the site for the Bridges' summer home.

Armand Hammer, later president of Occidental Petroleum with Doloris Bridges and James Hayes, executive councilor of Concord in the 1950s

Was it Illegal or Immoral?

So the question can reasonably be asked: Did Styles Bridges take the money? Did he trade his power and influence for cash payoffs? Jack Anderson, the preeminent national columnist, apparently thinks so. "I was very fond of him," Anderson said in a candid interview at Washington's University Club in 1986.

But I thought he was an incorrigible crook. By that, I mean, he took money under the table. I never had the impression that he took it for himself . . . that he lavished money on himself. I never had the impression that he lived the luxurious life. But what he loved was power, and he discovered that the key to power was money. He always had money to help out political friends.

In his interview, Anderson also commented,

I think that he felt that his motives were pure, and that he was serving the right causes, and taking the funds from people he would have supported anyway. I don't think he really considered himself corrupt . . . but he was. He was taking money in violation of the law. But so were a lot of Senators. The laws were so constructed in those days that you almost couldn't get elected if you obeyed the law strictly. So almost no one did. The Corrupt Practices Act had become mean-

Speaker Joe Martin and Senator Bridges confer with President Eisenhower

ingless. . . . It was kind of like Prohibition. It was against the law, but everybody did it.

While Anderson was on friendly terms with Styles, the columnist was not hesitant to blow the whistle on the senator. In a September 1956 column, Anderson reported that Bridges' office had received a leak regarding a Civil Aeronautics Board ruling that would have a very positive effect on Northeast Airlines stock. Bridges' staff, Anderson wrote, rushed out to buy the stock at a relatively low price, just hours before it jumped to thirteen dollars a share. This charge of insider trading was never confirmed.

Styles intervened on a more personal level on behalf of another wealthy contributor, Bernard Goldfine, owner of a New England woolen company and a client in the law firm headed by Norris Cotton. Goldfine's son was in the throes of being expelled from Dartmouth College, and Norris suggested that Goldfine contact Styles Bridges to see if anything could be done. Bridges wrote to the president of Dartmouth, and the wayward son was invited back to the college. For his services in this matter, Styles accepted a two thousand dollar cash payment, strictly as a "campaign contribution." However, Goldfine told Norris Cotton that he made numerous other cash payments to Styles, who in Goldfine's words "constantly stated that he could not get along on a senator's salary." It was also rumored that Goldfine was more than a little upset when Bridges' $35,000-a-year salary from the United Mine Workers came to light.

Did Bridges himself believe that he was doing anything illegal or immoral? A difficult question to answer. The senator was careful and close-mouthed about his financial dealings. He once wrote in a personal memo, "Never put anything on paper that you don't want the whole world to read." It was advice that the senator apparently took very much to heart. There are, however, a few revealing facts.

At his death Bridges left an estate of between $250,000 and $500,000. It was alleged that for years Bridges had in the least in his possession a sizeable amount of cash which was discovered shortly after Doloris Bridges' death, behind a bookcase in the cellar of Bridges' home. Joseph Millmett, a leading attorney from Manchester, was called in as an impartial party to help determine whether the cash rumored to be between fifty and one hundred thousand dollars, belonged to the Bridges estate. After reviewing financial records, Millmett decided that the money was not part of the estate, and as Styles was at the time of his death chairman of the Republican Policy Committee, the funds were turned over to the National Republican Party as campaign contributions. Fred Upton, probate attorney for the Bridges estate, denies the story, claiming that the valise contained only "a small number of un-negotiated checks."

Undisputed, however, is the fact that members of Bridges' staff, as well as friends, were given valises and asked to keep them at home. In the event of the senator's death, the valises were to be turned over, unopened, to Doloris. William Deachman III, a Bridges legislative assistant, said in an interview he did exactly that. And on the day before Styles' funeral, on November 28, 1961, over lunch at her home with Lyndon Johnson and his aide, Bobby Baker, Doloris declared that Styles "had left her a million dollars in cash, money that was never accounted for." When asked about the allegation, Anderson also had an opinion: "He certainly got money, and he certainly stashed a lot of it away. It's my guess that a lot of it was never found. That he stashed it away so safely that perhaps it's still lying in some hidden cache."

Why would a prominent United States senator, a man whose loyalty to his country and his constituents remains undisputed more than thirty years after his death, sell his power and influence? The answers are as complex as the man himself. It is reasonable, taking into account Jack Anderson's statements, to assume that Bridges himself saw little or no contradiction in his actions. A fervent anti-Communist, Styles would unquestionably have supported Chiang Kai-shek and the China Lobby whether there was money

The inscription on this informal photograph of Lyndon Johnson and Styles Bridges in a Senate Committee meeting reads: "To Styles Bridges, my mediating friend."

involved or not. In a letter to Alfred Kohlberg, another Bridges' contributor and former president of the American China Policy Association, who was himself disparaged in *The Reporter* article, Styles wrote: "It is indeed a pity that you and I and others who stand up for our convictions and fight boldly against the evil forces in the world today have to take personal abuse from those who constantly aid the evil forces."

How Important Was Money to Bridges?

Money was in fact a large issue, both in Styles' private and public life. After having lost his financial security in the stock market crash of 1929, Bridges was determined that such a disaster would not befall him again. According to the senator's financial records, he had at least thirty bank accounts throughout New England, as well as in Washington, where he would deposit dividend checks from his investments, sometimes in amounts of as little as two dollars. And, as it does today, money turned the political wheels in Washington during Bridges' tenure in the Senate. The list of registered political lobbyists and soft-money contributors runs into the thousands in today's Washington power circles. The money contributed by tobacco, insurance, and gun lobbyists, the pro-and anti-abortion factions, runs into the billions of dollars, and few politicians are exempt from soft money and PAC contributions. As Jack Anderson stated, "It was the way business was done." And it still is today. In order to get reelected, to keep their power structure intact, almost all national politicians do, in fact, take the money. Styles Bridges was probably more prudent than most.

But there is a dichotomy in Styles Bridges, who came to Washington as a man without wealth, without much formal education, a farmer from a rural New England state. In essence, Bridges was a small-town boy, who rose to a position on the Public Service Commission, a former Farm Bureau official, who became governor of New Hampshire, and eventually a powerful United States senator. A man whose genius was that he was as comfortable talking milk prices to a New Hampshire dairyman as he was speaking on the subject of national politics to esteemed members the congressional body. Styles Bridges, through the gift of his personality, found himself rubbing shoulders with the American elite—men from wealthy families, with Ivy League educations, for whom power and influence were assumed to be their natural birthrights. In the normal course of events, Bridges would have to be seen as a fish out of water when compared with the movers and shakers in the capital of the world's most powerful nation. In many ways, that was precisely the truth of the matter. But Styles had a secret weapon, one he used with great effectiveness: He understood people, from the New Hampshire dairyman to congressional leaders. And he was a quick study, a man who could identify problems and, through the power of his personality, effect solutions.

This gift first surfaced shortly after Bridges' election as governor in 1934, when at the age of thirty-six he became the nation's youngest governor. The Bridges initiatives during these years are both impressive and progressive, and this from a man whom many would later label "arch conservative." During his governorship, from 1935 to 1937, Styles managed to balance the New Hampshire budget, at a time when the state was deeply in debt. "What we need is a little of the old-fashioned New England thrift," he said in a 1934 Manchester speech.

But even in the throes of his cost-cutting measures, Styles never forgot that the people were the reason government existed in the first place. He initiated a new Agricultural Standards Act, set up the New Hampshire Planning and Development Board, passed legislation that greatly enhanced aid to mothers, as well as State unemployment insurance, workers' benefits, and old-age compensation. He also appointed the first female judge in the state's history. Under Bridges' leadership, New Hampshire became the first state to qualify under the Federal Social Security Act. Bridges himself would later make the comment, "They always spoke of me as a radical or a liberal

*Senators Bridges, Saltonstall, and Knowland confer on pending matters of importance
before the second session of the 84th Congress in 1956*

in my own state. But in Washington they call me a conservative." It was
during this period, one of the most productive of his life, that Styles did
some of his best work and developed the political instincts that carried him
to prominence on the national scene.

Undoubtedly Styles Bridges could have run for reelection as governor
of New Hampshire, and won easily. But it was another of Styles' traits that
he was always looking for a new challenge. Constantly seeking the next rung
on the ladder of success, Bridges changed jobs as easily as another man
might change coats. He moved from his position as an agricultural agent in
1922 to become executive secretary of the New Hampshire Farm Bureau,
ran a New Hampshire investment firm for Governor Bass, and was appointed to the Public Service Commission before defeating the powerful
George Higgins Moses for the Republican U.S. Senate nomination. He served
a single term as New Hampshire's governor before his successful run for the
Senate.

When he came to Washington as a minority senator in 1937, one of
only two Republicans to be elected that year in the wake of the Roosevelt
landslide, he quickly saw how the system worked—and it revolved around

money. As a staunch opponent of big government and the New Deal, Bridges entrenched himself as a Republican attack dog. One of his first initiatives in the Senate was to launch an investigation into alleged "TVA waste, mismanagement, and backstairs conspiracy," an unmistakable signal that opposition to Roosevelt's vision of big government had now arrived in Washington with a vengeance. Bridges also declared openly: "The billions of dollars that have been spent in America for relief might just as well have been thrown in the ocean for all the good they have done."

Importance of Doloris Thauwald Bridges

Then in 1941 another crossroads, one critical to explaining Bridges as a man, and as a politician. Late that year Styles met a Minnesota woman, Doloris Thauwald, who was working at a minor post in wartime Washington. Curiously, the two met at the infamous "House on R Street," which *The Reporter* article was later to call an elegant place where social climbing mixed with dubious business activities. John Porter Monroe, the resident of the House on R Street, was arrested for black-market activities during World War II, and served a two-year prison sentence. But as usual, Bridges distanced himself from the more blatantly illegal activities of his sometimes dubious associates, and claimed that he had attended only social functions at the notorious Washington residence.

Doloris' presence at the House on R Street undoubtedly had more to do with the social-climbing aspect of the festivities, than any unsavory business dealings. Coming from a family of modest means, Doloris' brother financed her move from Minnesota to Washington, where in February 1944 she became Mrs. Styles Bridges. A lot of harsh things have been said about Doloris, but the truth is she and Styles were married for over seventeen years, until the senator's death in 1961. Letters between the two reveal a mutual affection and an understanding of the often egregious world of a senator's personal and professional life.

It can also be said of Doloris that she was a strong, often domineering person. Although it is hard to imagine Styles Bridges, who was himself a vibrant personality, being intimidated by anyone, including his wife. Probably he wasn't. Theirs was a union of two strong personalities, and it is easy to imagine a lot of give and take in the Bridges household.

But Doloris would, on occasion, blow like a storm through the senator's staff, generating an unquestioned harsh opinion of her. Tom Shannon, a Bridges' staffer, remarked, "Doloris was terribly ambitious . . . and anyone who says they weren't afraid of Doloris on that staff is lying."

Gerry Zeiller, a Bridges legislative assistant, says about Doloris, "She would either play the senator, like she was the senator, or she would play

The New Hampshire Congressional delegation discussing the inaugural plans in 1957. From left are Senator Bridges, Congressman Bass, Senator Cotton, and Congressman Merrow.

the grand dame. She was not beloved by anybody on the staff. She used the staff for her social and personal use which really in those days was illegal. She had no endearing qualities that I can think of."

John Pillsbury, a New Hampshire lawyer who worked as a Bridges staffer in the early years of his career and would later run for governor of the Granite State, had an entirely different take on the couple's relationship,

Doloris was marvelous. She was a wonderful person and a great help to the senator. He was just crazy about her. And she was good for him. She knew how to calm him down and they were funny in a way. She liked to spend money and he didn't. I remember she outfitted their Washington apartment with new drapes and then threw a party that night, so that when Styles came home, she wouldn't be alone. She'd get around him in that way. Another time, when Styles was in Europe, she had a porch built on the house in New Hampshire. And then she got out of the way when he came back, until he could calm down. But it wasn't just scrapping between them at all, it was just the interplay of the two. They were both devoted to one another. And she was a terribly able person. She was very, very smart.

Another thing that can be reliably said about Doloris is that she enjoyed being the wife of a United States senator. She was very active on the Washington political scene, and was not hesitant to cart her famous husband off to dinner parties and the fashionable events of Washington society—events that the workaholic Styles often wanted no part of, Warrington said. "Doloris was indeed tough on the staff. She wanted to be an aristocrat, but wasn't. She pushed Styles into the Washington social scene." Senator Bridges was much more comfortable in the corridors of the Legislature, or giving a speech at a New England political gathering, than at a cocktail party with the fashionably elite. Some Bridges insiders even say that the senator often kept long hours in his Washington office to avoid fancy social gatherings. There may be some truth to those whisperings, but it is probably more correct to say that Styles Bridges liked being a United States senator at least as much as Doloris liked being married to one.

Bridges worked long and hard at his job, often putting in twelve- to fourteen-hour days. He enjoyed the work immensely, and understood the type of commitment necessary to do the job effectively. The Senator realized early on that power, once gained, had to be held tightly in order to be retained. John Warrington remembers one particular "Bridgism": "It was said that Styles Bridges was probably one of the five or six most powerful men in the world. He handled it well and said that you have to grasp power properly. 'If you grasp it like a bird and hold it too tightly you'll crush it,' Styles said. 'If you hold it too loosely, it'll fly away.' He was always very conscious how power should be controlled and exercised."

Bridges was always campaigning, always responding to his New Hampshire constituents. One especially effective tactic was what Styles called "the nice little note." Warrington, who was especially close to the senator, recalls:

Bridges believed in the value of "the nice little note"—a personalized letter. This was usually done by inserting a special paragraph in the middle of a form letter. For example, at the Rockingham County Fair a distinguished gentleman known as Pokey Fuller was the man who always mixed the clam chowder. The following week after Bridges had attended the fair, a "Dear Pokey" letter would be mailed, the middle paragraph commenting favorably on the chowder. The recipient never forgot this courtesy and Bridges dictated thousands of these personalized notes over the years.

While Doloris was married to the senator, Styles Bridges was also married to his work. He was tireless and deeply committed. But, unfortunately, being a United States senator or congressman in the 1940s and '50s was far from lucrative. Without question the jobs held power and prestige,

Senator and Mrs. Bridges leave for the Eisenhower Inaugural Ball of 1957

but not much money. The average U.S. Senator's salary in those years was $12,500 a year. Unlike most of his peers, Styles Bridges did not come from wealth. In many ways, he was a poor man playing a rich man's game. The problem of money, of maintaining dual residences in Washington and New Hampshire, was a burden. He had to support himself and Doloris in a manner befitting that of a powerful Washington politician, as well as providing for his children. And there was always another costly election campaign waiting just around the corner.

This is the true dilemma of politics, even today, when senatorial campaigns run into the tens of millions of dollars. Fund raising is a constant concern, and only the very wealthy are immune from the persistent pull of lobbyists with open checkbooks and bundles of ready cash. Styles Bridges, a common man from a relatively poor background, was perhaps more susceptible than most. Through tireless work, he found himself in extraordinary circumstances, at the threshold of power, which as a boy growing up in rural Maine he surely could never have imagined. And no man as driven to succeed as Styles Bridges would have let the minor inconvenience of money stand in his way—not in a city like Washington, teeming with lobbyists armed with seemingly bottomless resources. Thus, Bridges allowed himself to become involved with such notorious money men as Grunewald and the Chinese-based Kung family; with men like Armand Hammer, who were eager to support influential politicians, whose power did not quite match their bank accounts.

As his opponents were quick to point out, Bridges did support the nationalistic forces of Chiang Kai-shek in the fight against Communist China. He supported Armand Hammer in numerous bids for government contracts. He did attempt to intercede for Harvey Klein in the liquor dealer's troubles with the IRS. But in these dealings Bridges always attempted, on the surface anyway, to maintain the high moral ground. When Grunewald and Klein were eventually brought before grand juries Bridges was able to distance himself from them, and although his integrity was occasionally attacked, it was never truly tarnished.

And in the end, these political storms, which seemed too potent at the time, blew themselves out and Styles Bridges was left standing. The New Hampshire electorate, those who really mattered in Bridges' political life, ignored or disregarded the charges made against their personable and powerful voice in the Congress, returning Styles to his senatorial office by ever-increasing pluralities. In 1954, the year of *The Reporter* article, Styles won his senatorial election by claiming over 60 percent of the popular vote, beating his nearest rival by more than twenty percentage points. Bridges was a man of the people, and the people loved him. Whenever he returned to New Hampshire to speak, throngs of supporters turned out to hear him. Even when the taint of scandal touched him, Bridges was the dominant person in New Hampshire politics and a leader in the Republican Party.

The Good Politician

Overall, Douglass Cater's article in *The Reporter* brought together various observations that had been made over the years about Bridges' career, but it presented no evidence of criminal conduct, or even of activities that were particularly unusual among U.S. senators. What Cater did show was Bridges' lack of good judgment when faced with possibly compromising situations.

The Reporter article was not the only investigation of the Senator's activities. Ben Bradlee, a Washington reporter and columnist and subsequently editor of the *Washington Post*, writes in *A Good Life* (Simon & Schuster, 1995) that he personally conducted a first-hand investigation into Bridges' affairs: "I had come down out of the woods of New Hampshire at the end of 1948, convinced that Senator Styles Bridges was mixed up in a war surplus liquidation scandal of major proportions." Bradlee was never able to tie Bridges to the war-surplus scandal, however, and had to content himself with investigating the list of the senator's political contributors—men such as Alfred Kohlberg and the China Lobby.

Was Styles Bridges innocent of all the allegations thrown at him over the years? Or was he incredibly effective at covering his tracks?

No matter. Bridges' constituents didn't mind and the New Hampshire press did not attack him. His good qualities as a politician far outweighed whatever questionable dealings he might have had. His campaign style was direct, and most of his friendships were lasting. His ability to spot issues and address them concisely in language his supporters could understand gained him votes regardless of the controversies that surfaced. Bridges enjoyed and cultivated good relationships with both national and Granite State newsmen. Reporters were always greeted with a friendly smile and usually came away with good information. There was never a media crusade against the senator.

Robert Novak, syndicated newspaper columnist and political commentator for CNN (the Cable News Network), began his career as a Washington reporter. Novak recalled covering the hearings during which Robert S. McNamara was in the process of being approved as John F. Kennedy's Secretary of Defense. According to Novak:

> When I left the AP to become the Wall Street Journal's Senate correspondent in 1958, I was tipped that Senator Bridges was an absolutely fabulous source who should be cultivated. I found that to be completely accurate. So, by the time McNamara was up for confirmation in January 1961, I had been drinking at the Bridges well for over two years.
>
> It was natural , then, that I went to Bridges when the Senate Armed Services Committee was not releasing its settlement with McNamara (which was a big story for the Journal). He tried to explain to me but then threw the file on his desk in his Capitol hideaway office and let me figure it out for myself. It was not the first news exclusive that Bridges had given me; regrettably, it was one of the last.

Bridges' special friendship with William Loeb also gave him some measure of protection, as the *Manchester Union Leader* publisher could always be counted on for positive publicity.

Did He or Didn't He Accept Bribes?

The question of whether Bridges profited from his deals may never be answered. Cynics assumed that he did, and supporters assumed that he did not.

It is true, however, that receipts at the New Hampshire Savings Bank in Concord show that after her husband's death Doloris signed for "six large manila envelopes and one small letter-sized envelope," which had been kept in the bank's silver vaults, sealed and unopened at Bridges' request. Robert Hill, president of the bank, recalls that Styles, who preceded him as president and who had been on the Board of Trustees since 1935, left specific instructions that the envelopes were to be turned over to Doloris—and to Doloris only—in the event of his death. The contents of the envelopes were never revealed.

Those who contend that Bridges did accept bribes point to his estate at the time of his death, and ask how a politician could have piled up such a large amount of money. A partial answer is that Bridges was always frugal. His youthful poverty and his losses in the stock market crash of 1929 made him careful in money dealings. Profits from his investments were reinvested. His income tax returns reflect this policy, showing higher and higher amounts from dividends as the years went on.

The Reporter presentation infuriated Bridges, largely because it appeared during an election year. Duane Lockard writes in *New England State Politics* (Princeton University Press, 1959):

> The magazine sent press releases and copies of the article to all ten New Hampshire daily newspapers. Only one paper, the *Claremont Eagle Times,* saw fit to use the release. Even granting that the writer was out to show Bridges at his worst, it would seem that an impending attack on a senator in a national magazine would rate mention in the state news columns. In due time at least six of the newspapers carried editorials in defense of the senator.

It was also reported by Bridges' staffers that supporters were sent out to buy up all the copies they could find of *The Reporter* article as it hit the news stands.

Bridges investigated to see if libel could be pressed, or if writer Douglass Cater and the publisher, Max Acoli, had any Communist connections. Neither item could be proven and Bridges had to be content with a charge that the article was "a vicious smear." But he was careful not to deny any of its details.

While he could not sue for libel, he stated on August 8, 1954, "The insinuations and innuendoes are such that [the article] was written with malice and irresponsibility, as far as the truth is concerned." On August 19, he rose in the Senate to condemn the article as an attack upon the Senate itself. Conveniently ignoring the free-speech declaration he had signed some years earlier, he concluded, "It's time for every American to do a little thinking for himself. And it is time that we protect the fundamental institutions of democracy from being undermined."

Campaign ad for Bridges fifth term in 1959

Democratic contender Gerard Morin, Laconia's young mayor, jumped onto the magazine article and skillfully maneuvered its issues. He charged that while Bridges was involved in shady deals, he was not paying attention to the problem of attracting new industry to New Hampshire to help cope with an unemployment crisis. Morin asserted that Republican budget cutting was reducing jobs and that Democrats would work toward full employment. Bridges replied that his Senate Appropriations Committee had saved $16.7 million in federal spending in two years, and called upon voters to keep the Republicans in power, to allow for the complete balancing of the federal budget.

In New Hampshire, Bridges found the Republican campaign progressing favorably. Nixon toured the state with him, and local labor unions defied orders from their national headquarters not to support him.

Morin claimed the Republican Congress had "a record of broken promises and a crusade that never got started." He picked up some surprising Republican support. Charles W. Tobey, Jr., eager to settle a score with Bridges for the senator's failure to endorse his father in the 1949 campaign, organized a Republican group to campaign for Morin. He also toured the state urging voters to oust Bridges.

Bridges added strength to his campaign by going into Laconia to lambaste Morin and laud the Republican party. He emphasized that the Republicans had saved the country from Democratic principles by building up the military, attacking subversives, and reducing federal spending. At a Laconia rally, Bridges said, "We have been on a twenty-year spree. The hangovers and headaches have been painful, but we stand today strong, steady and clear-eyed after not quite two years of Republican rehabilitation."

When the election returns were tallied, Bridges had won a fourth term by his largest majority to date, defeating Morin by nearly 40,000 votes— 117,150 to 77,386. Lane Dwinell became governor; Norris Cotton was elected to launch a long Senate career; Perkins Bass also won, all of them by substantial majorities. Merrow had a narrow squeak in his congressional bid, topping McIntyre by only 468 votes, 54,052 to 53,584. McIntyre, who had run a well-fought campaign, asked for a recount, but called it off before the tally was completed. He and the Democratic party developed new life after the election, which was to bear fruit in following years.

On the national scene, the Granite State triumph was small consolation to Republican leaders. The GOP lost control of the Senate by one vote and the Democrats recaptured control of the House. As Bridges celebrated his personal victory, his disappointment showed. He commented, "The commitments of the Republican party cannot be effectively carried on in the years ahead under such circumstances."

The Republicans would never again win control of the Senate in Bridges' lifetime. Ahead lay the bitter debate over the McCarthy censure and continued international problems. Bridges would see younger senators, like Dirksen and Goldwater, take control of the party. Taft, Knowland, and Wherry were gone. Still, nobody suggested that Bridges was through as a national figure.

13

The Eisenhower Years

*"The Republican Party is the Party of liberty
. . . and everybody has the right to be heard."*

George Higgins Moses,
Senator from New Hampshire

O SOONER had the election returns been counted than the Senate was called back into session on November 8, 1954, to act upon the proposed censure of Senator Joseph McCarthy. The censure was recommended by a committee headed by Senator Arthur Watkins (R-Utah). By Senate tradition, a censure constitutes a severe reprimand, rather than dismissal or a fine, for having brought dishonor upon that body. Up to this time, the Senate had censured the following members since its creation in 1789: Timothy Pickering (Federalist-Massachusetts) in 1811; Benjamin Tappan (D-Ohio) in 1844; Benjamin Tillman (D-South Carolina) in 1902; and Hiram Bingham (R-Connecticut) in 1929.

Senator Aimer S.M. Monroney (D-Oklahoma) and Senator Everett M. Dirksen (R-Illinois), who was organizing an anticensure bloc, worked out a compromise whereby McCarthy would publicly apologize for his actions and the censure measure would be dropped.

Before that could happen, however, McCarthy let loose once again. Speaking at an anti-Communist rally, he accused the U.S. Senate of aiding the Communist cause and called the proceedings against him a "lynching bee." Those remarks so infuriated the procensure senators that they refused all compromise efforts. Senator Wallace F. Bennett (R-Utah) proposed additional censure charges.

203

The censure resolution denounced McCarthy for "affecting the honor of the Senate and acting contrary to Senatorial traditions." McCarthy had "intemperately abused [and] . . . destroyed the good faith which must be maintained between the executive and legislative branches of our system of government," the resolution went on.

While Bridges disapproved of McCarthy's attack style and even denounced his methods, he did not judge the man; and that led him to one of the most controversial votes of his Senate career.

As the debate opened, it became evident that some form of censure would be approved. A majority of senators viewed McCarthy as an embarrassment, a vicious political infighter who slapped a Communist label on anyone who opposed him, calling any critic a threat to the American democracy. Bridges, on the other hand, saw the censure as a threat to the Senate's freedom of speech and conscience. McCarthy was a victim of the same intolerance that he was charged with, he believed. He proposed several amendments to tone down the resolution, but these were voted down. He then called for the reconvening of the committee, saying it had not defined a censurable offense, but that objection was also swept aside.

The crucial vote was delayed when McCarthy was hospitalized with traumatic bursitis. After he returned to the Senate, on December 2, 1954, the censure was approved 67 to 20, with Bridges voting nay. Senator Bridges would contend to the end of his career that the censure was a mistake, but his fears of a curb on the Senate's freedom of speech were never justified.

Bridges Tries Peacemaking

As the 1955 session convened, Bridges had the pleasure of swearing in his New Hampshire associate Senator Norris Cotton, with whom he had been friends since the 1920s, as well as two other new senators—Joseph C. O'Mahoney (D-Wyoming) and Samuel J. Ervin, Jr. (D-North Carolina).

Of great concern to Bridges was the tension between the conservative and moderate Republican factions. He was to play a major role in the efforts to reunite these factions to aid in the passage of Eisenhower's programs, and to assure a Republican congressional victory in 1956. Bridges induced Leverett Saltonstall, the moderates' leader, to withdraw from the leadership contest and keep his post as party whip. This led to Bridges' election as chairman of the Republican Policy Committee. A 1946 law had established separate policy committees for the Senate majority and minority parties, the purpose being to coordinate the legislative agenda and discuss party strategy. Senate staff directors and senators themselves both met weekly to discuss key issues and explore new ideas for legislative action. (For more information on this subject, and on the Senate itself, visit the U.S. Senate Web Page at www.senate.gov.)

Knowland was reelected as the party's floor leader. At first, Bridges was expected to stick to the role of compromiser, but he became a tough chairman, whose goal was party unity at all costs.

When the 84th Congress convened, there developed a brief possibility that Bridges might continue as president pro tem, despite a one-member Democratic majority. A group challenged the seating of Senator O'Mahoney. If that had proven successful, it would have caused a tie vote, and Vice-president Nixon would have cast the tie-breaking vote, presumably for Bridges. But the challenge was thrown out, and Walter F. George (D-Georgia) became president pro tem.

Bridges managed to prevent moderates from ousting McCarthy from his committee assignments. In return, he added more moderates to the policy committee. Bridges declared that Republicans could not afford to characterize themselves as McCarthy Republicans or Eisenhower Republicans. As Bridges struggled to hold the GOP together, Eisenhower openly sided with the moderates. Conservatives began plotting to replace Ike in the 1956 election. The best that Bridges could accomplish was a shaky ad hoc unity.

Eisenhower had decided after the 1954 election that the Republican party needed a more liberal platform, one that would conform with the thinking of people who normally voted Democratic but who had crossed over to vote for him. He proposed a program that continued the liberal domestic policies of the New Deal and the Fair Deal, while promoting a conservative, but flexible, foreign policy. He coined the term "modern Republicans" to describe his philosophy.

Senate conservatives, who outnumbered moderates 27 to 20, voted against the Eisenhower proposals, which they saw as too much like what Republicans had opposed for years. Conservative Democrats joined them and defeated much of the president's legislation, especially in the areas of social welfare and civil rights. Bridges both praised and criticized Eisenhower's 1955 State of the Union address, winning him friends on both sides of the conflict.

After much research, Bridges cosponsored a bill with Harry F. Byrd (D-Virginia) for an amendment to the Constitution that would require a president to submit a budget based on the expected revenues from the fiscal year the budget represented. Critics favored exceeding revenues if necessary to keep social programs and a large defense establishment intact.

Pressing for his balanced-budget amendment, Bridges declared that, in addition to areas of wasteful spending in government agencies, the government misused excessive amounts of money in foreign aid. He summed up his position by saying, "This nation is prosperous. Our people are well clothed, well fed, well housed. We are in a period of abundant employment. There is no just reason why we cannot pay our operating expenses." Later, in a 1958 speech in Concord, New Hampshire, Bridges made a statement on the federal budget deficit, that still rings true today: "The need for cutting the budget, as urgent as it is, far transcends in importance the achievement of saving for a single year. If this huge budget goes unchecked at a time when we are enjoying our highest peak of prosperity, then we can share the unwelcome responsibility of establishing wild and undisciplined federal spending as a fixed, unchangeable pattern of American life."

Homage to the Old Man of the Mountain

While Congress debated Eisenhower's domestic program, the president moved swiftly to confront a crisis developing in the Far East. The Red Chinese had begun to harass the remnants of the Nationalist government entrenched on Taiwan over control of two other offshore adjacent islands, Quemoy and Matsu. Eisenhower sent military aid to Taiwan and declared that the United States would resist any invasion of the islands. Although saber-rattling incidents continued for years—and continue to the present—the Chinese refrained from invading Nationalist-controlled islands.

Eisenhower's firm action in defense of Taiwan won praise from Bridges, but when the president agreed to a summit conference with Soviet Russia —the first such meeting since World War II, Senator Bridges criticized the move, warning of Stalin's duplicity at the Yalta conference in 1944.

After Congress adjourned in June, Bridges escorted President Eisenhower on a combined vacation and political tour of New Hampshire through the White Mountains and the Lakes Region. Eisenhower was on hand for the commemoration of the 150th anniversary of the discovery of the Old Man of the Mountain. (The Postal Service also recognized the occasion by issuing a twenty-five-cent stamp commemorating New Hampshire as "the state that made the nation" by ratifying the Constitution on June 21, 1788.) He visited with Laurence Whittemore of the Brown Company, as well as with other New Hampshire political and business figures, and toured the Dartmouth College Grant area, a large wilderness preserve along the New Hampshire and Maine borders. The president hinted at a second-term bid, which would be launched in the Granite State's first-in-the-nation presidential primary in 1956.

In September, President Eisenhower suffered a heart attack, and was hospitalized for three weeks. While his life was never believed to be in danger, his incapacity caused a scramble for power within the White House. Ike's chief aide, Sherman Adams, was at odds with the vice president and did what he could to keep Nixon from participating in decision-making.

*In 1955 young Republicans honored Bridges for 25 years
of public service and the Democrats who crashed the party
presented him with a live donkey.*

As 1955 came to a close, New Hampshire paid tribute to Styles with a
testimonial dinner in Manchester to commemorate a quarter century in
public office. Warm sentiments and gifts poured in from all over the state,
and much to his amusement, a group of Democratic supporters presented
him with a live donkey.

Bobby Baker, Lyndon Johnson's secretary and legislative aide, tells a
story in his book *Wheeling and Dealing* (Norton, 1978):

On one occasion I was asked to transmit $5000 from Lyndon B. Johnson to a
Republican senator, Styles Bridges. [Bridges and LBJ had a long-standing friendship.] I don't know where the money came from. As was the Washington practice,
Johnson handed me the boodle in cash. "Bobby," he said, "Styles is throwing an
'appreciation dinner' for himself up in New Hampshire sometime next week. Fly up
there and drop this in the kitty and be damn sure that Styles knows it came from me.
And while you're up there, invent a lot of flowery compliments you've heard me say
about Senator Bridges."

The second session of the 84th Congress opened on January 2, 1956,
with the recovered president presenting a new farm policy, an ambitious
national highway construction plan (which was to become the mammoth
interstate highway system), and a balanced budget.

Bridges agreed with most of Eisenhower's election year proposals, but he helped defeat the president's request for reorganization of the military and the Defense Department. Eisenhower wanted to replace the Joint Chiefs of Staff with a general staff system, reducing civilian control in the Defense Department. Bridges saw the proposal as a step toward a military dictatorship and the termination of civilian control over the military. He also pointed out that the plan would weaken the defense role of the states' National Guard units.

Pointing out that Germany used the same military system in launching World War II, Bridges declared on the Senate floor, "Only defeat, disaster and enslavement await America if, following victory, we adopt the methods of the vanquished." Bridges formed a coalition of senators from both parties to defeat the measure.

For or Against Bridges?

The ability of special-interest groups to mount expensive campaigns to influence Congress to vote in their favor had become a common feature of Washington political life. Increasingly concerned about the pressures on Congress from a growing array of lobbyists, on April 1, 1955, in a speech in Chicago, Bridges stated, "No longer are the administration and the Congress free to make their independent decisions on the merits of any issue. . . . We are continually subjected to the lobbying and the influences of the pressure groups."

What particularly concerned Bridges was the way these groups used campaign contributions to reward or punish congressmen. In 1956, Congress decided to investigate and make public the extent of these lobbying operations, and to determine whether new laws were needed to govern their operations. Bridges was named to this investigative committee, which included senators John R. McClellan (D-Arkansas), Barry Goldwater (R-Arizona), Albert Gore, Sr., (D-Tennessee), and John F. Kennedy (D-Massachusetts). Unfortunately, partisan politics quickly came to the forefront. The committee became mired with infighting, when the liberal Senator Albert Gore, father of the future Vice-president, Al Gore, was denied chairmanship. Much of the blame for this, justly or unjustly, was laid at the feet of Senator Bridges, who played the political game as well as anyone who ever served in the U.S. Senate. The shades of light and dark in the political arena, the opposing viewpoints of Styles' influence on this committee, are reflected in two articles, each taking an entirely different slant on the Senator's position.

Tom W. Gerber wrote in the *Boston Sunday Herald* (March 25, 1956):

New Hampshire's Senator Bridges is one of the most powerful men in the United States. This 57-year-old former Maine farmboy seldom makes bombastic speech-

The New England Senatorial Delegation in 1959. From left, standing are Aiken of Vermont, Bush of Connecticut, Saltonstall of Massachusetts, and Cotton of New Hampshire. Seated are a youthful Kennedy of Massachusetts, Green of Rhode Island, Bridges of New Hampshire, and Margaret Chase Smith of Maine.

es. He never hurls charges that grab headlines throughout the nation. And he doesn't cut an imposing, regal figure. He speaks in a disarming New England twang that might give the unknowing an impression that he still is an unsophisticated farmboy. . . . But history well may mark Styles Bridges as one of the shrewdest political manipulators of all time. For he's possessed of an almost uncanny ability to grasp hidden facets, possible repercussions and consequences of any major issue. And it's partly because of this unseen talent he's called into consultation on nearly every knotty problem that confronts Republicans in the Senate. . . . For instance, he was chosen almost immediately as one of the GOP members of the eight-man select committee to look into lobbying and campaign contributions, the touchiest issue of the session so far. . . . One of the reasons he was picked without hesitation was because of his widely recognized ability in the deft art of political maneuvering. He could be counted upon to protect his party's interests—to see to it the Republicans shared in the glory or would not be publicly embarrassed. And the GOP investment paid off handsomely. For it was Bridges' manipulation that forced Tennessee's Senator Gore, about whom the Republicans were uncertain, to step aside when the committee chairmanship seemed assured him. . . . Bridges did this by using a set of rules, ironically proposed by the Democrats, as a lever of compromise.

Taking the opposing viewpoint, Russell Baker wrote in *The New York Times* (March 18, 1956):

Under sedatives administered by Senator Styles Bridges, the Senate's heroic fervor for investigating itself has diminished markedly in the last week. . . . From the beginning, Mr. Bridges, a New Hampshire Republican and a casting director's dream of the backroom politician, had shown no excess of zeal for the projected investigation of lobbying, campaign contributions and pressure on Congress. . . . Ever the realist, Mr. Bridges evinced an immediate sensitivity to the potential dangers of such an inquiry. These were obvious: Headlines about campaign contributions from pressure groups, Senatorial names lined to the Pharisees, and similar squalors calculated only to dry up the contribution wells and damage reputations in a critical election year.

These contradictory articles underscore the conflicting methods in which political commentary is presented. It is a fact, however, that the squabbling between Republicans and Democrats continued for the duration of the committee hearings, and in the end little was done. The problem of political contributions and lobbyist influence continues to this day, with reform in this critical area of representative government remaining elusive despite continuing public demand for legislative action.

On January 11, 1956, the Republican senators were called to a White House meeting to bolster party unity and plan strategy to win control of the Congress. Eisenhower was silent about his own election plans, so conservatives began talking about Senator Knowland as a likely presidential candidate, and his name was entered in the New Hampshire primary. Senator Bridges had long preferred to remain neutral in primary contests, but this year he could not do so. In his judgment, Eisenhower was doing a good job and deserved a second term. A year earlier Bridges had said, "I think it is fair to say that this administration probably satisfies neither extreme in our country. I am sure that the New Dealers are not pleased with it, and I imagine that the ultraconservatives are not happy either. In my judgment, the administration is following a constructive middle course."

If Eisenhower chose to run, Bridges thought, the conservative efforts to replace him would evaporate. If the president did not seek a second term, however, Bridges feared the Republican party would be split apart as conservatives fought moderates for the nomination. The end result might well be the nomination of a compromise dark-horse candidate, which could return the White House to the Democrats.

While the Senate's Republican partisans were fighting each other, Sherman Adams publicly warned Bridges and Knowland that they were ruining the party's chances for Eisenhower's reelection. That rebuke broadened a long-growing rift between Bridges and Adams.

Bridges jumped into the New Hampshire primary to secure the state's convention delegates for Eisenhower. If Ike should decide not to run, Bridges placed himself in a position to help control the convention with the

Senators Margaret Chase Smith of Maine and Styles Bridges. The inscription reads "To an outstanding statesman and leader, the honorable Styles Bridges, with esteem and best wishes."

Granite State delegation. Bridges and his slate of delegates easily defeated the Knowland supporters, and on February 29 Eisenhower announced his candidacy for reelection.

Some Government Problems

In the fall of 1956, a crisis developed in Egypt over use of the Suez Canal. President Nasser, in defiance of the international pact, closed the canal to shipping in retaliation for an Israeli incursion on the Sinai Peninsula. The Soviets backed Nasser but the United Nations did not, and sent troops in to open the canal. The UN also placed economic sanctions on Israel for its part in the conflict. Bridges and Knowland attacked that decision, because the UN had failed to impose such sanctions against the Soviets for brutally crushing an uprising of freedom fighters in Hungary. The issue revived Bridges' complaints about American aid to Yugoslavia and Poland, which had Communist regimes, advancing the argument for slashing foreign-aid funds in the new budget.

The 1956 election was relatively straightforward. Eisenhower and Nixon were rematched against Stevenson and Kefauver. Bridges toured the nation and warned that electing Democrats would be a return to the dark ages of President Truman. He stressed the economic stability and strength of the dollar achieved under the Eisenhower administration. To those concerned about Eisenhower's age—sixty-six—he pointed out that Truman had been elected president at the age of sixty-five and Winston Churchill had become British prime minister at seventy.

The 1956 campaign was surprisingly dull in New Hampshire. Democrats failed to muster a repeat of their 1954 showing. Governor Lane Dwinell and the state's other major Republican office holders, along with Eisenhower, won with large majorities.

Nationally, Eisenhower swept to an easy second term victory, but his party lost seats in the Congress. Democrats gained an additional Senate seat, giving them a 49-47 edge, and increased their majority in the House. In spite of this reversal, Eisenhower hailed his victory as a triumph for "modern Republicanism." He said, "Modern Republicanism looks to the future, which means it looks to that era—that time—in which our young are most interested."

In the Senate, conservative Republicans still enjoyed a 27-20 edge over moderates. Once again, Bridges found himself in the role of referee and peacemaker. Bridges kept his key post as chairman of the Republican Policy Committee. He almost became president pro tem again, when Frank Lausche (D-Ohio) refused to commit himself to the Democratic candidate. Lausche finally voted with his party, and Carl Hayden (D-Arizona) got the top Senate position. As in 1953, Bridges was elected by the senators of both parties as chairman of the Senate's Inaugural Committee.

On January 23, Bridges reintroduced his balanced-budget constitutional amendment, saying, "I have never sponsored a resolution which I thought had more potential as far as the future welfare of this nation is concerned, than is contained in this resolution." Almost as if to emphasize his point, Eisenhower filed his annual budget, a record $71.8 billion. Bridges vowed to find ways of reducing it over Eisenhower's objections, and his amendment gained some support, but eventually was buried in committee.

A dispute developed within the White House when Eisenhower suffered another heart attack. Vice-president Nixon was again rebuffed by Sherman Adams. This time Nixon demanded to at least preside at cabinet meetings. Bridges agreed with the vice-president's stand. The ensuing bitter dispute grew so acute that it might have become a constitutional issue, but Eisenhower recovered before an official confrontation occurred.

Eisenhower's 1958 budget rose to a record $74.9 billion, largely because of increased defense spending, and ran afoul of Bridges, who declared, "I never saw a budget yet that was not overstated in at least some of its various areas. My position, in short, will be billions for adequate defense, but not one cent for unnecessary frills."

One of Bridges' "frills" was foreign aid. His constant efforts to reduce, even eliminate aid abroad drew White House criticism, adding to party disunity. As the 1958 election neared, Republicans faced major campaign issues.

On October 4, 1957, the Soviet Union launched the world's first satellite, Sputnik. A month later, Sputnik II, carrying the first living creature to go beyond the Earth's atmosphere—a dog named Laika—was launched into space. (Unfortunately for Laika, the technology at the time did not permit bringing an object safely *back* to Earth from space, so the dog was euthanized ten days into the mission.) The Soviets' success in collecting data on how living organisms reacted in the space environment was a blow to American's technological pride. Moreover, the Russian missiles used to launch the space crafts had a far greater range and capacity than those of the United States, raising questions about the nation's defense program.

The Soviet space feats cast a shadow on Eisenhower's assurances in the 1956 election campaign that the United States was dealing with the USSR from a position of strength. When it became publicly known that the Russians had missiles with a five thousand mile range, capable of delivering a nuclear warhead—in contrast to American missiles, which were launched with small payloads and often malfunctioned shortly after take-off—the furor increased.

A crash defense program was needed, and Bridges proposed several solutions. One was to draft scientists into government service until the missile gap was closed. Each branch of the defense forces was trying to produce its own missile, without the knowledge or the experience of the others, and Bridges correctly laid part of the blame for the lag in missile development on interservice rivalry. He warned, too, of the danger of reckless spending in an effort to catch up with the Russians.

A number of bills were introduced in the Senate to deal with the issue. One established a national space policy, and provided grants to industry and universities to speed up development of missiles and space exploration. By 1959, after much effort, Americans were becoming competitive with the Soviet Union; and in 1961, Alan B. Shepard, a Derry, New Hampshire man, became the first American to fly into space. Styles was then a member of the Aeronautical and Space Sciences Committee, and took great pride in the achievement.

Americans demanded to know how the Soviets had become dominant in an area so important to the nation's defense, and Republicans suffered

In 1961 Alan Shepard of Derry, New Hampshire, became the first U.S. astronaut to fly in space. In this photo he briefs the Aeronautical and Space Committee with Styles Bridges in the center and Vice President Lyndon Johnson and President Kennedy at the far right.

serious political damage from the missile gap. In the summer of 1958, Bridges toured the country addressing the problem. He attacked Americans' complacency in accepting the illusion of national security and called for the sacrifice of material wealth to help finance building America's military might. "The time has clearly come to be less concerned with the depth of pile on the new broadloom rug, or the height of the tail-fin on the new car, and to be more prepared to shed blood, sweat and tears, if this country and the free world are to survive," he declared.

Bridges, who was from his earliest years a watchdog of budgetary excesses, also denounced the growth of American materialism at the expense of the economy. Materialistic Americans, he asserted at Suffolk University in Boston, have one thing in common. "They want something for nothing. They want to spend more than they make, reduce taxes and increase benefits. . . . They don't realize that freedom and bankruptcy are irreconcilable. These people are looking to Washington without realizing that the money they are demanding comes from taxes of the people and industry."

The Eisenhower years had brought substantial prosperity to the country, but the economy began to cool through 1957, dealing the Republican party another blow. By February of 1958, unemployment had risen to a sixteen-year high. Democrats were quick to propose a tax cut and increased government spending to improve the economy. Eisenhower insisted that reducing government spending would be a better idea. To many people, that sounded too much like President Herbert Hoover's ineffective program for combating the Depression thirty years earlier.

Eisenhower agreed to a plan for more public-works projects to create jobs, but Bridges opposed it, declaring that a tax cut and a balanced budget were the solutions to the weakened economy. He also proposed that nations receiving foreign aid be required to buy goods made in this country to stimulate business.

An upturn in the economy in June 1958 failed to revitalize the Republicans, and problems worsened when a key member of Eisenhower's staff became involved in a scandal.

The House had been investigating influence peddling for a long time, and in 1958 the probe focused on a free-spending industrialist from Boston named Bernard Goldfine (the same man whose son Styles had helped get back into Dartmouth). Among others, Adams was accused of accepting gifts from Goldfine, including a freezer and a vicuna coat. Many other politicians, including Bridges had accepted such gifts; but in Adam's case the gifts were in exchange for securing a hearing for Goldfine before the Federal Trade Commission.

Sherman Adams had built such power into his job as chief of staff to the president that he was virtually the "assistant president"; Bridges had attacked him for controlling the White House and barring many Republicans from visiting Eisenhower. His arrogance and high-handed manner had alienated party conservatives, who gleefully berated him for the Goldfine gifts. The House investigating committee ultimately concluded that Adams had not violated any law, but Eisenhower failed to support his chief of staff. Adams resigned and quietly returned to his New Hampshire home in Lincoln, where he built and ran the Loon Mountain Ski Resort.

The Man Behind the Scenes

Sputnik, the recession, and the Adams affair were major liabilities as the Republicans headed into the 1958 campaign. Ticket-splitting among American voters showed that they were voting on issues, rather than for party candidates, as Bridges had warned two years earlier. He emphasized that the Republicans needed to produce vigorous leaders with clear issues, but none materialized. Instead, several proven Republican vote getters, such as Knowland, announced they would retire in 1958. Eisenhower's declaration that those who had opposed his foreign-aid policy would get no support from him in the election further demoralized Republican candidates.

A hint of coming political change was seen as early as 1957, when Senator McCarthy died. In a special election called to replace him, Wisconsin

Republicans had a difficult time finding a candidate satisfactory to all sides. This led to the election of Democrat William Proxmire by a wide majority. With this upset, and from other issues being raised, the Democrats began to sense that 1958 might be their year.

Former President Truman opened the Democratic campaign with a speech attacking Eisenhower's policies and spoke of the prosperity the nation had enjoyed under his leadership. Bridges was chosen to go on national television to reply. Most of what Truman said was misleading and untrue, and he said, that Eisenhower had increased Social Security benefits and created a strong military defense. Bridges then launched another of his national tours in an attempt to unify the Republican factions, declaring that if Republicans did not unite, Democrats would take over the White House in 1960.

A party split was not evident in New Hampshire. The only primary contest there was for governor, to succeed Dwinell after two terms. Ex-governor Gregg decided to reenter politics and run. He was quickly challenged by Powell, house speaker W. Douglas Scammon, Senate president Eralsey Ferguson, and Elmer Bussey, perennial candidate, a loner who had never had a political organization. In the primary Powell beat out Gregg by a slim margin, 39,761 to 39,365. Bridges headed up the Republican state campaign and used the Flying Squadrons tactic of the 1930s to get the candidates closer to the voters in small rallies, both during the daytime and in evening meetings.

Granite State Democrats had put up another Laconian, former mayor Bernard Boutin, for governor. Boutin lashed out at the Republicans as responsible for the recession and the missile gap. Powell's campaign began to lag as most of the state's newspapers endorsed Boutin—some backing a Democrat for the first time in their history. Bridges concentrated all his efforts behind Powell, his former chief of staff, and the two men campaigned vigorously side by side.

Voting in the November 4 election was the heaviest in years. Boutin won in all but two of the state's thirteen cities, but lost to Powell by a narrow 106,790-99,955 margin. In contrast, congressmen Merrow and Bass were reelected by heavy majorities.

Nationwide, the Republicans suffered their worst defeat in many years. They lost forty-seven House seats, and another thirteen in the Senate. Most of the congressional losses were from the conservative side. New Democrats replacing conservative Republicans included Robert Bryd (West Virginia), Edmund Muskie (Maine), Eugene McCarthy (Minnesota), Vance Hartke (Indiana), and Philip Hart (Michigan).

Because of the repudiation of conservative senators, moderates demanded a larger role in the Senate leadership. Led by George Aiken (Vermont), they sought to fill Knowland's vacancy as minority leader with John Sherman Cooper (Kentucky). Dirksen was to be replaced as party whip by Thomas Kuchel (California). This confrontation once again put Bridges on the spot as a compromise for the leadership role, and once again he declined becoming the compromise candidate for floor leader because he considered his position on the major committees more valuable. He was again given the policy committee chairmanship, and Dirksen became floor leader, with Kuchel his aide, in the role of minority whip.

Senator Hugh Scott (R-Pennsylvania) tells a revealing story of Bridges' "quiet leadership." During the rancorous meeting in which Dirksen became floor leader,

> the moderates got together in George Aiken's office before the vote. We agreed to nominate John Sherman Cooper as floor leader against Dirksen, and to put Thomas Kuchel (R-California) up as whip. But we were in the minority, of course, and when the vote was taken Senator Dirksen won by a vote of twenty-one to fourteen. Dirksen then nominated Karl Mundt (R-South Dakota) to be the minority whip, bypassing Kuchel, and the fight was on. I remember Senator Aiken rising up and shouting. "You can't ride roughshod over us [the moderates] Everett Dirksen. This will be war! War, war, war!" For my part, I said to Dirksen, "We will offer you a velvet glove, or an iron hand, Senator. But you had better decide. We may not be a majority, but we can make or break your leadership. This is to be a united Republican party, and we demand to be included!" Meanwhile, as we were all ranting and raving—and I remember this quite clearly—I saw Styles moving around the room, speaking quietly to a number of senators. And when the vote was taken, Kuchel won twenty-one to fourteen. Styles had changed *the exact number of votes* by which Dirksen had won. It was a terrific example of leadership—a tribute to Styles Bridges' mastery of the political art.

Joyce Wiggin, Bridges' executive secretary for a number of years, recalled Styles being

> very much the man behind the scenes. Quiet, but extremely powerful. He was very warm, very interested in people. He had the knack to make the person he was talking to—from the president down to the man who shined his shoes—seem like he was the single most important person in the world. He loved gossip, loved talking to people, loved learning about people. That's what put him in good standing with his colleagues. He was just plain likable. You couldn't help but like him. He was a powerhouse in Washington because people liked him, and he genuinely liked people. He was very effective behind the scenes, and he didn't hesitate to call in the chips, if a favor was owed.

Bridges joined Dirksen and Kuchel in efforts to rebuild the Republican image for the 1960 presidential campaign. Satisfied that conservatives had been discredited in the 1958 election, moderates rallied behind Eisenhower and his 1959 budget. It was high, but balanced, with even some reduction in the national debt. It also contained a strong defense program and increased social-welfare benefits. Both sides of the Senate supported the new budget and with the cooperation of liberal Democrats, the Congress enacted several new laws, including a civil-rights statute. For his part, Bridges kept the Republican policy committee united. Behind the scenes, without fanfare or publicity, he worked to settle disagreements between Republican senators and the president.

Another Family Tragedy

Tragedy struck the Bridges family again in the spring of 1959, when the senator's younger brother, Ronald, a doctor of theology, was reported missing from the family's summer home in Pembroke, Maine. On Saturday, May 16, a neighbor, Ernest Mains, concerned that he hadn't seen Dr. Bridges since the day before, checked the property, but could find no sign of Ronald, who at fifty-three was in poor health and disabled by arthritis. A week earlier, Ronald had left his family at their Sanford, Maine home and had gone alone to the summer house. His concern deepening, Mains searched the premises, including the house and barn and the surrounding grounds. Finding no sign of Bridges, Mains called the police.

Further investigation revealed that Ronald Bridges' small boat was missing from its mooring on the nearby Pennamaquan River. A life preserver was found in Dr. Bridges' automobile. Fearing the worst, the police organized a search party. Dragging crews, planes, a Coast Guard cutter, and searchers on foot combed the area, with no result. The next morning a helicopter was called and divers scoured the river bottom. On the morning of the 17th, Ronald's fishing boat was found capsized. Half a mile downstream, a black loafer was washed up on shore, along with Ronald's cane, and a single paddle. The search was continued for the next two days, but given the smooth bottom and strong currents of the Pennamaquan, divers reported any body in the river would undoubtedly be washed out to sea. On May 21, the search effort was terminated.

When he had learned of the tragedy, Styles Bridges immediately left Washington with Doloris to join the search. Even after the official search effort ended, Styles spent several days cruising the basin with a Coast Guard party.

Predictably, rumors dogged the Bridges family. A young man who had been doing work around the estate stated in his report to the State Police that Ronald had seemed despondent, and had been drinking heavily on the day of his disappearance.

He was rumored to have been seen in the company of "several strangers" shortly before. The boat was described in the police reports as "unsafe and not suitable for the water conditions of the area." The reports also stated that "the doctor had a large sum of money on his person" the day before his disappearance.

In the face of the speculation and gossip surrounding the death of Styles' brother, his political enemies, including Congressman Perkins Bass, obtained copies of the official Police Report and related statements of the case, but the official finding remained accidental drowning.

Ronald Bridges' body was never recovered. The loss depressed the senator for several weeks, but he soon returned to his Washington office. As in the past, family tragedy did not keep him from his work for long.

Looking Out for New Hampshire

Bridges continued to monitor the military installations in New Hampshire. He kept a close watch on the Portsmouth navy yard, seeking commitments from the navy to keep its repair facilities open and to construct atomic submarines. He won an air force commitment to station a reserve unit at Grenier Airport in Manchester, which had been converted with the aid of federal funds into a municipal airport, with facilities for industrial use.

Bridges' efforts were directly related to the establishment of a missile-tracking station in New Boston. The huge air base adjacent to Portsmouth was dedicated in 1956, and a year later it was named for Karl Pease of Plymouth, a Congressional Medal of Honor winner who had been killed in the South Pacific during World War II. From the army, Bridges helped secure several Corps of Engineers dams at various locations in the state to improve flood control. He also helped obtain the Cold Regions Laboratory, which was established near Dartmouth College in 1959.

As John Pillsbury of Bridges' Washington staff noted:

> Bridges did enormous things for New Hampshire. . . . If there was a cold region laboratory, he wanted it for Dartmouth College. If there was to be a Strategic Air Command Airport, he wanted it for Portsmouth. He was helpful in getting General Electric to Somersworth. Always very conscious of that part of his duty, he was probably the most effective senator New Hampshire ever had or ever will have.

Bridges' responsiveness to his constituents led to the upgrading and construction of several civilian airports around the state with federal cooperation, along with an FAA center in Nashua. He also arranged for a Small Business Administration office to open in Concord.

Bridges had long fought federal trade bills that threatened New Hampshire's shoe and textile industries. Favoring foreign production of these products would create "boom towns in Japan and ghost towns in New England," he said.

The senator's work on behalf of his New Hampshire constituents also continued. When a railroad locomotive fireman snatched a child from the path of a train in Rindge, he saw to it that the man received the president's medal for heroism. By personally appealing to the State Department and the president to intervene, he helped saved the life of army private John Vigneault of Manchester, who had been condemned by a German court for murder. The Germans were persuaded to commute the sentence.

In one celebrated international incident, Bridges came to the aid of Mrs. Reuben Rajala of Keene, whose young nephew, Alfred Ensio Lahti, was a hostage in the U.S. Embassy in Moscow. While the boy had been born in the Soviet Union, his father was an American, making the child a U.S. citizen. When Alfred's parents were caught up in one of Stalin's ongoing purges, the boy, at seventeen months of age, was secreted in the U.S. Embassy to prevent him from falling into the Communist state's hands. There he languished for five years, as authorities wrangled over his citizenship. In response to Mrs. Rajala's request for help, Bridges pursued the matter, writing innumerable letters to the State Department and the U.S. Ambassador in Russia, pressing for action. World War II complicated the matter, as did the fact that the Russians considered anyone born within their borders a Soviet citizen. The issue dragged on, but Bridges kept up his letter-writing campaign, demanding that the State Department make every effort to resolve the dispute. On January 10, 1947, the senator's efforts proved successful, and Alfred was finally united with his aunt in Keene.

The veteran senator always paid special attention to letters from his constituents. With the aid of his staff, all correspondence was given full attention and answered, many with "the nice little note" attached. Some letters were requests for patronage; many simply sought information. Bridges tried to return to New Hampshire at least once a month to meet with its citizenry.

Bridges was also instrumental in getting the main altar at the Cathedral of the Pines, in Rindge, declared a national memorial. The Kancamagus Highway in the White Mountains wilderness was constructed with a federal grant that he sponsored.

Several honors came to Bridges as his fourth term came to an end. In 1960, he was awarded the coveted Pettee Medal by the University of New Hampshire for distinguished service to the state. The legislature named a section of Interstate 93, starting near his East Concord home, in his honor.

The Election of 1960

As early as 1958, Bridges announced he would seek a fifth term in 1960. Within his own party he had no opposition, except for Judge Albert Levitt of Hancock, a political unknown. In early 1960, Bridges came out

Senator Styles Bridges introducing former president Herbert Hoover at the 1960 Republican Convention in Chicago

for Vice-president Richard Nixon to succeed Eisenhower. Nixon's only serious opponent was Governor Nelson Rockefeller of New York, a moderate. Rockefeller's main New Hampshire support came from Sherman Adams and a few others, but when it became known that Bridges was for Nixon, Rockefeller's support vanished. Nixon swamped Rockefeller, 65,204 to 2,750, in the 1960 New Hampshire presidential primary.

Bernard Boutin still dominated the Democratic party, and he endorsed Senator John F. Kennedy for president, who won the primary endorsement. Quite a few Catholic Republicans crossed over in the primary to vote for Kennedy, alerting the Republican leadership to the need for extra effort in the election campaign.

Boutin had promised in 1959 that his party would put up a strong candidate against Senator Bridges in 1960. On July 22, 1960, Professor Herbert W. Hill of Dartmouth College announced his candidacy for the Senate seat. Hill was a well-known speaker in academic circles, and like Bridges, advocated a strong defense and a realistic foreign policy. Personable and a capable phrase maker, Hill waged an attention-getting campaign.

Powell and Gregg had a rematch of their 1958 contest for governor. A record turnout of voters braved the rains of Hurricane Donna on primary day, and Powell again edged Gregg by only 1,011 votes—49,119-48,108.

THE UNITED STATES NEEDS U. S. SENATOR

STYLES BRIDGES

PRESIDENT EISENHOWER SAID THIS TO SENATOR BRIDGES: "I WANT TO STATE ONCE AGAIN HOW HIGHLY I VALUE YOUR OUTSTANDING SERVICE IN THE UNITED STATES SENATE . . . YOUR STATE AND OUR NATION ARE BETTER OFF TODAY BECAUSE OF YOUR TIRELESS DEVOTION TO THE CAUSE OF GOOD GOVERNMENT. AND IT IS MY HOPE THE GOOD PEOPLE OF NEW HAMPSHIRE WILL OVERWHELM-INGLY SUPPORT YOU."

Front cover of Bridges flyer distributed during the 1960 senatorial campaign

Senator Bridges and New York Governor Nelson Rockefeller in earnest conversation at the Chicago Republican convention

Bridges spent most of the 1960 campaign traveling with the Republican Flying Squadron and speaking for their entire slate of candidates, rather than for himself. He never seemed to worry about Hill, and countered the friendly educator's campaign by speaking of his own seniority in the Senate and his philosophy of limited government. The senator's supporters were confident of another Bridges' victory.

Hill's chief issue was the need for more federal aid to education. He pointed to the teacher shortage and said New Hampshire also had a shortage of suitable classrooms. He also charged that the Eisenhower administration had failed to revitalize national defense to cope with Soviet Russia's belligerence. He spoke of the bright promises being made by Kennedy and called Bridges the "senator from yesterday."

Bridges countered Hill's charges by saying that local control over education was better than bureaucratic federal supervision, which would ultimately mold the minds of students. He pointed out that the missile gap between the United States and the Soviets had been closed through Republican leadership. Kennedy would not be able to keep his campaign promises, Bridges warned, because Congress would never approve them.

Bridges 1960 campaign poster

Senators Cotton and Bridges of New Hampshire meet with Vice President Nixon on January 5, 1960 to urge him to enter the New Hampshire presidential preference primary. He did and won, but his bid for the presidency was unsuccessful until eight years later.

He also contended that Nixon's experience was far better than Kennedy's, and he would be more effective in dealing with world and domestic problems.

The 1960 campaign was one of the cleanest in Bridges' career. The only charge of unfairness came in October, and it was precipitated by Doloris Bridges. As she traveled the campaign trail, she charged that Kennedy was "soft on communism." That brought loud protests from the Democrats, but Hill declined to make an issue of the statement.

In the November 8 election, Bridges swamped Hill, winning a fifth Senate term by a record majority of almost 60,000 votes—173,521 to 114,024. It was a fitting climax to one of the most successful political careers in Granite State history. This victory was by 60.3 percent of the total vote, following the Bridges pattern of ever-increasing victory margins—52.2 percent in 1936; 55.2 percent in 1942; 58.2 percent in 1948; 60.2 percent in 1954.

Governor Powell easily won a second term, with both Merrow and Bass returned to Congress. Nixon, as expected, also carried New Hampshire, but by 20,000 votes fewer than Bridges' total.

Nationally, the Republican party was defeated. Kennedy and his running mate, Lyndon B. Johnson, beat out Nixon and Henry Cabot Lodge, who had entered the U.S. Senate from Massachusetts with Styles in 1936. In the electoral vote tally, he actually received less than 50 percent of the popular vote. For Nixon, this was the first of several unhappy setbacks he was to suffer in the early 1960s. The narrowness of the margin of victory, however, would hamper Kennedy's legislative efforts. As Bridges correctly predicted, "The closeness of the race should have a sobering effect on Mr. Kennedy, because it certainly does not indicate general approval of his programs."

Adding a special good feeling to Bridges' fifth term achievement, Hill, a gentleman to the end, sent him a congratulatory telegram calling him the "champion vote-getter in this state."

Historian Leon Anderson paid tribute to Senator Bridges' dedication to the Republican party in the *Concord Monitor*:

> Senator Bridges did much more than win a fifth term at Washington, by a record-smashing majority in the recent Presidential election. State House election records reveal he also saved the Republican State Committee from bankruptcy. . . . Final reports on the campaign show the committee spent a gross of $109,380 . . . of which $33,000 came from wealthy contributors in New York, California and Texas, thanks to Senator Bridges. Never before in GOP history has a New Hampshire campaign been so heavily financed by nonresident cash.

Actually, Senator Bridges turned better than fifty thousand dollars in cash to the state committee, for he induced quite a number of instate contributors to give their cash to the committee, rather than to himself, for the Republican cause.

14

The Final Year

*"Soon now we shall go out of the house and
go into the convulsion of the world, out of history into history and the awful responsibility
of Time."*

Robert Penn Warren,
All the King's Men

ENATOR BRIDGES' fifth term lasted just
less than a year. He continued to
be a vigorous champion of his
beliefs and a successful politician to the end. President Kennedy was no
stranger to him, as they had served together in the Senate and were both
New Englanders. Bridges probably understood Kennedy better than any
other president he served with, but politically, he was as distant from the
White House as ever.

In January 1961, Bridges welcomed back his former assistant, Scott
McLeod, as counsel to the Republican minority on the Senate Appropriations
Committee. McLeod had served as Eisenhower's ambassador to Ireland.

Senate Republicans again elected Bridges as chairman of the party's
policy committee, and once more he used this position to help keep conservatives and moderates somewhat unified. Both sides expressed displeasure
with Nixon's showing, their chief complaint being that he had not campaigned hard enough. Without a Republican president, Bridges' Senate role
became more important than ever.

Dirksen continued as leader of the moderates, and with the aid of such
men as Jacob J. Javits (R-New York) and Leverett Saltonstall (R-Massachu-
setts), he fought to keep conservatives off the key committees. Led by Barry

227

Goldwater (R-Arizona), the conservatives hit back, and Bridges stepped into the breach. He blocked an effort to remove Goldwater from the Senate Elections Committee, then let the moderates know that he was prepared to back Rockefeller in the 1964 presidential election. This support of Rockefeller would have been a big step away from the strong conservative position long held by Senator Bridges. As a result, moderates ended their antagonism and party unity was again restored.

The first session of the 87th Congress opened with Vice-president Johnson presiding as Senate president and his long-time Democratic colleague, Mike Mansfield (D-Montana), as majority floor leader. The first order of business was confirming President Kennedy's appointees, and all but one were approved without argument.

Bridges opposed the nomination of Chester Bowles as undersecretary of state, largely because of Bowles' seeming lack of support for Nationalist China. Bowles declared that the American recognition of the former Chinese government, now entrenched in Taiwan, was irrevocable, and that satisfied a majority of the Senate, which approved his appointment.

Bridges gave his usual scrutiny to the budget and produced a line-by-line analysis identifying areas where reductions were possible, and once again alleged waste in foreign-aid proposals. For a third time, he introduced his measure for a balanced-budget constitutional amendment, and for the third time it attracted little attention.

Kennedy's first State of the Union address to Congress included specific recommendations on various issues. Bridges was chosen to give the Republican response. He pointed out that while Kennedy's vision was one of a nation on its knees, the Republican leadership in the 1950s had made the country prosperous and strong militarily. Above all, Bridges declared, the Republicans had made the government financially sound, and Kennedy's proposals threatened that stability.

Kennedy had made a major issue out of the missile gap in his campaign. Upon becoming president, however, he discovered that the Republicans had been correct in stating that the nation had closed the gap. When the Defense Department refused to acknowledge this, Bridges demanded a senatorial investigation to determine the truth. He was joined by Richard Russell (D-Georgia), but the rest of the Democrats stalled on the issue. Bridges' efforts gradually forced the administration to admit publicly that its campaign rhetoric had been in error.

The Cuban Danger

A dominating issue in Kennedy's first years in office was the question of what to do regarding Cuba. In late 1958, Fidel Castro and his band of guerilla fighters overthrew the Fulgencio Batista dictatorship after a long struggle. Throughout 1959, Castro strengthened his hold on the island, while appearing to be granting freedom to its people. At the same time, he began executing members of the ousted government. Indications pointed to the emergence of a Communist dictatorship only ninety miles from American shores. Bridges observed, "Regardless of the reasons for the executions in Cuba, what is happening amounts to mass murder, and I, for one, am appalled that the so-called liberators of that country would permit such ruthless reprisals."

Castro's radical philosophy became more apparent when he began seizing U.S. property on the island. Bridges openly accused Castro of being a Communist and proposed an amendment to the foreign-aid bill denying aid to any country that took over American property without proper compensation. The Senate killed the measure, however.

When it became clear that Cuba had indeed become a Communist dictatorship, Bridges demanded that something be done about it, because of the island's proximity to the United States. In a speech on the Senate floor, he recalled how China had been allowed to become Communist. Now communism had become entrenched off American shores. Bridges concluded,

> Patience is a fine virtue, but if it is carried to an extreme, as a guide for the conduct of diplomatic relations with an upstart dictator. . . . [It is] likely to prove just as dangerous and unfruitful as 'waiting for the dust to settle' in China. . . . I do not believe that any government which continues to confiscate American property, to insult Americans . . . can be anything other than a great threat to us and the free world.

The Kennedy administration acted in April of 1961, by launching the ill-fated Bay of Pigs invasion. Planned by the CIA and carried out by Cuban nationals, the invasion proved to be a disaster. American and Batista forces were defeated within forty-eight hours, and the ensuing public outcry assured Castro that there would be no interference with his regime. Although in the following years the CIA continued its clandestine attempts to disrupt the Cuban government, and even to assassinate Castro, he remains in power.

In May of 1961, Bridges repeated his call for an embargo of Cuba and another direct invasion, if necessary, but he was ignored. Castro continued to be Kennedy's nemesis and eventually caused a major Cold War confrontation—the Cuban missile crisis, in 1962.

The Berlin Crisis

Berlin was another crisis center. In 1961, that divided city was physically split by the erection of a wall to keep refugees from escaping to the Western sector. As the Soviets tightened their grip on the eastern half of Berlin, they closed all access to the city.

The Senate considered several ideas to deal with the Berlin situation. Senator Mansfield proposed that the capital be made an "open city"—one that is not occupied by foreign forces—even though that designation had proved unworkable during World War II. Bridges demanded that the administration disavow Mansfield's statement. Secretary of State Dean Rusk was called to testify and reassure the Senate Foreign Relations Committee that Kennedy had no intention of following Mansfield's suggestion. Bridges, siding with the president, piloted a heavy defense-appropriations bill through the Senate, and supported Kennedy's request to call up the army reserves to display strength to the Soviets.

In his role as Republican spokesman, Bridges denounced the Democrats as a "new generation" government that was fostering old ideas from the New Deal. He also pointed out that Kennedy had not been very successful in getting Congress to act on his proposals. Once again, Bridges worked to create a Republican program that would win congressional control in the 1962 election. Unfortunately, the senator would not live to see the victory.

In August of 1961, after leading a successful floor fight to prevent American recognition of the Communist People's Republic of Mongolia, Bridges was hospitalized for pulmonary congestion. His health had frequently been threatened by his tendency to overwork, but he usually was able to recover quickly and return to his Senate duties in a few weeks. In September, Bridges convalesced at his Wolfeboro summer home and his East Concord residence. He seemed to be recovering, but on September 21, Styles suffered a heart attack.

His doctors in Concord ordered him to rest completely, but he was soon issuing an attack on Kennedy's "New Frontier," accusing the president of manipulating the economy to create a false prosperity for the 1962 election. Although he appeared vigorous in public, in private Bridges was extremely tired and many friends thought he might resign from the Senate.

Bridges was released from Concord Hospital on November 3, and received good wishes from around the nation. His old nemesis, Harry Truman, led the list of well-wishers. By the end of the month, Bridges appeared improved and was discussing Republican plans for the 1962 Congressional session and the 1964 presidential race. Bridges thought Kennedy was vulnerable. The president's leadership seemed to be losing strength, and Bridges felt good about the next presidential election campaign.

Styles thought that Nixon could make a comeback in 1964, if he could win the California governorship in 1962. Nixon lost the election, however, and immediately called a bitter press conference announcing his retirement from politics, in which he made his famous declaration, "you won't have Dick Nixon to kick around anymore."

Meanwhile, Rockefeller looked increasingly attractive as presidential material. When conservatives pressed him, Bridges, always looking ahead, replied, "I've never been for Rockefeller—he's much more liberal than I. But I'm a practical man and I want to win in 1964."

The End of an Era

In the early evening of November 25, 1961, the senior senator from New Hampshire had been home from the Concord Hospital for three weeks, and seemed to be recuperating from his heart attack. Styles was in good spirits, looking hale and hearty, as he shared a drink with John Warrington, his executive secretary. The men sat alone in what is now the Bridges House, the official home of New Hampshire governors.

The senator was unusually positive and upbeat, and was looking forward to the convening of the 87th Congress in January of 1962, which would mark his quarter century of service in the United States Senate. Bridges was the senior Republican in the U.S. Senate, the ranking Republican member on all Senate committees. He was known affectionately as the Gray Eminence, the Dean of Senate Republicans, an authentic American Tory. He and Warrington had both lost their fathers at an early age, and that helped form a bond between the two. They enjoyed bantering into the night, discussing practical politics, which both men loved.

As the fire burned down in the fireplace, they talked about a project the Senator had long been considering, a "white paper" on the future of the Republican party. As chairman of the GOP policy committee, Bridges planned to present this policy statement to the new Congress, which would take a most positive Republican position, encompassing all the major problem areas around the world. As the discussion continued, Warrington outlined his ideas on the statement, and Bridges showed typical quiet enthusiasm.

Hours had passed when John realized it was getting quite late, and he still had to return home to Nashua. In parting, he joked that he worked for a hard taskmaster and needed to be back at the senator's house early the next day.

At approximately 5:40 A.M. on the 26th, the ringing of the bedside phone in the Warrington home pierced the cold winter darkness, startling John and his wife awake. John sat bolt upright in bed, listening with disbelief as Doloris Bridges calmly told him, "John, the senator died in his sleep, about five o'clock this morning. Please come to Concord as soon as you can."

He had not wept since his father's funeral, but the tears flowed copiously now. Warrington had been like a son to the senator, and was overcome by the news of his death.

Henry Styles Bridges, one of the most fascinating political figures in the past one hundred years of New Hampshire history, was gone, dead at the age of sixty-three. Granite State politics would never be the same.

Eulogies for Styles Bridges

Washington correspondent Robert Pfeifle wrote in the *Overseas Report* of December 8, 1961:

From the President of the United States to the elevator operator in the new Senate office building, the news of the death of revered Republican Senator Styles Bridges saddened the nation's capital, as eulogies echoed from every corner of the land. . . . The conservative wing of the Republican Party will surely miss the counsel and leadership of Styles Bridges in its continuing struggle with the liberals for legislative dominance. It was a struggle which undoubtedly played a part in sapping his energies, although he never shied from active participation in any fight which he considered to be in the best interests of his state and country. No more could be expected of any man.

President Kennedy made a personal phone call to the senator's widow, and issued a statement as he arrived in Washington from Hyannisport: "The nation will mourn the loss of Senator Bridges, a great patriot who devoted his life to the continuing strength of our country. He was a distinguished advocate of his state, his region and his nation."

Former President Eisenhower said, "During my years of close association with [the senator] in government, I came to know how deeply he was dedicated to the good of our nation."

In California, former Vice-president Nixon declared, "Styles Bridges was one of the most effective political leaders ever produced by the Republican party."

Senator Barry Goldwater stated, "His death was a great personal loss. Senator Bridges was one of my best friends and most trusted advisers."

Chaing Kai-shek, leader of the Chinese Nationalists, whom Bridges long supported, wired condolences from Taiwan.

Long-time family friend and speech writer Alex Hillman wrote in the *National Review*, "Bridges was a proper and principled conservative who believed in an open society—open to talent and industry, but a society restrained by the wisdom of the past, and by a certain enlightened pessimism as to Man's nature and the precepts of natural law."

Senator Cotton said, "Our grief at the loss of a beloved friend is overshadowed by our country's loss." Publisher William Loeb wrote, "The country boy from Maine to the end was the same plain speaking, unaffected man who was known as Styles to thousands of his friends in the Granite State. . . . [New Hampshire] has lost a great pillar of our state. But more than that, they have lost a dear and beloved friend."

A private family service was held in the small East Concord Congregational Church, with Vice-president Johnson representing President Kennedy. Two days later, an elaborate state service was held in the historic Hall of Flags in the State House in Concord, the first funeral rite to be held there. An honor guard stood around the bier, while several thousand mourners filed by and paid their respects.

Top congressional leaders paid homage in the service. Senator Dirksen delivered the principal address. John McCormack, speaker of the house, and Governor Powell also eulogized Bridges. Teddy Kennedy also spoke on behalf of his brother, the President. A combined choir from the Keene and Plymouth state colleges and the University of New Hampshire rendered "The Battle Hymn of the Republic" from an adjacent hallway. The Senate chaplain, Dr. Fred B. Harris, gave the benediction.

An estimated four thousand people attended the service, including Styles' mother, eighty-six-year-old Alina Bridges, as well as his sister Doris. The old marble flooring beneath the hall had to be shored up with steel posts to accommodate the crowd.

Historian Leon Anderson, then the *Concord Monitor*'s veteran political editor, wrote:

New Hampshire will long remember and miss Senator Styles Bridges. . . . Much is being said and written through the nation about him, now that inevitable death has taken this Maine farm boy of humble origin, who rose to international prestige and national power, as another of Concord's illustrious adopted sons. The nation's great have joined in homage to his public service, and the friendships which have been the hallmark of his career. But we will remember Styles Bridges most of all for his humility in the midst of all his success. He continued to the last to be a plain person, a simple neighbor, without pretension or fanfare. . . . Senator Bridges was one of those rare men who was able to rise to heights, walk with the high and mighty, and yet retain and practice the modesty and humility which made it easy and enjoyable for the rest of us to know and share his personal friendship. We know full well, of course, that Styles Bridges never pleased everyone. For the very nature of politics, his chosen life, denied such attainment.

The Aftermath

Ironically, the man who held party unity above all else in his political life was to shatter that principle by his death. Party leaders quickly scrambled to get in line to succeed him, and the competition became so bitter that it influenced New Hampshire's politics for years.

Vice President Lyndon Johnson escorts Doloris Bridges from the East Congregational Church in East Concord following the memorial service for Styles Bridges in 1961.

It was Governor Powell's official duty to appoint an interim senator until the 1962 election, and he was barraged with suggestions. Former governors Dale and Blood were mentioned, along with ex-senator Upton. Powell considered appointing himself, then ruled himself out without explanation. It was known that he entertained ambitions toward a national office, and during his term as chairman of the National Governors' Conference he had been mentioned as a possibility for vice-president.

The strongest suggestion came from William Loeb. He editorialized in his *New Hampshire Sunday News*, "New Hampshire could pay no stronger tribute or respect to its greatest son, Styles Bridges, than to send Mrs. Bridges to take his chair in the United States Senate."

Loeb's demand infuriated Powell, causing a major rift. Some of Doloris Bridges' friends suggested that if she were given the interim appointment, she would retire by the 1962 election, with appreciation for the honor. But Powell apparently understood better, for Doloris Bridges would become a major political factor for the next several years.

On December 7, 1961, only eleven days after Bridges' death, Governor Powell stunned New Hampshire by announcing the interim appointment of the state attorney general, Maurice J. Murphy, Jr., of Portsmouth, to the Senate. Murphy had been Powell's administrative assistant. Although many Bridges supporters were dismayed by the surprise choice, Powell had made an adroit political move: In one stroke, he had appointed a loyal supporter, broken with Bridges' immediate political forces, freed himself from Loeb's dominating influence, and set himself up as the ranking leader of the Republican party.

Whatever his own hopes and aspirations, Powell's appointment of Murphy devastated Republican unity, and led to a series of Democratic victories. Loeb was especially upset. He accused the governor of "disloyalty and ingratitude towards Senator Bridges" for not naming Doloris, and he openly broke with Powell, whom he had zealously supported for years.

The Washington Vacuum

Senator Bridges' death had an immediate effect in Washington as well. The 1962 session of Congress was marred by bipartisan infighting, as it seemed that no Great Compromiser stepped forward to take Styles' place. (Once in the 1950s, John Warrington relates, he and several other Senate Republicans were in the cloakroom when Mark Trice, secretary of the Senate, entered and asked if "the senator" was in the room. Seeing that Styles was not present, the men responded that "the Senator" was not there. It was obvious to everyone who Trice was looking for, without anyone asking,

87th Congress
2d Session

𝕾𝖙𝖞𝖑𝖊𝖘 𝕭𝖗𝖎𝖉𝖌𝖊𝖘

Senator Norris Cotton of New Hampshire moved that the following resolution be adopted and the motion was seconded by Senator Everett McKinley Dirksen. The resolution was then unanimously adopted by the Republican Minority Conference on January 10, 1962:

Whereas Almighty God in His infinite wisdom has taken from us our beloved former colleague, Senator Styles Bridges, and

Whereas throughout his twenty-five years of service as a Member of the United States Senate he rendered statesmanlike service to our Nation and to the State of New Hampshire, and

Whereas he rendered distinguished service as President Pro Tempore of the United States Senate, Republican Leader, Chairman of the Republican Policy Committee, and Chairman of the Committee on Appropriations of the Senate, and

Whereas he was our affectionate friend and esteemed colleague, ever ready to give of himself, of his efforts, and of his wise judgment:

Now, therefore,

Be It Resolved, That we, the Members of the Republican Conference of the United States Senate, express our sense of great loss at his passing, and

Further, That a copy of this resolution be transmitted to Mrs. Doloris Thauwald Bridges, that she may be assured of our deep respect for her and of our condolences to her upon the passing of our friend, her husband.

Attest:

Chairman of the Conference

Secretary of the Conference

The resolution marking Senator Bridges' death unanimously adopted by the Republican Minority Conference on January 20, 1962

Which senator?) For the first time in twenty-five years, Congress convened without "the senator" present.

Margaret Chase Smith, then senator from Maine, made the following comments in a speech in Brunswick, Maine:

> When Styles Bridges, a native son of Maine, who was born in West Pembroke, Maine, died in November of 1961, a very serious vacuum was created in the Republican ranks of the United States Senate . . . That vacuum was deeply felt in this year's 1962 session. Not only was there no one to step in to take the place of Styles Bridges on the Republican side—but many Democrats in the Senate deeply felt the void of leadership caused by his death. It will be many years before any Republican will reach the position of power, influence and leadership in the Senate that Styles Bridges did.

The New Hampshire Fallout

Senator Murphy had hardly stopped celebrating his appointment when he had to begin campaigning to retain his seat in the 1962 election. But conservatives rallied behind Doloris Bridges, moderates coalesced behind Congressman Perkins Bass; and then Congressman Merrow also jumped into the contest.

As the campaign progressed, it led to a showdown between Doloris Bridges and Perkins Bass, as Maurice Murphy and Chester Merrow fell behind. Doloris' claim to her late husband's following was obvious. She had campaigned with him frequently accompanied by their youngest son, John, who had become well known in the state. On every possible occasion, she stressed, "I alone among all of the candidates am on public record for ten years of having supported that which he believed in."

Emphasizing her conservative views did not appeal to some of the old Bridges supporters, who included many moderates. Bass also wooed them. He recalled how Bridges had been closely allied with his father, the progressive governor Robert Perkins Bass, in his early political career.

Not since the Tobey-Powell battle of 1950 had a Republican primary contest been so hard fought. The result was a Bass victory by only 1,492 votes—31,037 to 29,545. Senator Murphy finished with 24,204 votes and Merrow trailed with 14,417.

Doloris demanded a recount, which gave her a net loss of 32 votes, while Bass dropped 22. The recount led to several legal suits and countersuits over election practices.

Meanwhile, Democrats united behind Thomas McIntyre, a Laconia attorney, to oppose Bass. Despite several personal appeals by Senator Cotton, Doloris Bridges refused to endorse Bass. It became apparent that she continued to believe in her political potential and felt that if McIntyre

*Senator Bridges shortly before his death with Perkins Bass, who later defeated Bridges'
widow Doloris in a Republican primary in 1962 for her late husband's Senate seat.*

became senator, she could unseat him in 1966; whereas if Bass won the
seat, it would be difficult to beat him in the next primary. Doloris' decision
did give the election to McIntyre. (The strategy, however, did not prove
successful. Doloris lost in the 1966 Republican primary, finishing fifth among
six candidates, with Loeb supporting the victor, retired general Harrison R.
Thyng of Barnstead.)

The bitterness of the 1962 senatorial primary spilled into the gubernatorial race, as conservatives blamed Powell for the fracas. Powell confidently
predicted that he would be renominated, and would become the first
governor to win three consecutive terms since the state government had
gone on a biennial basis, in 1879. His prediction did not come true, as John
Pillsbury of Manchester, a former Bridges aide, a popular seven-term state
legislator, and publicity director for the Public Service Company, captured
the nomination by a surprise vote of 55,784 to 42,005.

However, under Pillsbury the Republicans could not present a united
front. Attorney John W. King of Manchester, a two-term state legislator, became the first Democrat to win the governorship in forty years, swamping
Pillsbury by more than 40,000 votes.

Powell and Pillsbury had a rematch in the 1964 primary and Pillsbury
won again, only to lose once more to Governor King. From then on,

Powell repeatedly bid for the governorship and the Senate, but failed each time.

Other members of Senator Bridges' staff fared well after his death. When Merrow vacated his First Congressional District seat, Louis Wyman, a former Bridges' aide won it by defeating J. Oliva Huot, the Democratic mayor of Laconia. Two years later, Huot unseated Wyman, but Louis regained the seat in 1966 and held it until 1974, when he became a candidate for the Senate, losing to Democrat John A. Durkin of Manchester, a former state insurance commissioner, in the closest Senate election in Granite State history. After a prolonged recount, in which a Wyman victory margin of 355 votes was changed to a 10-vote edge for Durkin, a rematch election was ordered, which Durkin won by a substantial margin.

James Cleveland ran up an impressive congressional record after winning the Second District seat vacated by Bass in 1962. After six state Senate terms, this Republican moderate served nine terms in Washington and retired in 1980.

Gregg tried once again for the governorship in 1966 and won the Republican nomination, only to lose to Governor King—making King, instead of Powell, the first governor to win three consecutive biennial terms. Gregg returned to his family business, but continued in politics behind-the-scenes. His son, Judd Gregg, served as governor from 1989-'93, in the U.S. Congress from 1981-'89, and as U.S. Senator from 1993 to present.

Merrow retired from politics after his 1962 defeat, then in 1970 turned Democrat and failed twice to unseat Congressman Wyman. Senator Cotton filled the role of being New Hampshire's senior senator for thirteen years, but never attempted to take over Bridges' role as the state party leader. While Cotton served three terms in Congress and twenty-one years in the Senate, he never achieved the national prominence that Bridges earned. Cotton retired in 1974, after winning his final term in 1968 by a landslide over Governor King.

Doloris Bridges left the political scene after her 1966 defeat, and died in 1969 after a long and debilitating illness. Of her three sons, only John showed an interest in politics. He bid for public office himself, serving in the New Hampshire House of Representatives from 1971 to 1973, representing Bedford and Litchfield. In his first year John Fisher Bridges was deemed to be "one of two outstanding freshmen legislators." John also served on the executive council under Governor Meldrim Thomson, Jr., of Orford, from 1973 to 1975. In 1975, when Wyman left his First District congressional seat to run for the Senate, John Bridges ran for the position, but he lost the Republican nomination to David Banks of Chichester, an automobile dealer, who then was defeated in the election by Democrat Congressman Norman E. D'Amours.

The Concord Heritage

Before his death, Senator Bridges willed his East Concord brick residence to become New Hampshire's official governor's house, effective after the death of his wife. The legislature accepted the gift, including the furnishings and spacious surrounding grounds. Governor Walter Peterson of Peterborough was the first chief executive to occupy the historic structure. Governor Thomson induced the legislature to vote a substantial appropriation to remodel the spacious adjoining barn into a meeting room, along with a small office space, a fieldstone fireplace, and a custodial security room.

A portrait of Senator Bridges hangs in the governor's residence, which is situated on a knoll from which one can see Interstate 93. In the distance, just three miles away, is the dome of the New Hampshire State House, where Styles served as governor from 1935 to 1937. The access lanes from Concord to the Vermont state line bear Styles Bridges' name—U.S. Senator Styles Bridges Highway.

The governor's residence has become a lasting memorial to Styles Bridges. The house, located on Mountain Road in East Concord, was built in a simple architectural style known as Greek Revival, popular in the early 1800s. Furnishings include many of the antique pieces that Styles loved to collect, late-eighteenth-and early-nineteenth-century American chests, tables, and chairs. Several are of New Hampshire origin, including a tall clock made in the Concord-Hopkinton area; Queen Anne chairs from the Portsmouth area; a pine and maple slantfront desk from the central part of the state; and a yellow-painted rocker made by Abijah Wetherbee of New Ipswich. The Bridges also left a significant collection of English Georgian silver, displayed in the dining room. Two sets of china are available for special functions, including a gold-edged Bavarian "Diplomatic" crested set, with the official U.S. symbol of the eagle, the type used at the White House and at American embassies, which was purchased by Senator Bridges during his tenure in Washington.

It is a bit of historic irony that the official residence of the chief executive of New Hampshire was bequeathed to the State not by one of the wealthy elite, but by a man who rose from humble beginnings—according to Leon Anderson one of the poorest governors the State of New Hampshire ever had—to become one of the Granite State's most prominent public figures. In 1979, the State Historical Commission erected a large metal marker in front of the house, which reads:

Bridges House, Governor's Residence: This house, on land long occupied by Revolutionary Veteran Joshua Thompson, was built by Charles Graham about 1836.

The Bridges House in East Concord, now the official residence of New Hampshire governors, was willed to the state by Styles Bridges before his death.

Styles Bridges, Governor of New Hampshire (1935-37) and U.S. Senator for 25 years thereafter, lived here from 1946 until his death. Left to the state upon the death of his widow, it became in 1969 the Governor's official residence.

New England College in Henniker, a dozen miles west of the Bridges house, which long was his favorite educational center, named its educational and cultural center Bridges Hall. In 1963, New England College established the Styles Bridges Chair in Government. The Memorial Fund dinner to establish the chair was attended by such notables as John W. King, governor of New Hampshire; U.S. senators Barry Goldwater and Norris Cotton, Styles' friend and colleague for close to forty years; and Doloris Bridges, her son, John Fisher Bridges, and numerous family and friends. The dedication read in part, "The Styles Bridges Chair in Government will serve as a lasting symbol to the ideals set in pattern through the years of service in the Senate of the United States by the man whose greatest reward was in making government service enriched by his efforts; the nation is more secure by his devotion and the lives of us all better for having known a truly great man."

Epilogue—What One Man Can Do

OVEMBER 28, 1961 was a cold, raw day in Hopkinton, New Hampshire. At about 5:30 in the afternoon, just as the sun was setting, my father, John Carl Kiepper, finished the evening milking. The fresh milk was poured into forty-quart cans at the milkhouse, and my father headed for the house. He stomped his boots by the back door, asking my mother, Sarah, if dinner was ready. He took off his coveralls, washed up, and sat down for dinner.

They finished eating by 6:30 and dressed in their Sunday finery for the drive to Concord. He backed the 1951 Chevrolet truck used to deliver milk to West Hopkinton and Henniker, and picked up my mother.

As they drove down the Hatfield Road to Route 9, toward Concord, my father remarked, "Styles Bridges has been our Senator for as long as I can remember. We should go to the State House to honor his passing." My mother, who had been active in the Hopkinton Republican Club, agreed. Because of the press of traffic, my father parked the truck three blocks from the State House, and they walked to the State House rotunda.

My parents, dairy farmers, stood quietly in the long line at the front door of the Capitol as it moved slowly toward Senator Bridges' open casket in the Hall of Flags. A full military honor guard stood around the casket.

John and Sarah Kiepper were typical of the four thousand New Hampshire citizens who came from all walks of life across the state to pay their final respects to the Senate leader. This was a time for what my father called the "little guy" to honor the Senator who represented all the people.

Styles Bridges' Room in the Capitol

Twenty years later, Styles Bridges had not been forgotten. On March 12, 1981, Senate Room S-113 at the United States Capitol was officially designated the "Styles Bridges Room." The bill to name S-113, the Republican Senators' Dining Room, for Senator Bridges was sponsored by minority leader Senator Howard Baker, Jr., and cosponsored by Senators Gordon J. Humphrey and Warren B. Rudman, both of New Hampshire.

The room was dedicated in a ceremony in Washington on June 24, 1981. More than a hundred people gathered in the ornate dining room, one of the most exclusive places in the capital, where only Republican senators are allowed to dine. The *Manchester Union Leader* described the room "as truly fitting of the former senior senator from New Hampshire. . . . The room's ceiling is ornately painted in revolutionary motif, depicting decorative shields, floral arrangements, and elegant trimmings. On the walls hang beautiful mirrors trimmed in heavy gold-leaf, while the room is enclosed with exquisite velvet drapes, giving it an aristocratic, sophisticated, air of distinction."

In attendance were two of the senator's children: Styles Bridges, Jr. and his wife, Marion, along with their daughter, Christy, and Mr. and Mrs. John Bridges, as well as other friends and family members of the late senator. Among the dignitaries were senators Baker and Rudman; Strom Thurmond, president pro tem of the Senate; Theodore F. Stevens, assistant majority leader; John Tucker, New Hampshire house speaker; as well as James Hayes, dean of the New Hampshire Executive Council for more than twenty years; and former U.S. senator Maurice Murphy, who replaced Bridges following his death.

The ceremony was conducted by Senator Humphrey, New Hampshire's senior senator, who quoted from the memorial address delivered by Senator Norris Cotton on the death of Senator Bridges: "Styles Bridges, to a greater degree than any other person I have ever known in all my life, had a talent, a gift, a genius, a friendship. He had that kind of natural love for his fellow men that caused him throughout his life to exemplify the teaching of the Master who said, 'Thou shall love the Lord thy God with all thy heart, and with all thy soul, with all thy strength, and with all thy mind, and thy neighbor as thyself.'"

Humphrey wore a large "Styles Bridges for President" button from the 1940 election, which he later presented to Bridges' granddaughter, Christy Bridges.

One of those in attendance, Scott A. Trendell of Laconia, New Hampshire, wrote in letter to the *Manchester Union Leader*: "S-113, the Styles Bridges Room, exudes the esteem and respect of Senator Bridges and will continue to do so far past our lifetime, for the legends of Styles Bridges are still echoed throughout Washington and New Hampshire. Senator Styles Bridges has staked his claim for the State of New Hampshire which he

The Styles Bridges Room in the Capitol in Washington, D.C. was dedicated in June, 1981 by New Hampshire senators Gordon S. Humphrey and Warren B. Rudman.

loved so deeply. The significance of this dedication makes this 'A Great Day For New Hampshire.'"

In his remarks, Senator Rudman captured the mood and sentiments of all those who were touched by the remarkable presence of the man who gave so much to New Hampshire and the nation, as he put what could well be the capstone on *the Senator's* life: "If Styles Bridges stands for anything, he stands for the proposition that one good man from one small state can make a difference."

Appendices

Styles Bridges, Biographical Notes

Chronology

1898	Born September 9, in West Pembroke, Maine
1916	Graduated from Pembroke High School
1918	Graduated from the University of Maine
1918-19	Instructor, Sanderson Academy, Ashfield, MA
1920-21	County Agricultural Agent, Hancock County, ME
1921-22	Member, Extension Staff (Soils and Crops Specialist), University of New Hampshire
1922-24	Executive Secretary, New Hampshire State Farm Bureau Federation
1923-36	Secretary and Business Manager to former Governor Robert P. Bass
1924-26	Editor, *Granite Monthly Magazine*
1924-29	Secretary and Director, New Hampshire Investment Co.
1925-37	Lieutenant, Reserve Corps, US Army
1928-29	Vice-chairman and Director of Speaker's Bureau, Republican State Committee (NH)
1930-34	Member, New Hampshire Public Service Commission
1935-37	Governor, State of New Hampshire
1937-61	United States Senator from the State of New Hampshire, from January 3, 1937 until his death in office, November 26, 1961
1940	Nominated for President of the United States, Republican National Convention, Philadelphia, Pennsylvania
1947-48	
1953-54	Chairman, Senate Appropriations Committee
1947-61	Director, Rumford Printing Company
1948-50	Trustee, United Mine Workers of America Welfare and Retirement Fund
1951	Alternate Delegate, signing of Security Treaty between the United States and Japan
1952	Republican Floor Leader in the United States Senate
1953-54	President Pro Tempore of the US Senate
1953-57	Chairman, Joint Congressional Inaugural Committee
1955-61	Chairman, Republican Policy Committee
1960	Awarded Holmes Pettee Memorial Medal by the Alumni Association of the University of New Hampshire
1961	Died November 26, at his home in East Concord

Committee Appointments

Chairman, Joint Committee of the Congress on the Legislative Budget
Chairman, Subcommittee on Aircraft Procurement
Chairman, Joint Committee on Foreign Economic Cooperation
Aeronautical and Space Sciences: 1959-61
Appropriations: 1937-61
Armed Services (Military Affairs until 1947): 1937-61
Buildings and Grounds: 1939-41
District of Columbia: 1939-47
Education and Labor: 1939-47
Foreign Relations: 1945-47
Interoceanic Canals: 1937-43
Post Offices and Post Roads: 1937-41
Privileges and Elections: 1937-47
Special Committee to Investigate the Civil Service System: 1939-41

Other Honors

Senator Bridges was a trustee of the Robert A. Taft Memorial Foundation; representative to the San Francisco Conference, which drew up the United Nations Charter; trustee and treasurer of the Putnam Agricultural Foundation; member, Advisory Council, New England College; president and trustee of the New Hampshire Savings Bank. He was also the recipient of numerous honorary degrees, including the M.A. from Dartmouth College; L.L.D. from the University of New Hampshire and University of Maine; D.C.L. from New England College, as well as awards, citations, tributes, and commendations too numerous to mention. He was senior republican Senator in point of service (at the time of his death) and a leader of the party's conservative wing.

Selected Bridgisms

1) Pay as you go. 2) Plan for tomorrow. 3) A dollar looked pretty big to me when I was a boy, it looks about the same size to me now. 4) Unemployment insurance is not a cure-all, but it is the single greatest constructive step from the staggering burden of relief. 5) The small industries are the life blood of New Hampshire. 6) Fight the cause of the under-dog. 7) A state should observe the ordinary precautions of the prudent citizen, who does not spend more than he can reasonably earn, and who does not borrow more than he may ultimately be able to pay. (*Yankee* magazine, May 1936)

Understanding the United States Senate

The Constitution of the United States is very specific regarding the United States Senate. Article 1, Section 3 states: The Senate of the United States shall be composed of two Senators from each State, chosen by the Legislature thereof, for six Years; and each Senator shall have one Vote.

Immediately after they shall be assembled in Consequence of the first Election, they shall be divided as equally as may be into three Classes.The Seats of the Senators of the first Class shall be vacated at the Expiration of the second Year, and of the second Class at the Expiration of the fourth Year, and of the third Class at the Expiration of the sixth Year, so that one third may be chosen every second Year; and if Vacancies happen by Resignation, or otherwise, during the Recess of the Legislature of any State, the Executive thereof may make temporary Apppointments until the next Meeting of the Legislature, which shall then fill such Vacancies.

No person shall be a Senator who shall not have attained to the Age of thirty Years, and been nine Years a Citizen of the United States, and who shall not, when elected, be an Inhabitant of that State for which he shall be chosen.

The Vice President of the United States shall be President of the Senate, but shall have no Vote, unless they be equally divided.

The Senate shall chuse [choose] their other Officers, and also a President pro tempore, in the Absence of the Vice President, or when he shall exercise the Office of President of the United States.

The Senate shall have the sole Power to try all Impeachments.When sitting for that Purpose, they shall be on Oath or Affirmation.When the President of the United States is tried, the Chief Justice shall preside: And no Person shall be convicted without the Concurrence of two thirds of the Members present.

Judgment in Cases of Impeachment shall not extend further than to removal from Office, and disqualification to hold and enjoy any Office of Honor, Trust or Profit under the United States: but the Party convicted shall nevertheless be liable and subject to Indictment, Trial and Judgment and Punishment, according to Law.

Article II, Section 2, states: The President shall be Commander in Chief of the Army and Navy of the United States, and of the Militia of the several States, when called into the actual Service of the United States; he may require the Opinion, in writing, of the principal Officer in each of the executive Departments, upon any Subject relating to the Duties of their respective Offices, and he shall have Power to grant Reprieves and Pardons for Offences against the United States, except in Cases of Impeachment.

He shall have Power, by and with the Advice and Consent of the Senate, to make Treaties, provided two thirds of the Senators present concur; and he shall nominate, and by and with the Advice and Consent of the Senate, shall appoint Ambassadors, other public Ministers and Consuls, Judges of the Supreme Court, and all other Officers of the United States, whose Appointments are not herein otherwise provided for, and which shall be established by Law: but the Congress may by Law vest the Appointment of such inferior Officers, as they think proper, in the President alone, in the Courts of Law, or in the Heads of Departments.

The President shall have Power to fill up all Vacancies that may happen during the Recess of the Senate, by granting Commissions which shall expire at the End of their next Session.

Amendment XVII to the Constitution states: The Senate of the United States shall be composed of two Senators from each State, elected by the people thereof, for six years; and each Senator shall have one vote. The electors in each State shall have the qualifications requisite for electors of the most numerous branch of the State legislatures.

When vacancies happen in the representation of any State in the Senate, the executive authority of each State shall issue writs of election to fill such vacancies: Provided, That the legislature of any State may empower the executive thereof to make temporary appointments until the people fill the vacancies by election as the legislature may direct.

This amendment shall not be so construed as to affect the election or term of any Senator chosen before it becomes valid as part of the Constitution.

These quotations from the U.S. Constitution are from the 2000 edition of *Our American Government*, published by the U.S. Government Printing Office, by authority of H. Con. Res. 221, 106th Congress, House Document 106-216.

This booklet is available from your congressman or U.S. senator and could be requested for use in high school social studies classes.It is an excellent reference, and should be in every student's personal library.

The Senate of the United States: A Bicentennial History, by Richard A. Baker, Director, U.S.Senate Historical Office (Robert E. Krieger Publishing Company, Malabar, Florida; 1988) is another excellent basic source for a fuller understanding of the U.S. Senate. It provides a comprehensive account of the personalities and issues that for nearly two centuries shaped "the world's greatest deliberative body." It offers a narrative survey of the Senate's development from its constitutional origins through the late 1980s, and is enriched with first-person observations from national figures ranging from James Madison to Robert C. Bryd.

Frequently Asked Questions About How the Senate Works

1. *When is a senator on the floor?* United States senators have many conflicting demands on their time. Each senator is a member of several committees, which may be holding hearings. Senators also work in their offices in the Senate office buildings, where they meet with constituents, representatives of the executive agencies, their staff, or others concerned about legislative business. Generally, the only senators on the floor at a given time are those prepared to speak on the issue at hand. Since the proceedings are televised, other senators can follow the debates from their offices, just as the public can watch them at home. Senators can quickly be notified of the need to return to the floor to establish a quorum or to cast a vote, by a series of bells that ring throughout the Capitol and the Senate office buildings.

2. *Who is presiding?* The Constitution designates the vice-president of the United States as the president, or presiding officer, of the Senate. Because of other demands on their time, the vice-presidents generally preside only on rare occasions when they might be needed to cast a tie-breaking vote. The Senate elects a president pro tempore—usually the senior member of the majority party—to act

in the vice-president's absence. The president pro tempore frequently presides at the opening of a day's session and prepares a list of senators from the majority party to preside hourly, throughout the day, on a rotating basis.

3. *When does a senator speak on the floor?* Through floor speeches senators seek to explain their legislation, to convince other senators to support their bills, and to leave a legislative history of a bill for executive agencies and the courts to interpret after the law is enacted. They announce their positions on legislation, nominations, and treaties and offer their reasons for casting their votes for or against. Their remarks are broadcast to all Senate offices and to viewers at home. Reporters of debates are also recording everything said on the floor for publication in the next day's *Congressional Record.*

4. *What is a quorum call?* From time to time, debate is suspended for a quorum call, which will last for a few minutes or longer. During this period, the clerk will slowly call the names of all senators. There are two types of quorum calls. The most frequently used quorum calls simply suspend floor proceedings while awaiting the next scheduled speaker. Such quorum calls may also occur while the managers of the legislation under debate confer to seek compromise or to draft amendments to the bill. "Live" quorums, by contrast, are designed to bring enough senators to the chamber to establish that a majority is present to conduct business. Such quorums are sometimes employed by senators seeking to delay or otherwise prevent passage of legislation and are frequently demanded during filibusters.

5. *What is a senator's salary?* As of January 2000, each senator receives an annual salary of $141,300.

6. *Where can I find out more information about past United States senators?* The Senate Historical Office can provide information about former United States senators, as well as information about the history of the Senate. You can contact the Senate Historical Office at 202-224-6900, by e-mail at historian@sec.senate.gov, or by writing the office at the following address: Richard A. Baker Ph.D., Director, Senate Historical Office, United States Senate, Washington, D.C. 20510-7108.

The Conservative in America

The conservative starts with the proposition that men are the creatures of God—but the imperfect creatures of God-and that being the creatures of God their primary task is to come to those moral concepts that bring them into line with their Creator.

It is only through long and tortuous struggle that man can finally realize himself fully. Man is imperfect.He contains within his being good and evil, and life is a struggle to realize the one and to defeat the other.

The conservative knows that man is a bundle of paradoxes—the brave and the coward—the kind and the cruel—the generous and the mean—the noble and the ignoble, all wrapped into one. That is the humanist approach. The realistic approach to man believes that men are not the creatures of a blueprint made by visionary liberals who insist that he live up to some a priori concept, but recognizes man for what he is—always inspired by the knowledge that because man is God's creature he is capable of the divine spark . . .

The conservative has serious doubts about man and pure reason. He knows that man cannot pierce the veil. That man is finite and his reason always faulty. That man cannot live by reason alone just as he cannot live by bread alone. He believes that the accumulated experience of the race, handed down by his forefathers, is the true wisdom of the people. He hates to disturb anything which is at rest. He believes that experience is the best guide to action. . . . The conservative will not change things for the sake of change itself, but only if there is a clear and present need for change —and then if there is reasonable assurance that the change is not for the worse. . . . He will prescribe for the body politic only after long and exhaustive study and then with great fear and trepidation. . . .

The conservative is deeply conscious of the fact that he and his generation are part of the endless stream of man under God, living, trying, accomplishing and dying. The conservative recognizes that this is the essence of man's growth—not the sudden, violent change based on the blueprint of some reckless mind. (Excerpts from an address by Styles Bridges to the "Great Issues Course" at Dartmouth College on October 16, 1955.)

Bibliographical Note

Because of space limitations I have followed in the footsteps of the noted historian Robert Leckie, and have not included the enormous number of footnotes a text of this type usually entails. Rather, the source material is indicated in what the University of Chicago's *Manual of Style* calls the parenthetical method of notation and resource listing. That is, sources from outside the Styles Bridges Papers, such as newspaper articles and Leckie's *Delivered from Evil*, are cited within the body of the text itself. All other quotations are either from taped interviews of the participants in this biography or have been gleaned from the many thousands of pages of speeches, letters, and legislative material found in the Bridges Papers, on file at the New Hampshire State Archives in Concord, New Hampshire. A registry of these papers, compiled by the author, can also be found at the State Archives office. The tapes themselves, which provided much of the background and insights into Bridges' character, are the product of interview sessions spanning over thirty years, and are available at the Archives office. A listing of the interview subjects, with dates, appears opposite.

Biographies can often be long, ponderous works, and while valuable in their context, often lose the reader in a flood of footnote and source explanations. This is particularly true when detailing the life and times of a man like Styles Bridges. As the book is directed not only toward readers of biographies but also students at the secondary and college level, I have attempted to write a swiftly moving narrative, free of the so-called "stop-and-go" reading which plagues many of the works in this genre.

Taped Interviews

Aiken, George	04/19/80	McIntyre, Thomas	07/09/88
Anderson, Frank	04/09/81	McQuaid, Joe	10/30/96
Anderson, Jack	04/01/86		02/12/98
Baker, Bobby	10/11/88	Menzel, Gail	10/15/96
Bartholemew, John/Hazel	08/14/80	Merrow, Chester	07/25/72
Bass, Perkins	04/16/79	Millmett, Joseph A.	11/19/97
	02/04/80	Munroe, Hank	07/25/96
Bellush, Bernard	05/03/70	Murphy, Maurice J., Jr.	06/19/81
Bowles, Raimond	08/23/88		07/27/88
Bridges Dedication*	06/24/81	Mates, Benjamin	12/10/85
Bridges, Doris**	08/26/69	Orr, Dudley	07/26/88
Bridges, John F.	07/30/81	Perkins, Mildred	08/14/80
	12/11/95	Pillsbury, John	06/03/81
Bridges, William	10/15/96	Powell, Peter	06/28/00
Brown, Jim/Jackie	09/30/97	Riedel, James	02/25/86
Chandler, Jack	02/18/73	Sargent, Sarah	11/10/97
Chennault, Madame	06/17/82	Scott, Hugh	06/21/82
Cole, Stacy	03/25/99	Shannon, Tom	01/19/80
Conway, Mrs. George	02/04/73	Shapiro, Milton	07/26/88
Cotton, Norris	04/17/79	Smith, Margaret Chase	07/10/89
Dagostino, Mike	02/04/97	Sokul, Beatrice	01/13/97
Deachman, William III	07/28/81	Teague, Bert	07/26/73
Dunlap, Phil	11/21/95		11/21/95
Dwinell, Lane	12/02/72	Treat, William	06/17/88
	12/21/96	Trice, Mark	01/17/81
Eddy, Richard W.	11/26/72	Upton, Robert F.	07/27/88
	07/13/87	Upton, William W.	10/07/70
Everett, Douglas	07/25/96	Warrington, John	10/07/80
Fong, Hiram	11/21/81		06/15/87
Gaskell, James	09/28/96		02/08/89
Hayes, James	07/26/88	Waterman, Guy	02/22/97
Johnson, Ted	07/30/72	Wiggin, Joyce	10/15/70
Keenan, Francis	08/14/80		09/14/79
King, William	02/03/80		12/12/95
Landon, Alf	09/15/68	Wyman, Louis	09/12/98
Loeb, Nackey	04/26/73	Zeiller, Gerald	09/12/98
Loeb, William	07/26/87		

*(US Capitol)
**(interview notes only)

Sources

Primary Sources

A History of the United States Senate Republican Policy Committee 1947-1997. Prepared by Donald A. Ritchie, Historian, U.S. Senate Historical Office. (U.S. Government Printing Office, Washington, 1997.)

Abell, Tyler (ed.). *Drew Pearson Diaries* (New York: Holt, Rinehart and Winston, 1974).

Allen, George E. *Presidents Who Have Known Me* (New York: Simon and Schuster, 1950).

American National Biography, DAB; U.S. Congress, Memorial Services for Henry S. Bridges, 87th Congress, 2nd Session, 1962. (Washington, D.C.: United States Government Printing Office, 1962).

Bass, Honorable Robert Perkins, Papers, Collected at Dartmouth College Library, New Hampshire. A Register of His Papers in the New Hampshire Historical Society, Edited by James J. Kiepper. (Concord, New Hampshire: New Hampshire Historical Society, 1974).

Bradlee, Ben. *A Good Life: Newspapering And Other Adventures* (New York: Simon & Schuster, 1995)

Bridges, Doris A. *Growing Up Way Downeast, A Memoir of Childhood On the Coast of Maine*, Gail Menzel, ed. (Mt. Desert, Maine: Windswept House Publishers, 1997).

Bridges, Styles. *Papers of Styles Bridges*, U.S. Senate. U.S. Senate 1949-61, Staff files of Dorothy Territo, Congressional File 40 (428). Also found at New England College, Henniker, NH [Papers: ca – 1923-1961) (124 boxes, ca. 100,000 items + 190 scrapbooks, photographs, memorabilia) Majority of the collection consists of reprints and secondary material. Guide in repository. Papers also at New Hampshire Historical Society in Concord, New Hampshire correspondence 1933-1950 scattered in various collections. (Papers also includes copy of the Federal Bureau of Investigation's File on Senator Styles Bridges.)

Bridges, The Honorable Styles, "On 18 years in the Senate" (Box 31/NIN – Review of voting With Conclusion of 83rd Session of Congress.)

Bridges, The Honorable Styles, "The Third Term." *Current History* 51 (June 1940), pp. 38-39 & 61-62.

Bridges, The Honorable Styles, *Address on the Conservative and Government*, Given at Dartmouth College on October 16, 1955.

Bridges, The Honorable Styles, "Protest Against the Use of the Fifth amendment to the Constitution As A Shield for Communist Instructors," *Congressional Record*, June 2, 1953.

Bridges, The Honorable Styles, "Voting Record of Hon. Styles Bridges On Yea and No Votes with Index and Chronologically Arranged. Covering Period from: 1] January 5, 1942 - December 16, 1942; 2] January 6, 1943 - December 21, 1943; 3] January 10, 1944 - December 19, 1944; 4] January 3, 1945 - December 21, 1945; 5] January 14, 1946 - August 2, 1946. Compiled by C. A. Loeffler, United States Senate.

Buchanan, Patrick J. "Growing Peril To U.S. Sovereignty," February 26, 1999 (http://www.theamericancause.org) The American Cause, Patrick J. Buchanan, Chair, McClean, Virginia.

Buckley, William F., Jr. *Excerpts From An Address To The Conservative Party of New York On The Occasion of its Second Anniversary* (Privately printed by Alex L. Hillman for his friends, 1964).

Buckley, William F., Jr. *Up From Liberalism* (New York: Hillman Books, 1959).

Cotton, Sen. Norris *In The Senate. Amidst the Conflict and the Turmoil* (New York: Dodd, Mead & Company, 1978).

Devine, Donald. "Why Are We Conservatives," January 20, 2000. [http://www.conservative.org/columnists/devine01202000.htm) (American conservative Union, 1007 Cameron Street, Alexandria, VA 22314, acu@conservative.org]

Eisenhower, Dwight David, President. First Inaugural Address of Dwight D. Eisenhower, Tuesday, January 20, 1953. (The Avalon Project at the Yale Law School, http://www.yale.edu/lawweb/avalon/presiden/inaug/eisenl.htm]]1997: The Avalon Project, William C. Fray and Lisa A. Spar, Co-Directors.)

Goldwater, Sen. Barry. *The Conscience of a Conservative* (New York: MacFadden Books, 1964).

Goldwater, Sen. Barry M. and Jack Casserly. *Goldwater* (New York: Doubleday, 1988).

Groves, Leslie R. *Now It Can Be Told* (New York: Harper & Row, 1962).

Kennedy, John F. *Profiles In Courage* (New York: Harper & Row, Publishers, 1964).

Kiepper, James J., *Taped Interviews with Associates, Friends and Colleagues of Senator Styles Bridges* (conducted between 1968 and 1982).

Madison, Frank. *A View From The Floor, The Journal of a U.S. Senate Page Boy* (Englewood Cliffs, New Jersey: Prentice-Hall, 1967).

Martin, Joe. *My First Fifty Years in Politics, As told to Robert J. Donovan* (New York: McGraw-Hill, 1960).

Merrow, Chester E. *My Twenty Years In Congress* (Concord, N. H.: Rumford Press, 1965).

Miller, Clem. *Member of the House, Letters of a Congressman*. Edited by John W. Baker (New York: Charles Scribner's & Sons, 1962).

Novak, Robert D. *The Agony of the G.O.P. 1964* (New York, Macmillan Co., 1965).

Reagan, Ronald W., President. "Great Quotes From President Reagan" (found at the Ronald Reagan Home Page, http://reagan.webteamone.com/speeches/quotes.html).

Rudman, Hon. Warren B. *Combat, Twelve Years In The U.S. Senate* (New York: Random House, 1996).

Smith, Margaret Chase. *Declaration of Conscience*, William C. Lewis, Jr., (ed.) (Garden City, New York: Doubleday & Company, 1972).

Smith, Papers of Hon. Senator Margaret Chase Smith, Maine. Margaret Chase Smith Library, Northwood University, Skowhegan, Maine.

Robert Alphonso Taft, Late A Senator From Ohio. Memorial Addresses (Delivered in Congress, 83rd Congress, 2nd Session,) (Washington, D.C.: United States Government Printing Office, 1954).

Tobey, Charles William, United States Senate, New Hampshire, Papers. (Dartmouth College, Hanover, N. H.) (papers: 1933-1953, 175 feet: includes photographs and comprehensive correspondence).

Town Meeting, Vol. 15, No. 32 (Town Hall, Inc., New York, New York, Dec. 6, 1949). "Should We Recognize the Chinese Communist Government?", Moderator: George V. Denny, Jr., Speakers:, John K. Fairbank, George G. Cobean, Styles Bridges, Charles M. Cooke, Jr.

Truman, Harry S. *Memoirs*. Volume 1, *Years of Trial*, Volume 2, *Years of Trial and Hope* (Garden City, New York: Doubleday & Company, 1955).

Truman, Margaret. *Harry S. Truman* (New York: William Morrow & Company, 1973).

Webster, Honorable Daniel, "Webster speech titled 'Seventh of March'," Reading No. 33. Richard Allan Baker, Director, U.S. Senate Historical Office (Robert E. Krieger Publishing Company, Malabar, Florida, 1988), pp. 185-6

Williams, Papers of Senator John J., of Delaware. Special Collection, University of Delaware Library, Newark, Delaware (re: files related to Styles Bridges).

Winant, John Gilbert. *Letters From Grosvenor Square, An Account of A Stewardship* (Boston: Houghton Mifflin Company, 1947).

Secondary Sources

Adams, Henry H. *Harry Hopkins, A Biography* (New York: G. P. Putnam's Sons, 1977).

Allen, Gary, with Larry Abraham. *None Dare Call It Conspiracy* (Seal Beach, California: Concord Press, 1971).

Allen, Robert S. and William V. Shannon. *The Truman Merry-Go-Round* (New York: The Vanguard Press, 1950).

Austin, Erik W., *H. Styles Bridges: The Road To Conservatives. 1930-1938* (unpublished master's thesis, Dartmouth College, New Hampshire, April, 1965).

Belknap, Jeremy. *History of New Hampshire* (3 volumes) (New York: Arno Press, 1972).

Bellush, Bernard. *He Walked Alone, A Biography of John Gilbert Winant* (The Hague: Mouton, 1968).

Bisson, Wilfred. Comp. With assistance of Gerry Hayden. *Franklin Pierce: A Biography* (Westport, CT: Greenwood Press, 1993).

Bixby, Roland. *Standing Tall, The Life Story of New Hampshire of Senator Norris Cotton* (Crawfordsville, Indiana: Lakeside Press, 1988).

Cash, Kevin. *Who The Hell is William Loeb?* (Manchester, New Hampshire: Amoskeag Press, Inc. 1975).

Churchill, Winston *Coniston* (New York: The Macmillan Company, 1906).

Dahl, Robert A. *Who Governs? Democracy and Power in an American City.* (New Haven: Yale University Press, 1961).

De Toledano, Ralph. *The Winning Side, The Case For Goldwater Republicanism* (New York: MacFadden Books, 1964).

Drury, Allen. *Advise and Consent, A Novel of Washington Politics* (Garden City, N.Y.: Doubleday & Company, Inc., 1959).

Duncan, Dayton. *Grass Roots* (New York: Penguin, 1991).

Early, Eleanor. *Behold The White Mountains* (Boston: Little, Brown, and Company, 1935).

Ewert, William B. (Compiled by). *Robert Frost New Hampshire* (Durham: Friends of the Library, University of New Hampshire, 1976).

Federal Writers' Project. *New Hampshire, A Guide to the Granite State* (Boston: Houghton Mifflin Company, 1938).

Frost, Robert. *Collected Poems, Prose & Plays.* Edited by Richard Poirier and Mark Richardson (New York: Literary classics of the United States, Inc., 1995).

Gallagher, Edward J. *George H. Moses: A Profile* (Laconia, N.H.: Citizen Publishing House, 1975).

Garraty, John A. and Mark C. Carnes (eds.). *American National Biography* (New York: Oxford University Press, 1999) Vol. 3, pp. 524-525.

Gill, Gillian. *Mary Baker Eddy* (Cambridge, Mass.: Perseus Books, 1998).

Guide to Research Collections of Former United States Senators, 1789-1982 (U.S. Senate Bicentennial Publication #1), (97th Congress, 2nd Session, Senate Resolution 306, Senate Doc: 97-41).

Guide To the Records of the United States Senate at the National Archives, 1789-1989 (Bicentennial Edition). (Robert W. Coren, Mary Rephlo, David Kepley, and Charles South, eds., Prepared by Walter J. Stewart, Secretary of the Senate of the United States, 1789).

Halberstam, David. *The Fifties* (New York, Villard Books, Random House, 1993).

Henry, Laurin L. *Presidential Transitions* (Washington: The Brookings Institution, 1960).

Hill, Evan. *The Primary State, An Historical Guide to New Hampshire* (Taftsville, Vermont: The Countryman Press, 1976).

Hillman, Alex (Submitted by). "Report On Mission To England and Italy, April 5 – April 27, 1948," To The Senate Appropriations Committee, Honorable Styles Bridges, New Hampshire, Chairman. United States Senate.

Houseman, Gerald L. *City of the Right* (Westport, Conn.: Greenwood Press, 1982).

Irwin, Will. *Herbert Hoover, A Reminiscent Biography* (New York: Grosset & Dunlap, 1928).

Kiepper, James J. (Prepared by) *Styles Bridges: A Register of His Papers In The New England College Library* (Manuscript Register Series, Register Number 1, January 1972; Manuscript Collections, New England College, Henniker, New Hampshire).

Kirk, Russell, "Kirk's Six Canons of Conservative Thought," (found at http://www.townhall.com/hall_of_fame/kirk/kirkhome.html).

Kirk, Russell. *The Conservative Mind* (Seventh Revised Edition) (Washington, D.C.: Regnery Publishing, Inc., 1999).

Kirk, Russell. *A Program For Conservatives* (Chicago: Henry Regnery Company, 1954).

Lamont, Lansing. *Day of Trinity* (New York: Atheneum Press, 1965).

Lockhard, Duane. *New England State Politics* (Princeton, N.J.: Princeton University Press, 1959)

Lord, Walter. *Day of Infamy* (London: Bantam Books, 1982).

Mahood, H. R. *Pressure Groups In American Politics* (New York: Charles Scribner's & Sons, 1967).

Mayo, Lawrence Shaw. *John Langdon of New Hampshire* (Port Washington, New York: Kennikat Press, 1970 reprint of 1937 edition).

Mazo, Earl and Stephen Hess. *Nixon, A Political Portrait* (New York: Popular Library, 1967).

McCullough, David. *Truman* (New York: Simon & Schuster, 1992).

McMaster, John Bach. *Daniel Webster* (New York: The Century Co., 1902).

Mitchell, Edwin Valentine. *An Encyclopedia Of American Politics* (Garden City, New York: Doubleday & Company, Inc. 1946).

Morrison, Elting E. *Turmoil and Tradition – A Study of the Life and Times of Henry L. Stimson* (Boston: Houghton Mifflin, 1960).

Morrison, Elizabeth Forbes and Elting E. Morrison. *New Hampshire: A Bicentennial History* (New York: Norton, 1976).

Neal, Steve. *Dark Horse: A Biography of Wendel Willkie* (Garden City, N.Y.: Doubleday & Company, Inc., 1984).

New Hampshire, State of. *Manual of the General Court 1935*, Governor H. Styles Bridges. Prepared by the Department of State, No. 24, Concord, New Hampshire.

New Hampshire, State of, *Manual for the General Court 1997*, Governor Jeanne Shaheen. Prepared by the Department of State, No 55., Concord, New Hampshire.

New Hampshire Women Legislators 1921-1971, Golden Anniversary. (Concord: the Evans Printing Company, 1971).

New Hampshire. The State That Made Us A Nation (A Celebration of the Bicentennial of the United States Constitution.) (Peter E. Randall, Publisher, Portsmouth, New Hampshire, 1989). (A publication of the State of New Hampshire.)

Official Congressional Directory, 83rd Congress, 1st Session, March 1953, (Washington, D.C.: United States Government Printing Office, 1953).

Oshinsky, David M. *A Conspiracy So Immense: The World of Joe McCarthy* (London: Collier Macmillan Publishers, 1983).

Palmer, Fredrick. *This Man Landon* (revised and enlarged edition) (New York: Dodd, Mead, 1936).

Paul, Karen Dawley (Compiled by). *Guide To Research Collections of former United States senators 1789-1995)* (Washington, D.C.: United States Government Printing Office, 1995) (Senate Do. 103-35, 103d Congress, S.Con Res.5, US Senate).

Quatannens, Jo Anne McCormick (compiled by). *Senators of the United States, A Historical Bibliography* (Washington, D.C.: United States Government Printing Office, 1995).

Reeves, Thomas C. *The Life and Times of Joe McCarthy: A Biography* (London: London, 1982).

Republican National Convention, Official Report of the Proceedings of the Twenty-Second, Philadelphia, 1940 (Published Under Supervision of Harold W. Mason, Secretary of the Convention) (Washington: Judd & Detweiler, Inc., 1940).

Rossiter, Clinton. *The American Presidency* (New York: Signet Key Book, 1956).

Russell, Francis. *The Shadow of Blooming Grove, Warren G. Harding In His Times* (New York: McGraw-Hill Book Company, 1968).

Sewell, Richard. *John P. Hale and the Politics of Abolition* (Cambridge: Harvard University Press, 1965).

Shadegg, Stephen. *What Happened to Goldwater? The Inside Story of the 1964 Republican Campaign* (New York: Holt, Rinehart and Winston, 1965).

Sheed, Wilfrid. *Claire Boothe Luce* (New York: Berkley Books, 1982).

Sherman, Michael (ed.). *The Political Legacy of George D. Aiken, Wise Old Owl of the U.S. Senate* (Woodstock, Vermont: The Countryman Press, Inc., 1995).

Solberg, Carl. *Herbert Humphrey, A Biography* (New York: W. W. Norton & Company, 1984).

Speece, Glenn Harrison. *After Roosevelt* (New York: The Alliance Press, 1936).

Squires, James Duane. *The Granite State of the United States: A History of New Hampshire from 1623 to the Present*. 4 Vols. (New York: American Historical Co. 1956).

Swain, Martha. *Pat Harrison, The New Deal Years* (Jackson: University Press of Mississippi, 1978).

Swanberg, W. A. *Luce and His Empire* (New York: Charles Scribner's & Sons, 1972).

Thompson, Jr., Meldrin. *Live Free or Die* (Oxford, New Hampshire: Equity Publishing Corporation, 1979).

Thorne, Melvin J. *American Conversative Thought since World War II, The Core Ideas* (Westport, Conn.: Greenwood Press, 1990).

Williams, T. Harry. *Huey Long* (New York: Alfred A. Knopf, 1969).

Wright, James. *The Progressive Yankees Republican Reformers in New Hampshire, 1906-1916* (Hanover and London: University Press of New England, 1987).

Magazines

American Mercury (New York, New York); Vol. LXXVI, January 1953; Vol. LXXVI, Feb. 1953, No. 350; Vol. LXXVI, March-April 1953, No. 351; Vol. LXXVI, May 1953, NO. 352, June, 1953.

Bellush, Jewel, L. "Robert Bass: Progressive Strategist," *N.E. Quarterly*, Vol. 35, Dec. 1962, No. 4, p. 9.

Bridges, Styles, Member, United States Senate, and Sen. Estes Kefauver, and Stephen McCormick, "What's Ahead for the New Congress?", *The American Forum*, Vol. XIX, Sunday, January 15, 1956, No. 3, p. 11.

Flynn, John T., "Bridges and Bird vs. the 'Good' Public Debt", *American Mercury*, October 1954, pp. 51-55.

Kiepper, James J., "Campaign History: A Political Powerhouse," *New Hampshire Editions*, Feb. 1996, pp. 30 & 32.

_____, *Rural Electrification*, March 1956.

_____, "Commit: When Is A Conservative A Liberal," *Washington Newsletter*, Dec.1955, Vol. 5, No. 9 (Published by the National Federation of Republican Women).

_____, "The Watchdog Committee and How It Watches," *Newsweek*, Dec. 12, 1951.

Wertenbaker, Charles, "The China Lobby," *The Reporter*, 15 April 1952, Vol. 6, #8, pp. 2-24.

Newspapers

The Argus-Champion (Newport, N.H.) July 15, 1954: "Doubtful Journalism"

Baltimore Sun: July 30, 1959: "Liberals Hit For Silence on Book Ban" January 24, 1961: "Bridges Attacks New 'Gag' On Anti-Soviet Talk; Burke Text Cut, White House Says"

Berlin Reporter: October 27, 1960: "Bridges Urges Full Break With Cuba"

Boston Daily Globe: July 4, 1958: "Women Aides Given Checks" by Robert Healey

The Boston Herald: April 14, 1953: "Grunewald Reply Involves Bridges" by Clayton Knowles
April 23, 1953: "Leftists Accused of Ignoring Truth in 'Smear' of Bridges" by David Lawrence
July 24, 1954: "N. H. Campaign Now Expected to Hit Climax in Mid-August" by Oliver Jenkins
February 13, 1956: "Senate Weighing Full Probe of All Gas Bill Lobbies" by Coleman B. Jones
March 25, 1956: "Bridges Holds Great Powers In U.S. Senate" by Tom W. Guber
August 25, 1960: "Senate Votes Cuba Squeeze, Would Deny US Aide To Arms Suppliers"

Boston News Bureau: May 22, 1940: "Bridges Urges Strong National Defense"

Boston Post: January 1953: "Bridges Named GOP Leader In Senate" by J. A. O'Leary
April 20, 1954: "Bridges Sees Fall of Asia Fatal to Defenses of U.S."
May 11, 1954: "Bridges Lauds McCarthy, Advises End To Hearings"; Bid of GOP Is Doomed, Mundt Vote To Decide Issue" by John Kelso
January 24, 1954: "Bridges Fifth N.H. Senator To Get High Senate Honor" by John Kelso
July 13, 1954: "Editorial: The Big Smear In New Hampshire" by John Fox
July 15, 1954: "Editorial: The Big Smear In New Hampshire" [continued] by John Fox
July 16, 1954: "Editorial: The Big Smear In New Hampshire" [concluded] by John Fox
April 3, 1955: "Role Played by Alger Hiss at Yalta Is Revealed by Senator Styles Bridges" by John Kelso
November 1955: "Senator Styles Bridges Under Pressure To Halt Full Exposure of Yalta Papers" by John Kelso

Boston Sunday Herald: March 8, 1953: "Speedy Cleanup of State Dept. Personnel Pledged by McLeod" by John Kelso

July 18, 1954: "Two Top N.H. Nominations Going Begging for Contests" by Oliver Jenkins
January 16, 1955: "Battle of Liberals; Conservatives Near" by Bill Cunningham; "Round About" by M. E. Hennessey
April 1, 1956: "Senator Bridges Calls for Reappraisal of Whole U.S. Foreign Aid Program" by John Kelso

Boston Traveler: November 17, 1960: "Sen. Bridges, The Man Who Beats All Comers!"

Brooklyn Eagle: June 11, 1940: "U.S. Neutral No More, Bridges Asserts Here"

Chicago Tribune: June 11, 1940: "Bridges Assails Roosevelt For LAG in Defenses"; July 30, 1959: "Hits 'Liberals' For Silence On Book Removal" by William Moore; March 30, 1961: "Bridges to Kennedy: Bar Reds from Laos Cabinet" by Robert Young; April 2, 1961: "Bridges Tries, Tho Warnings Go Unheeded" by Williard Edwards

The Christian Science Monitor: May 18,1940: "Dark Horse Who Won't Stay Hitched" by Charles Bargeron; July 26,1954: "Magazine Catapults Bridges Into Controversy"; February 13, 1956: "Senate Maps Fully Lobby Probe"; March 9,1956: "Unwelcome Project, Senate Lobby Probe Stalls" by Richard L. Strout

Claremont Eagle: July 24,1954: "Open Forum: Against Bridges" by Harold Foisy

Colorado Springs Gazette-Telegraph: March 4, 1954: "Byrd-Bridges Amendment"

Columbus Evening Dispatch: August 14, 1951: "Why Our Government Must Economize" by Styles Bridges

The Commercial And Financial Chronicle: October 1, 1953: "We Must Stop Socialistic Trends And Return To Solvency" by H. Styles Bridges, U.S. Senator from New Hampshire; January 19, 1956: "Hon. Styles Bridges, U.S. Senator From New Hampshire"

Concord Monitor: December 17, 1951: "Senator Bridges Is Linked To Tax Case, Grunewald Said He Acted for Him, Oliphant States." By Cecil Holland and George Beveridge; March 21, 1952: "Bridges Named In Tax Probe"; December 2, 1953: "Powell Tells Of Red Probe"; April 9, 1954: "Indochina Crisis Forces US To Restudy Foreign Aid – Bridges"; July 10, 1954: "The State Is My Beat" by Leon W. Anderson; July 13, 1954: "Letter: Status of Bridges" by Ralph H. Morse.; July 14, 1954: "Letters: Backs Bridges" by W. M. Hungerford; "The State is My Beat" by Leon W. Anderson; July 17, 1954: "Letters: Resents Attack" by Victor T. Keegan; "The Miners's Fund" by Dorothy S. Rollins; July 19, 1954: "Gregg Feels Article True On Bridges"; July 20, 1954: "Lebanon Newspaper Reprints Anti-Bridges Article In Full"; July 21, 1954: "Gregg Backs Sen. Bridges"; "The State Is My Beat" by Leon W. Anderson; July 22, 1954: "Letters: Likes Bridges" by Winnie Hoyt Reille; "Letters: Like Bridges" by Dwight D. Eisenhower; November 18, 1954: "Bridges Warns Of Terrific Peace Offensive Launched By Russians" by Lawrence Fernsworth; "Condemning Of Reds In Censure Set"; December 14, 1955: "Bridges Against Income Tax Reduction, Wants U.S. Budget Balanced by Next Congress"; March 7, 1956: "Bridges Tells Probe Views"; March 10, 1956: "A Secret Society"; October 23, 1957: "White House Aide's 'Ill Bauble' Crack Draws Fire From Angry Sen. Bridges"; September 8, 1960: "Bridges Rages at Lax Security"; March 31, 1961: "Juggling of Books Claimed"; April 26, 1961: "Bridges Expects Kennedy to Consult With GOP Leaders Before Cuba Policy Decided"; January 12, 1981: "N.H. Sen. Bridges' bid for GOP Presidential nomination recalled," Commentary by James J. Kiepper

Coos County Democrat: November 2, 1960: "Re-elect Sen. Styles Bridges"; November 13, 1953: "Sen. Bridges Still Opposes Red China's Entry into U.N."; February 9, 1954: "Creeping Socialism's Autocracy Broken, Bridges Tells Republicans"; August 21, 1954: "Reporter Replies To Response of Sen. Bridges"; November 18, 1954: "Senate Weighs Delaying McCarthy Censure Debate"

Detroit Free Press: January 12, 1954: "What Killed Senator Hunt? The Untold, Tragic Story" by Drew Pearson

The Evening Star: July 9, 1954: "Bridges Hires Counsel On 'Reporter' Article"; July 26, 1954: "A New Hampshire Interlude" by Doris Fleeson

Exeter News Letter: July 13, 1954: "Down In Our Conner" by James P. Lynch; July 22, 1954: "Unfortunate Reference"; June 26, 1958: "Extension of Communism Greatest Threat to U.S."

Foster's Democrat: December 2, 1953: "Powell Credits Bridges With Uprooting Reds"; August 25, 1954: " 'The Reporter' Answers Bridges"; October 26, 1960: "Mrs. Bridges Says Kennedy 'Soft on Communism' "

Hillsboro Messenger: July 15, 1954: "Editorial Comment: Bridges Falling Down?"; "State House Journal" by Enoch Shenton

The Houston Post: April 29, 1957: "GOP Reverses Trend To Socialism, Says Bridges"

Kearsarge Independent: July 16, 1954: "Capitol and State Streets, Opinion" by Ralph H. Morse

Keene Evening Sentinel: August 20, 1954: "Bridges Blasts Magazine For 'Smear, Vicious Attack' "; December 19, 1955: "Bridges Lists 10 Guideposts To Freedom"; February 16, 1956: "Chairman Asks Probe of Political 'Gifts' "

Labor: June 17, 1954: "Senators Threaten Libel Suits As New Weapon To Gag Unfavorable News Stories"

The Laconia Evening Citizen: August 21, 1951: "Editorial Comment: A Sad Commentary"; July 9, 1954: "Magazine Doubts Bridges Will Resort to Courts With Libel Allegations"; "Continued Sale of Reporter Despite Threat of Legal Action"; "Mercury Magazine Announces Article Lauding Bridges"; July 10, 1954: "Chandler Calls Bridges Article 'Dastardly' "; July 12, 1954: "Morin Deplores Move to Suppress Bridges Article"; July 13, 1954: "Smear by Political Rival Caused Senator Hunt's Suicide" by M. Childs; "Publisher Fox Calls Article in Reporter 'The Big Smear in NH' "; July 15, 1954: "Gene Daneli: Public Street Rally"; July 17, 1954: "Daniell Dares Bridges To Have Him Arrested?"; "We Enter the Hall of Fame"; July 19, 1954: "Headlines Bridges' Article with Comment 'Country Boy Goes Wrong' "; July 21, 1954: "Of Sen. Bridges &Wm. Loeb"; "Lebanon Daily Reprints Reporter Bridges' Article"; July 24, 1954: "Woodsville: Editor Wants Gregg to Oppose Bridges"; July 26, 1956: "Arouses Sympathy for Bridges"; August 2, 1954: "The Story of Styles Bridges: 'He Has Brought N.H. Honor, Dignity, Respect' "; September 28, 1954: "Few Senators Reveal Stand On Census" by G. Milton Kelly

Los Angeles Examiner: June 6, 1940: "People Not Being Fooled," Styles Bridges; June 11, 1940: "Training Favored by Sen. Bridges"

Manchester News: March 11, 1956: "McClellan Chief, Bridges Is Lobby Vice-Chairman"

Manchester Observer: October 1954: "Sen. Bridges Long National Leader"

Manchester Union Leader: October 3, 1938: "Change In Neutrality Law for U.S. Put Forward by Senator Bridges in Talk At Concord"; May 22, 1940: "Bridges Urges Cleanup of '5th Column' "; August 27, 1949: "Bridges Accused Of Fund's Misuse"; "Blames Bridges and Lewis For 'Unsound' Fund Policy"; September 15, 1949: "Bridges' Charge of Inconsistency"; October 3,1950: "Bridges Charges 'Sell-Out' by State Dept. To Reds"; June 13, 1953: "Smears On Bridges"; "Editorial" by Dorothy S. Rollins; September 19, 1953: "Bridges Scores Apathy On Red Threat To U.S."; December 2, 1953: "Powell Discloses Bridges' 1947 Move Rooted Out State Dept. Subversives"; "Agents Listed 81 Cases, One Girl Ex-Red Employee" by J. Leo Dery; January 29, 1954: "GOP Gets 'Loyalty' Pledges" by D. Frank O'Neil; "N.H. To Build Atomic Sub"; May 11, 1954: "Bridges Ask Clear Cut Foreign Policy"; June 7, 1954: "Bridges Would Use A-Bomb In Indochina"; June 11, 1954: "Bridges Says People Want Hearing Over" by Herman A. Lowe; July 8, 1954: "Attack On Bridges Brings Libel Moves"; July 15, 1954: "Pro-Communist Attack on Bridges"; July 16, 1954: "Bridges Is Right"; July 17, 1954: "Hails Bridges Statesmanship"; July 19, 1954: "Charges Against Bridges 'Appear True' - Gregg"; July 20, 1954: "Praise for Bridges"; "Attack on Bridges Roundly Criticized"; "Charges Against Bridges Appear True Says Gregg"; July 21, 1954: "Apology Letter To Sen. Bridges Put In Record" by Herbert A. Lowe; "Gregg Surprised at Reaction To Statement on Bridges"; July 24, 1954: "Under The State House Dome" by D. Frank O'Neil; August 3, 1954: "Asks 'Bridges Support' " (Dwight D. Eisenhower); August 21, 1954: "Bridges' Support of Democracy Emphasizes Flexibility"; "The 'Reporter' Defends Their 'Facts and Ideas' "; September 17, 1954: "Sen. Bridges Wins D.A.R Award For Americanism" by Meg Gerahty; September 22, 1954: "Bridges Raps Senate Session On McCarthy, 'Strongly Opposed' to Censure, Parley Prior To Election" by D. Frank O'Neil; October 6, 1954: "Bridges Demands End To Appeasing Soviets"; October 26, 1954: "Bridges Warns Grange Red Peril

Creeps On" by Fred E. Beane; November 3, 1955: "Mrs. Bridges Warns GOP Women Many Displeased With Party" by Meg Geraghty; November 12, 1955: "Bridges Warns Russia Is Still Greatest Potential Enemy of U.S."; December 9, 1955: "Honor Senator Bridges At Testimonial Here" by D. Frank O'Neil; December 15, 1955: "Need Yankee Hard-Headedness In U.S. Foreign Policy – Bridges" by Robert J. Drury; January 14, 1956: "Bridges Wants Budget Balanced, Debt Pared" by Herman A. Lowe; January 19, 1956: "Bridges Backs Dulles Position On Taking Risks To Keep Peace" by Herman Lowe; March 12, 1956: "Bridges Raps Aid To Nations Helping Reds" by Herman A. Lowe; March 13, 1956: "Commentary" by William Loeb; "Bridges Puts Country First"; March 31, 1956: "Bridges Demands Speed In U.S. Missile Programn by Herman A. Lowe; April 6, 1956: "Bridges To Ask Senate Restore State Probes" by Herman A. Lowe; April 12, 1956 "Bridges Introduces Bill To Regain State Rights To Act Against Sedition"; November 5, 1957: "Bridges Set To Ask For U.S. Missile Czar"; "Johnson Gloomy After Briefing By Experts. Bridges Wants Czar"; July 4, 1958: "Powell, Teague and Others Acknowledge Yuletide Gifts"; November 27, 1959: "'Liberals' vs. 'Conservatives'"; September 8, 1960: "Bridges Assails Security" by Paul Dietterle; October 25, 1960: "Kennedy's Record on Communism Very Soft, Mrs. Bridges Declares" by Meg Geraghty; October 27, 1960: "Bridges Is Cited For Courageous Public Service"; "Bridges Raps 'Stone Age Views' Of Jackson On Women's Rights" by D. Frank O'Neil; November 18, 1960: "Hill Believes Bridges Holds 'Seat for Life'"; "Bridges Says Jack Lacks Mandate" by D. Frank O'Neil; May 1, 1961: "Bridges Says FDR Confided Atomic Bomb Secret To Him"

The Michigan Times: October 7, 1960: "Senator From Granite State Is all-American" by Frank D. McKay

Nashua Telegraph: August 8,1951: "Bridges And Economy"; December 15, 1951: "Bridges Says Contact With Bureau, 'Proper and Correct'"; December 2, 1953: "Powell Says FBI Listed 81 State Dept. Subversives"; June 7, 1954: "Bridges Sees No Prospect of Involvement" by Jack Bell; August 21, 1954: "Magazine Says Bridges Denies All But Facts"; November 6, 1960: "Senator Bridges' Record and Services to State Expected to Win Him Huge Vote" by John Stylianos

Nevada State News: July 15, 1954: "Pure Politics"

New Bedford Standard Times: October 6, 1958: "Bridges Warns Of Danger U.S. Faces In Communism"; "Bridges Hails Citizenry At Reception"; May 3, 1959: "McCarthy Paid Tribute As Bust Is Dedicated" [Associated Press]

New Castle Herald Tribune: September 18, 1953: "Bridges Says Sound Dollar Is Returning"

New Hampshire Sunday News: June 14, 1953: "John F. Bridges, Senator's Son, Takes Bride In Salem"; January 3, 1954: "Bridges Warns H-Bomb Can 'Vaporize' Entire large city; poses gravest U.S. problem." By Sen. Styles Bridges; June 18, 1954: "Big Smear Attack On Bridges Backfires," by Maurice McQuillen; December 18, 1955: "Bridges For Home-Front Liberties" by Herb Allen; February 26, 1956: "N.H. Solons Clamp Lid On Hush-Hush Payrolls, Won't Say How They Spend Big $200,000 Kitty" by James Stack; March 4, 1956: "Bridges, Cotton, Merrow Mum On Payrolls"; March 11, 1956: "U.S. Funds Go To Political Aides, Publicity Men" by James Stack; March 18, 1956: "U.S. Senators Fail To Hide Outgo in Secret Federal Payrolls"; December 11, 1960: "Bridges Has GOP Reins" by Jack Bell; January 28, 1996: "Guest Commentary – Styles Bridges: A Conservative Ahead of His Time" by James J. Kiepper; January 5, 1997: "From The Farm To The Corner Office: How A Crop-And-Soil Expert Became Governor" by James J. Kiepper

The Newport-Lake Sunape Times: September 3, 1953: "Sen. Bridges Report New Era in U.S. Fiscal"; "New Hampshire's Report Shows Largest Appropriations Cut In Single Session In History"

Newark Star Ledger: October 28, 1955: "Bridges hits Dems on 'Legacy'"

New York Times: February 12, 1956: "Case Inquiry Told Oil Concern Head Put Up $2,500 Gift" by John D. Morris; March 11,1956: "McClellan Heads New Lobby Panel, Ending Deadlock" by John D. Morris; March 18,1956: "Senate Lobby Inquiry Will Tread Carefully, Senator Bridges Pulls the Strings To Tone Down Investigations" by Russell Baker; July 4, 1958: "Inquiry Lists 33 U.S. Employees As Recipients of Goldfine's Gifts"; August 25,1960: "Senate Cuts Off U.S. Aid To States Assisting Castro" by E.W. Kenworthy

Oakland Tribune [California]: February 13, 1940: "'Free U.S.!' Plea of Sen. Bridges"

Philadelphia Evening Ledger: June 11, 1940: "Senator Bridges Answers"

Philadelphia Inquirer: February 13, 1940: "Bridges Demands Economic Freedom"

Portsmouth Herald: July 17, 1954: "A Fox Gone Astray"; February 23, 1956: "Sen. Gore Seen Heading Probe of Vote Purchasing"; October 6, 1958: "Bridges Opposes Surrender Of Offshore Islands"; July 29, 1959: "Bridges Frowns On Idea of Khruschev Visit"; March 31, 1961: "Bridges Insists No Reds to Share Control of Laos"; "Goldfine Confesses All" by Drew Pearson; "Goldfine and Friends" by Drew Pearson

Providence Journal (Rhode Island): June 15, 1940: "R. I. Republicans To Meet Bridges"

Rochester Courier: November 20, 1958: "Honor Senator Bridges For Leadership in Americanism"

South Bay Breeze [Redondo Beach, California]: June 15, 1940: "Secret U.S. Bomb Sight Is Reported Stolen"

Times-Herald: September 3, 1950: "'Me-Too' Senators of East Thwart Republican Policies" by John Fisher

Transcript: August 10, 1938: "Bridges Says Nation Must Decentralize"; July 22, 1954: "Letter From the Editor: Bridges vs. Bridges" (letters in support of Bridges) United States Senate News; May 24, 1948: "Sen. Bridges (question of war and peace)"

Vallejo News: June 15, 1940: "Senate Hears Nazis Have U.S. Secret Air Bombsight"

Valley News: July 21, 1954: "Grunewald, Good Friend" by Douglas Cater; August 21, 1954: "'The Reporter' Challenges Sen. Bridges"; September 25, 1954: "Bridges and Dirksen Said To Have Stopped Recall"; November S, 1954: "Bridges Declares He Won't Approve McCarthy Censure"

Washington Daily Mirror: August 8, 1954: "Max Ascoli's Magazine Got a Strange Plug"; April 4, 1956: "Washington Glamor Gals: A Senator's Siren" by George Dixon; August 12, 1954: "When Kohlbeg and Taylor Met, Taylor Turned Quickly Away"; August 17, 1954: "The English Press Is Indifferent About the Treason of Communism"

Washington Evening Star: March 21, 1952: "Perjury Action Asked Against Malony" by Cecil Holland"; January 6, 1953: "McCarthy Discloses Letter By Truman Thanking Grunewald" by Cecil Holland; April 23, 1953: "Sen. Bridges Is Smeared" by David Lawrence; October 27, 1960: "Growth of A Smear"

Washington Post: October 6, 1950: "Anyhow, Nobody Can Say I'm Being Partisan," Political Cartoon by Herblock; December 12, 1951: "Grunewald Case Long Neglected" by Drew Pearson; June 30,1954: "Smears and Tears Plague The Senate" by Marquis Childs; August 20, 1954: "Bridges Flays Magazine as 'A Disgrace'"; November 18, 1954: "McCarthy's Heads Are Counted" by Drew Pearson; February 13, 1956: "Full Inquiry Into 'Gifts' Is Promised" by John W. Finney; February 21, 1954: "Sen. Bridges Defends Aid To Indo-China"; February 26, 1956: "Corruption, Wide Support Given Election Cleanup, But Primary Fight Looms"; March 2,1956: "Leaders End Deadlock, Lobby-Election Inquiry Gets Back On Track" by Murrey Marden; March 12, 1956: "Editorial: Now Let's Have The Facts"; March 13, 1956: "8 Congressmen Face Indictment" by Drew Pearson; April 9, 1957: "Cairo Suicide Poses Question for Dulles" by Marquis Childs; November 23, 1958: "Ring Out the Old" (editorial); May 2, 1959: "Bridges Protégé Probe Scandal" by Jack Anderson; March 30, 1961: "Goldfine Reveals More Dealings" by Drew Pearson; March 31, 1961: "Goldfine Was Celebrity – Collector" by Drew Pearson; May 30, 1998: "Barry Goldwater, Patriot and Politician" Special to the *Washington Post* (also found at http://www.washingtonpost.com)

Washington Star: May 31, 1954: "McCarthy vs. Eisenhower" by Constantine Brown; February 14, 1956: "Record Shows Oil Money No Novelty in Campaign" by Douglas B. Cornell; March 11, 1956: "Lobby Probe"

262

Index

264

of 1936, 46-49; Flynn nomination, 102-104; For or against Bridges? 208-211; Foreign aid, 123-125; Freshman senator, 68-69; Gentleman farmer, 26-27; Goal - Governor's office, 29; Gubernatorial campaign, 1924, 21-22; Campaign, 1934, 32-33; Helping folks at home, 174-175; Hiroshima destruction, 114-116; Homestead, illus., 6; Hoover, J. Edgar, friendship with, 141-142; How Bridges worked, 183-186; Hunt affair, 145-147; Hunting Communists, 122-123; Illegal or immoral? 187-190; Illustrations, iii, 8, 11, 12, 18, 30, 35, 37, 45, 53, 54, 58, 59, 62, 63, 66, 69, 80, 82, 90, 92, 94, 96, 109, 110, 117, 124, 128, 129, 137, 141, 152, 156, 158, 163, 164, 167, 168, l69, 171, 176, 177, 178, 179, 180, 184, 188, 189, 192, 194, 196, 200, 207, 209, 211, 214, 221, 222, 223, 224, 225, 235, 238, 244; Inauguration as governor, 34-37; Labor unrest, 72-73; "Little Boy Blue," 52-64; MacArthur vs Truman, 155-159; Man behind the scenes, 215-218; Manhattan project, 1-2, 101-102; Marriage to Ella May Johnston, 14; Marriage to Sally Clement, 22; Marriage to Doloris Thauwald, 105-108; McCarthy charges, 140-141, 143-145; McCarthy's end, 173-174; Middle of the roader, 49-51, 65-83; Money important to Bridges? 190-193; Move to New Hampshire, 15; Moving Republican Party forward, 77-79; Name change, 85; National security problems, 119-120; New Deal, 39-40, 44, 51; New Hampshire fallout following Bridges' death, 237-239; Newington Air Force Base, 174-177; Old Man of the Mountain, 206-208; Pay as you go basis, 31-32; Peacemaker, 204-206; Post-war adjustment, 117-118; Postal investigation, 73-75; President Pro Tempore of Senate, 167-169; Presidential aspirations, 84-87; Presidential election, 1944, 109-111; Presidential primary, 89-95; Public Service Commission, 24-25, 26; Reelection, 1946, 119-120; Ronald Bridges' death, 218-219; Room in capitol, 242-245; Roosevelt tries to pack Supreme Court, 69-71; Sally's death, 79-83; Security problems, 138-140; Senatorial race, 1936, 57-64; Sources, 255-262; Styles Bridges' Chair, 241; Styles Bridges' room, 242-243; Taped interviews, 253; Textile industry crisis, 41-43; To run or not run, 53-57; Tobey-Powell fight, 150-155; Toward second term, 97-99; Trusteeship in UMW, 136-138; TVA challenged, 75-77; War clouds, 87-89; Washington vacuum, 236-237; Waste blueprint, 121; Women's political importance, 46-47; Working for Farm Bureau, 18-19; World War II begins, 96-97

Brown, Albert O., 33
Brown, Fred H., 21, 26, 67, 77, 83
Bryan, William Jennings, 10
Bullitt, William C., 123, 133
Bush, Prescott, illus., 169, 209
Bussey, Elmer, 179, 216
Byrd, Harry F., 205; illus., 156
Byrd, Robert, 216
Byrnes, James F., 123, 124

Callahan, William J., 59, 62
Capper, Arthur, 68
Carroll, Charles E., 31, 32
Carroll County Independent, 49
Cartledge, Elmer V., 67, 98
Castro, Fidel, 228-229
Cater, Douglass, 182, 197, 199
Chambers, Whittaker, 130
Cheney, Thomas F., 32
Chennault, Claire, 135
Chicago Daily News, 55
Childs, Marquis, 146
China crisis, 132-133
China lobby, 147-148
Churchill, Winston (of New Hampshire), 131
Churchill, Winston (of England), 123, 212
CIO, 72-75
Clark, Daniel, 169
Claremont Eagle Times, 199
Cleveland, Grover, 74
Cleveland, James C., 118, 239
Clinton, Mollie, 84
Coal miners' strike, 118-119
Cohn, Roy, illus., 144
Cold war, 122
Concord heritage, 240-241
Concord Monitor, 31, 152, 226, 233
Connally, Tom, 88, 97
Connery, William P., 73
Conservative in America, 252
Converse, Edward, 85
Conway, George, 85

270

Designed by A. L. Morris,
the text of this volume was composed in Garamond Light
and printed by J. S. McCarthy / Letter Systems
in Augusta, Maine on Monadnock Caress Text.
The jacket and endleaves were printed on
Strathmore Americana Text,
and the binding in ICG Holliston Arrestox
and Rainbow Colonial
was executed by New Hampshire Bindery
in Concord, New Hampshire.

Styles Bridges

has been published in a limited first edition
of one thousand copies,
each of which has been numbered
and signed by the author.
This is copy number

439

and is here signed.

James J. Kiepper